A PASSAGE TO OBLIVION

Books by Gian Quasar

A PASSAGE TO OBLIVION

SCARLET AUTUMN

DISTANT HORIZONS

SOMA

RECASTING BIGFOOT

THEY FLEW INTO OBLIVION

INTO THE BERMUDA TRIANGLE

GIAN J. QUASAR

A Passage to Oblivion

The Last Voyage of the U.S.S. *Cyclops*

BRODWYN, MOOR & DOANE
PUBLISHERS
2014

Library of Congress Cataloguing-in-Publication Data

Quasar, Gian Julius

A Passage to Oblivion:
The Last Voyage of the USS Cyclops

1. US Naval Auxiliary. 2. Disappearance of the USS *Cyclops*. 3. Investigation.
Bibliography. I. Title.

ISBN 978-0-9888505-6-9

Contents

USS *Cyclops*

Foreword

The greatest mystery in the United States Navy, and perhaps one of the greatest in the annals of the sea, is the disappearance of the huge US supply collier *Cyclops* in the closing months of World War I. Mystery does not surround the vessel because she was suspected to have been just a wartime loss. In the placid waters of the tropic Windward Islands she was sailing far from the war zone. Here she was out of reach of U-boats and mines. Expectedly, she signaled herself "All well" and heading home to Baltimore. Yet she never arrived. An intensive investigation by the US Navy uncovered more than just 309 missing men; they discovered hints of treason and mutiny.

For 95 years this dramatic story has been lost. The great vessel disappeared in the area we today call the Bermuda Triangle. Fate's obscene taste for coincidence has caused us to remember the ship only in regards to the many others that have vanished in those seas. But the *Cyclops* is an entirely different matter; the truth so obscure that now, close on to a hundred years since the vessel vanished, this work is the first to go behind-the-scenes and finally document the known facts and explore the possibilities of what quickly came to be considered "The Greatest Mystery in the Annals of the Navy."

No nation can tolerate mutiny. It destroys the ranks. It cripples commerce. It is so rare that only one case has been celebrated. England was agog with the heroic return of William Bligh and his small party of men in 1790. They had not only remained loyal and survived the mutiny on the HMS *Bounty*, but Bligh had performed an epic feat of seamanship in getting their small boat to Timor, over three thousand miles from where they had been put adrift by the mutinous crew under First Mate Fletcher Christian. Heroism more than anything creates fame. It was this exceptional achievement that catapulted the saga of the *Bounty* into history. The image of mutineers throwing breadfruit over the stern castle while Bligh shook his vengeful fist from the longboat remain with us over 200 years later.

Yet for the *Cyclops* there would be no deserved fame, immortal novel or moral story. Wartime secrecy is not to blame. The case of the *Cyclops* had lit the spreadsheets. Nor was it ultimately the aura of the Bermuda Triangle. That came decades later and only provided a convenient and superficial epilogue. It was her end— she vanished. This ultimately sealed her fate as a great sea mystery and sealed her last voyage from critical eyes. Yet the last voyage was merely the crescendo of several voyages more strained, bizarre and contentious than the last voyage of HMS *Bounty*. But there were no known survivors to tell the tale. Bligh did not come back after an heroic trip to Timor to demand that action be taken. Nor would any ship innocently put in at *Cyclops'* own Pitcairn's Island to discover the mutineers.

As a result, officially the United States Navy still insists it has never suffered a mutiny. It is nevertheless undeniable that for years the Navy acted upon that belief in the case at hand. More time, in fact, was devoted in trying to find out what had happened than it took an 18th Century British navy to pursue and bring to book the mutineers on the *Bounty*. In the classic sense, however, the US Navy could not pursue. The world was at war in 1918, with America and the allies fighting against the Kaiser's Germany. Rumor, intelligence circle scuttlebutt, probability, said the *Cyclops* had made off for a German port. So long as the war raged, Pitcairn was beyond their grasp. They pursued in the only way they could, in the form of backtracking. Even years after the war, more than one admiral boarded a ship to scour a remote island or track down the claims of a note in a bottle.

The end result of all this is an epic sea yarn in its own right. It is one that is far more complex than any 18th Century "I've had enough" mutiny. There are elements that add darker nuances to it than those that could ever exist in the case of the HMS *Bounty*. The world was at war. The *Cyclops* was also carrying a special cargo, and it was a tempting prospect. It was manganese ore. For World War I it was breadfruit. It may not have fed slaves like that for which Bligh so cruelly sacrificed his men, but it fed armaments production. It was highly desired by both sides, but Germany's supply had been strangled by the British and American navies. There was no hope of getting any except by hijacking it. A key part of the *Cyclops'* crew had really only been crude merchant mariners, some of them pro-German, until war automatically enrolled them in the Naval Reserve, with which they never truly adjusted.

The *Cyclops* too had a demeaning captain. We tend today, and in this author's opinion quite wrongly, to gloss the character of William Bligh by showing that he was not like the brutal film incarnations as played by Charles Laughton or Trevor Howard. Be that as it may, the master of the *Cyclops*, George W. Worley, *was* a real life version of those dramatized roles. He had been hated. William Bligh was nothing compared to him. He had a brutal, bizarre and, just before this final voyage, an unchecked reign of terror. On the last major voyage trouble came to a head. Forty of his men took the brazen step to sign a petition calling for an investigation. They accused him of drunkenness, brutality, and being unfit for command. Most of the men, and all of the contention, were still aboard when the *Cyclops* sailed on her final voyage from which she and any shred of flotsam never returned to tell the tale.

These facts cannot be divorced from the *Cyclops'* outback route. For the first time since the problems aboard started coming to a head, she had a course far from any Navy influence or fleet duties. It was a tropic cruise. She had left Rio de Janeiro, a distant, exotic place back then, then she would sail along jungle coasts of South America, then hug the islands of the West Indies until coming off the coast of Florida en route to her destination of Baltimore. There were to be no stops on her route home. Yet there was. An unscheduled stop.

The great vessel had unexpectedly put in a call at the West Indian island of Barbados. Here her gruff captain, George Worley, surprised the US Consul, Brockholst Livingston,[1] with a request for him to pay for more supplies. The consul was irked and immediately disliked Worley in manner and appearance. It was so palpable that Livingston warned his superiors that it may have tainted his dramatic conclusion about the vessel's ultimate fate. After the vessel was reported overdue, he investigated and discovered that Worley had taken on more supplies than he could possibly have needed. On top of this, he realized his feelings were not isolated. He heard a startling rumor from the dockworkers, those who had had the closest contact with the men who had sailed her. They said a failed mutiny and an illegal execution at sea.

Despite confidential memoranda trying to temper any initial overreaction to Livingston's secret communiqué, Office of Naval Intelligence's opinion continued to be molded toward the worst possible scenario. Interviews with dozens of officers and men who had sailed the vessel before, and a close investigation of George Worley, uncovered a volatile atmosphere had been brewing on the vessel for quite some time. The ship had been a nest of pro-Germans— America's current enemy— and the ship's eccentric and brutal captain was the perfect trigger to set off a tinderbox.

In addition, several elements came together to create greater suspicion. There was no bad weather. There were no enemy submarines so close to the Americas. And most of all there was no SOS. And this was unusual. Since wireless, no US Navy ship had sunk without getting off an SOS, no matter how terse. Why should the *Cyclops* be first? More specifically, why should the ship disappear? After all, we do not speak of a sinking. There was no wreckage. More to the point perhaps, why

---

[1] Apparently the same as Charles L. Livingston.

should a vessel about which the last US official to have had contact with the captain and ship, and as a result feared mutiny, be the first to send no SOS *and* vanish?

The question kept repeating through Navy investigators' minds. Altogether Office of Naval Intelligence, FBI, and State Department investigations amassed a huge dossier of interviews with former crewmen, officers, diplomatic attachés, official scrutiny of weather reports, loading reports, German communiqués, and everything else they could lay their hands on to try and shed any light on the matter.

But although this dossier is massive, it is only a collection of hundreds of strings where the ends were never tied off, for the end of the war stifled the investigation. The Navy's attitude had already been stoked by the most sensational theory— treason. When after the war the vessel was not found in a German port, as had long been rumored, the Navy's reaction was to close the case. The reaction, however, was not in response to the evidence but to the quashing of the most popular theory.

Such an ironic epilogue to what the whole nation had long suspected was the most sensational saga in United States maritime history only caused the massive amount of documentation to be archived. Original investigators either went on to other assignments or were released from service. As information continued to leak in over the years, it leaked into various hands. All the information was therefore never balanced by any one investigator. Had that been the case, some of the belated information would have stirred the old worries of mutiny and treason.

Today it is possible to do what the various investigators could not do. The Navy meticulously preserved everything. Thousands of pages are in boxes 1068-1070 of the Modern Military Branch of the National Archives. After examining these documents, the original Navy investigators' questions seem even more pertinent now. I discovered why the Navy had great interest in the case behind-the-scenes long after the war was over. Though their response could no longer be refined, for years they took seriously any slim report of a survivor. I first found these documents in 1992. Now 22 years later I am able to put back together much of the final voyage of the U.S.S. *Cyclops* and its aftermath.

Outside of the Bermuda Triangle, history has only given us two belated epilogues. In 1975, a diver reported he had come accidently upon an unknown wreck off the Carolinas. He described it in picturesque terms— a large ship conveniently sitting on its keel with tall derricks encrusted with coral rising from the deck; the image of the *Cyclops.* In response, debunkers of the Bermuda Triangle dug up an old 1919 newspaper column blaming the loss on a gale off the Carolinas. The gale was no secret. Though after the brouhaha had faded, some newspapers may have tried to anticlimactically blame the gale— second stringers are notorious for their lust for irony— the Navy knew the *Cyclops'* speed and knew she could not have been near the area of the gale at the time in question. Anybody familiar with how a ship sinks knows that it rolls under the surface, the force of the sweep ripping off the superstructure. Both the gale and the diver's impossibly dramatic image become only ludicrous footnotes in the true pursuit of the *Cyclops'* fate.

Other than that, in 1969 there was a little piece in the *Naval Institute Proceedings* that stirred the old fears. *The Cyclops Mystery* was written by Conrad A. Nervig. He had been a passenger officer on the voyage south to Rio and was there transferred, thus being spared the return voyage on which the *Cyclops* vanished. Although Nervig wrote of his voyage 51 years after-the-fact, his article was anchored by his terse notes in his daily log. Worley fancied himself a "bucko" captain, and Nervig tells us that he should have been born 100 years before, for he was "a perfect example" of those "tyrannical sailing-ship captains who considered their crews not as human beings but only as a means of getting their vessels to the next port." But he was a comical, gaunt incarnation of one. He would visit Nervig nightly on the Dog Watch dressed only in his woolen underwear and wearing a derby hat and poking about with his walking cane.

Unbeknownst to Nervig, this burlesque image was added to by other sailors. Worley was not just eccentric. He was increasingly coming under the influence of alcohol. Comparison with the voluminous and thitherto unpublished papers at the National Archives proves Nervig's memory to have been quite reliable. Yet though reliable, it is not detailed. But when added to the recollections of many seamen, which were interviewed as a part of the Navy investigation, a horrifying picture of Captain Worley and life aboard is formed.

The voices that will speak to us are not substitutes. They are those who like Conrad Nervig speak firsthand of their travails aboard the *Cyclops* and as such they speak not by substitution but by proxy for those lost. None who vanished with the *Cyclops* have left us a word of the final voyage. The great, lumbering vessel was carrying the fleet mail home, and all accounts, from every man jack aboard every ship in Admiral William Caperton's South American squadron, were silenced. There is no letter home, opened after the ship vanished, to clue us in to some vignette or detail. None are left today, parchment in hue and ink faded, the edges of the paper accumulated as dust in the folds, blowing away effervescent like sand when opened, embodying the faded hopes and dreams of lads gone now 95 years ago.

Not all who will speak are those who had been transferred and spared. Some of those lost speak to us from earlier voyages. From the voyage off France, the one that had caused the men to take action, Quartermaster James Ryan of Virginia wrote his wife. She showed his parents. They were shocked to see him declare contemptuously that his "skipper" was a "Hun." Nothing had changed aboard when the vessel sailed off into oblivion. The last thing Consul Livingston picked up from Barbadian dock gossip was that the crew referred to their hated master as a "damned Dutchman"— a term back then which did not mean a Hollander but a Deutches Man . . . a German.

For all intents and purposes Worley was of English heritage and born in San Francisco. He appeared a coarse oaf who walked with a genteel mahogany cane. But combined evidence tells us he was actually far more subtle than his appearance and just plain lucky to be spared exposure by the mores of the Auxiliary Service at the time. It was indeed a different era, and Worley knew enough to always use an intermediary to do his brutal and often bigoted will. On one of his earlier commands, the *Abarenda*, it took the gross beheading of his evil toady to stop his "deep water style" of terror. Worley was blackmailed, tried for negligence, found innocent, but he stormed out of the Navy Auxiliary. He soon came back. Now, just prior to the *Cyclops'* final voyage, he had been called before the mast again. He said this would be his last voyage. He said he was leaving the Navy. He quickly sold his home and car.

The potential of all this can only be appreciated by understanding this unique period in time, for all actions will sprout from the rich nutrient that is the stage— the Auxiliary Service of the US Navy in 1918. It was not the US Navy of today. It was a melting pot of merchant seamen and barnacled South Seas skippers. But the most colorful part of the backdrop to the story of the *Cyclops* is the moment in time. The adventurous days of the old high seas were meeting a mechanized world, but they were not yet conditioned by that world. It was still the seas of the High Barbary. The square-rigger was no longer king. The barkentine was all but extinct. But foc's'le still served and quarterdeck still ruled. Ships were cold, dank dreadnoughts with old teak decks and mean masters. They belched coal as their fuel. They needed coal, and the Navy needed whoever could handle and ship it well. The Navy needed ships like the *Cyclops* and, more importantly, it needed its hodgepodge crew and "bucko" captain.

1

BETWEEN A GIANT STRIDE

"The Cyclops was the most seaworthy of her sister ships, but she rolled to wide angles."
— Capt. W.J. Kelton, *Neptune*

THE U.S.S. *CYCLOPS* MOVED AMIDST THE fleet like a giant lobster. Her tall derricks for loading coal looked like hideous talons. They appeared to reach out and clutch the warships. There she would remain latched onto them until those claw-like derricks pushed her off and she ambled with her ungainly rolls port and starboard to another warship, clutched it and began the process all over. Though long and sleek, the *Cyclops* was not elegant. At 520 feet, she was as big as any of the dreadnaughts that she serviced, but she was the ugly duckling— coal stained derricks, deckhouse, and a bridge that looked more like a prison tower standing on giant stilts.

Well named the ship was— a one-eyed monster. Though she had a crew of over 225 men, the *Cyclops* had like her namesake only one eye, and this was her captain, Lt. Commander George W. Worley. Here high on the flying bridge he strode back and forth, seldom ever treading beyond its elevated confines. Though the *Cyclops* was one of many Naval Auxiliary supply ships, she stood unique and independent of them all because of her master. Photos of the officers of other ships might show them proudly stiff in Navy uniforms; wrinkled perhaps, but at least looking Navy. Photos from George Worley's past aboard his ships might show a man with a predatory hawk-like visage. Such an appearance was so natural for him he could have this look even while in a casual stance. There was something about his looming size and bull neck; something about his Navy tunic unbuttoned and his t-shirt clinging to his Brahman figure. Something about weasely officers by his side, one with tunic unbuttoned and a blackjack stuck in his waist.

A photo such as this, sepia with age, brings to life the voyages of the U.S.S. *Cyclops*. It is a brief step in the path of George Worley's career in the US Navy Auxiliary Service and also a brief glimpse through a very narrow window in the march of progress at sea. Few then, and even less today, would know what the Naval Auxiliary Service was as opposed to the Navy proper. It represented the withered end of a long tradition of trader warships. *Cyclops* wasn't owned by the Navy but by the Bureau of Navigation, and her hands aboard were civilians. She went where the government chartered her whether it was to service the fleet or to haul the most ignoble cargo.

The early 20th Century was, like the US Naval Auxiliary Service, a strange hybrid. It was at the cusp of the modern world. Yet it was not that world. Mindset and machinery are vastly different things. Flesh and blood are not hammered into existence on the anvil. The spirit of progress that infected this age flowed like a torrent, but as with all torrents it left eddies in the side of its current where progress encountered obstacles— old attitudes, tried and frankly obsolete methods.

The sea, by its very nature, was the greatest obstacle. The sea is never at the cusp of progress. It is an unavoidable medium for transportation. For fishermen it is a field for reaping without ever having sowed. For some nations it is also a moat of protection; for others it is a wall that must be assaulted. Ultimately, the sea dictates the design of ships, and the confined nature of a ship dictates life aboard. This life is often very narrow, and it often creates very narrow minds. Purpose is to tend the ship and make sure she is able to perform her mission.

By the end of the 19th Century the industrial revolution had finally rendered the old wooden sailing ship obsolete and replaced it with steel, cold hard steel. But caged within these steel mammoths was the old world of the sea— a defined caste system and a stifling hierarchy.

Lawlessness comes with isolation, and a ship skirts one while she sails through the other. Long before Marconi was able to tether a ship to her owners by invisible wireless signals, captains alone had bent a crew to their will and held the ship together, even on voyages 10,000 miles from home, from a friendly port, or passing ship. These captains today might have first learned the sea as a cabin boy aboard the old sailing schooners, whalers, and barnacled old packets. It was not that long before when steel steamships were the oddity. Now they dominated the sea, in appearance at least. But as with their quickly obsolescing but far more elegant cousins, the master was the master, the last absolute monarch left on Earth.

Some captains had not lost their barkentine view of seamen. They were runaways, outcasts, thieves, ex-convicts, losers, and those that could adapt to this environment had become "leather monkeys." Not a very grand species, leather monkeys. They were fit only to climb the ratlines and tend the sails at the barking orders of their officers. Steel mammoths may no longer have had ratlines upon which to crawl, but the species was made to adapt to other duties. Instead of catering to the wind, they were set to cater to steam, which meant engines instead of masts, oil instead of rope, coal instead of canvas.

Steam, that ethereal wisp, was the soul that created a new body. It had freed the Navy from the wind. Warships thus need not look much like an evolution of the old sailing ships of the line. They became strangely archaic. In truth, they looked like old Roman galleons. Up toward the bow a tall pilot house was like the battle tower, now with a tall mast on it and a very visible crow's nest tickling the heavens. Around or on this pilot house was a platform where the captain could clutch the railing and direct the raging battle action. Steel casements amidships opened to reveal gunners feeding their thundering cannon. They were no longer mounted on a wood cradle with wheels as in Nelsonian days. They were bolted in the deck and mounted on a swivel.

Only one historical event gives us a window into this unique period— the Spanish-American War of 1898. The US Navy's "Great White Fleet" earned its name from its color. The hull was painted white, the color of peacetime. They sported ramming bows and were trimmed with gilt bronze bald eagles or red-white-and-blue battle shields of the Republic. Red trimmed the waterline. Above deck all of it was painted mustard yellow— smokestacks, bridge, masts, crow's nests. Round, mustard colored gun turrets revolved their huge black cannons over old fashioned teak decks.

It must have been a beautiful sight to see these luxurious steel galleons cleave a blue-green sea, the raging bald eagles emerging from the froth that licked the ornate bow and screaming in blood lust at the enemy. Bursts of smoke and thunderous echoes added to the pageantry. But it was war, whitewashed and painted many colors under bright, beautiful battle flags and belching clouds of dirty coal.

The US Navy of World War I evolved not from the tall ships but from this strange interlude of gilded Roman galleons. Ships only became bigger. They would remain the colors of wartime— gray and bleak. The beauty was gone. But the mentality remained the same— broadside to broadside, scrub the decks, quarterdeck over foc's'le.

Ritual too was unaltered. At dress, the officers looked as if they should be mounting the poop of an old colonial frigate or man-o-war. They had their folded bicorn hat with its gold braid. Their long blue coat extended to their knees, corners no longer pinned behind to form tails as in the Revolutionary days but the shoulders still cringed under enveloping and broad gold epaulets. Their pants were no longer pantaloons with tight hose showing off their calves, but officers still slung their cutlass by their side.

At war they were far more utilitarian. The tunic was blue, snug, with a mandarin collar, and only down to the hips. No epaulets. The rank was in little gold insignia thereon. Pants were blue, shoes black, and the hat was the small bell crown, and the visor small and a glossy black. In the tropics the entire ensemble was white. To this day, the US Navy keeps to this color scheme and tradition.

This, the daily uniform, fit much better aboard an Auxiliary ship like the *Cyclops*. Coal stains were not so ignoble on it. Grease and grime did not soil tradition. It could be unbuttoned to help cool the Dante's inferno the ship would become or, for some officers, to make it better to reach the blackjack tucked in their belt.

By World War I the US Navy, you might think, would not be permeated by such a crude lot. This was and always had been the Navy of John Paul Jones. This was the Navy of gallant lads and gentleman captains of the Academy. True though this is, the US Navy of wooden walls and ironsides in its day had been little different than other navies in commissioning and giving charter to privateers in time of war. Privateers were their own strange hybrid. They were pirates for a cause, cavorting for a single patron, profiting off any enemy; their saltwater captains, their rummy crews, turned into respectability by the Republic's commission.

It was not such an oddity therefore that in the late 19th Century, with a generation of admirals and captains and politicians all from the days of wooden walls and schooners, that the Navy should form the Naval Auxiliary Service. Not for war. God forbid that a huge battlewagon should be entrusted to a gallant clodhopper. But sailorly skills, no matter how they were come by, were of great need. South Seas tramp skippers were its captains. Old seamen of 'A roving's been my ru-i-n' were its crews. They wore the uniforms of the US Navy, if lucky to get them, but their cradle had not been the academy nor was a parchment commission their charter. They were part and parcel every bit of the old privateer stock, but in this modern world they need not be given a cutlass by charter. They were rather incongruously given an oilcan and coal derricks for feeding the fleet. A crass, crude, boiling pot of contention was given a Navy gray whitewash, with officers little better than press gangers of bygone days.

In appearance it worked. Only during refueling did the two meet. It was then a rehearsed, impressive sight. The *Cyclops'* huge derricks would swing over with agile swiftness huge "clamshells" of coal. Dirty streaks of black dust fizzled in their wake and floated down. Everything and everybody was soiled with coal. "Soup hounds" passed around coffee and hotdogs, both coated and tainted with the taste of coal. *Cyclops* continued to feed. The warship continued to ingest. Men aboard both ships worked furiously, except the band aboard the warship. They sat on a gun turret and played on while the soup hounds passed around coffee and hotdogs here too.

By the second decade of the 20th Century, the Naval Auxiliary Service was an integral but not yet integrated part of the new, fast Navy. Its skin and bones rubbed shoulders with the ornate grandeur of the new Navy— a Navy of brass bands playing while refueling— but its flesh and mind was dangerously of many nations and yet no nation. The sea gives birth to no sons. It does not command loyalty. It flies no flags. Only ships fly flags, and at a time like the early 20th Century modern travel had created a flux of world immigration, largely to America. Despite the flag any ship flew, the crews were a melting pot of many nations.

Perhaps no other navy was as inviting or as tolerant of this as the US Navy, for in the early 20th Century the United States was itself basically a hodgepodge of many nations. At least 15% of its citizens were foreign born, and one may safely guess that an even greater percentage of foreigners were in the Service. When America went to war with Germany in 1917, thousands of Germans were in the Navy and Auxiliary Service. Along with them were Greeks, Turks, Russians, Japanese, Britons, Spaniards, Italians, "Asiatics" and Filipinos. Every accent and language rang over the decks of US ships. Every nation had its dregs wearing improvised uniforms of the US Navy.

With the advent of World War I, the Naval Auxiliary began to experience changes. As a body it was automatically enrolled in the US Naval Reserve Force. But the Navy also saw fit to take precautions and transfer and spread out as much of the Auxiliary men as possible. Desertion had been a problem for the US Navy in times of stress, largely because of the many foreigners within it. Commodore Dewey's Asiatic Squadron, for example, had lost about 150 men, mostly foreigners, before the Battle of Manila Bay in 1898. And this had been the only foretaste the modern Navy had before World War I of how some froth might boil over from the melting pot.

Scattering and replacing created another bit of incongruity. It brought actual Naval officers into the ranks of the Auxiliary. It is not so remarkable then that some well-connected lads found themselves serving aboard the *Cyclops* rather than on the other end of battleship broadsides. Such a lad was Carroll G. Page. He was an Ensign now, the first rung on the officer ladder. He was young, chubby face, and, of course, circumspect due to the fact he was a Senator's grandson. Not just a Senator. He was the grandson of Vermont's self-made hide dealer Carroll Smalley Page, who was now Chairman of the Senate's Naval Affairs Committee. His name may not have had the distinction of the new Second Officer, Clarence Roosevelt Hodge, but both had to adjust equally to life aboard the Navy's finest modern collier.

Adjustment wasn't necessary just because of the crude lot of "feather merchants" who were throughout the ranks. George W. Worley was at the center of everything that worked and did not work on the *Cyclops*. Few spoke of their surly master aboard, but no one was ignorant of his unique, eccentric personality. Like the Service, George Worley owed his step into the Navy thanks to the Spanish-American War when he with his ship, the square-rigger *St. Mark*, was pressed into service during the Battle of the Philippines in 1898. Through rumor, gossip, or even his own carefully placed storytelling, all knew Worley had started out at sea as a 15 year old cabin boy. He was from San Francisco— a seafaring town— and he was in every sense of the phrase from the world of Jack London.

San Francisco was a boisterous boom town in the late 19th Century— especially the aptly named "Naughty Nineties." It had gotten rich off being the main port of entry into California from all the ships tapping the China trade. It also had something better than Sutter's Creek. It straddled the main shipping road for the gold leaving California's Gold Rush. Frisco's rolling hills were dotted by huge and frankly ostentatious Victorian mansions. It was the Venice of the time: a sea power with coarse merchant princes.

Naturally, San Francisco had its proletarian side, too. And one, perhaps far more of historic interest, was the Barbary Coast. The Barbary Coast was the docks. Everything a ship or crew needed, everything a shipper needed, could be found in this crude district on the Bay. The name was no doubt derived from the infamous Barbary pirates of old and the very connection of the name with barbarism. Very apt indeed. There was nothing exotic about it unlike with Chinatown next door. The architecture was unadorned brick wall and old west wooden porches, and its smell was tar, brine, and boiling fish. Horses trotted by the colorful street cars that would eventually become cable cars. Sailors waited about for a packet to Mandalay, Manila, Tahiti, or Zamboanga. More than one walked along with an eye patch and a few hobbled on a wooden leg. They wore striped shirts, dark hats, thick pea coats, and sooty and sweaty kerchiefs were tied around the neck.

George Worley wasn't one of them. But he catered to them. He owned a tavern that declared him on its colorful shingle to be a sea captain. Seafarers naturally put in here. Lewd dance girls plied their trade to bawdy piano tunes. But Worley was little good in business. He drank as much as his guests and he was indifferent as to how he balanced the books. Jeremiah Bourk, who will figure in the story later, got his first impressions of Worley here. "When I first saw him, he was attempting to manipulate cards while I was watching the game in which he participated in his own saloon. His reputation for honesty and integrity was poor."

Yet the tavern was a great meeting place for him too. Here, amidst the dregs skulking over a dram, he made his leap back into the sea. It sounded far more profitable than being a saloon keeper. He studied navigation, but never did very well. A sea captain dropped dead during one particularly revealing high kick of the Can Can, and George Worley seized the opportunity. He knelt down. After a careful survey with shifty eyes to see if the coast was clear, he removed the captain's papers and slipped them into his own breast pocket. Perhaps that's an un-forgivably tongue-in-cheek tableau I have painted for the reader, but we will learn it is not altogether inaccurate, though understandably a bit figurative. George Worley was dead, you see, and Fred Wichman, the crusty saloon keeper of "Captain Wichman's Roadhouse" became George W. Worley, and by a stroke of fate he ended up in the Navy Auxiliary, a night school navigator with his past completely unverified.

But the Barbary Coast and its dockside tavern standards would follow and dog his commands. The incident aboard the *Abarenda* in 1908 is just one case in point. Now given his first command, the night school navigator had set it all in motion when he made a big noise about wanting to run his ship "deep water style" and that he needed a "bucko" mate. We have an idea of Worley's standard for bucko first mates from the days when he was First Mate to Captain Shunliffe on the U.S.S. *Nero*. Henry Haley remembered him: "He was the worst excuse of a man that could be imagined unless you could compare him to noble Kaiser Wilhelm. He was overbearing and very brutal to his men, a big bull neck German." For the *Abarenda*, Worley got what he wanted, another German, Witchardt by name—one of the vilest men in the Service. But the results didn't end with the First Mate's head rolling out of the machine shop. The macabre beheading affected Worley's life at sea thereafter. Scuttlebutt said that the man responsible was really "lying in wait" for Worley and got the First Mate by mistake. Whatever the truth of it, thereafter Worley festered on his bridge. He was given command of the *Cyclops* fresh off the slips in 1910, but still he had not changed his routine. He slept and ate in his emergency cabin adjacent to the bridge rather than his larger and formal cabin aft where he was more vulnerable.

The years 1908 and 1914, the beginning of The Great War, were separated by a major disaster, the sinking of the *Titanic*. Yet it had not changed George Worley's maverick ways. His radioman was real USN Navy. Worley hated the regular Navy. He got in a tiff with the radioman and cashiered him from the ship. Many times after that he would have no radioman on duty— illegal after the *Titanic* sank in 1912. After war was declared, it was potentially dangerous for any neutral ship, such as a US supply vessel. U-boats could easily misidentify any ship and sink it. But Worley still hadn't changed. As late as 1915 he still commanded the ship his way. On one occasion he even chased all of his men and officers off the bridge, placed "an ignorant Greek seaman" at the helm and commanded the ship on through the night wherever he desired to go.

It is amazing that a man who was so little liked and given to such odd vagaries continued to command such a key supply ship. It is perhaps a testament to how separate the Auxiliary Service was from the real Navy that no superior knew of Worley's eccentric way of command. On paper he looked quite good, except for some strange glitch in 1908 when he had left the Service for a short time before coming back and being reinstated. If wisps of the Witchardt beheading or anything else still reached superior's ears, it was over pipe yarns and tales of the sea sort of thing. If any of them believed the rumors they could shrug them off, for the truth behind them could be Worley's own notorious sense of humor. It is most certain none were ignorant of this.

On one notable occasion in 1910 he made Fleet news when it got around that he kept a tame lion on board. The hoax, begun by Worley himself to scare his crew, finally reached the Bureau of Navigation's ears. He was sent a written order to put it ashore. He was always making jokes, and no doubt his jokes diluted the truth of the disturbing stories that constantly filtered from the ship's crew.

The unique confection of his humor, brutality and eccentricities had yet another ingredient. George Worley was a heavy drinker. He had his own concoction called "Deep Sea Punch" and drank it when he wanted. On one occasion he came aboard the USS *Hannibal* while at anchor in Boston and threatened to clean up the deck with her captain, R.G. Easton. Executive officers calmed him down and told him that the captain wasn't aboard. One, Lt. Burkhart, had served with Worley before. He escorted him into town and dutifully hung off him until reasonably sober. However, a better prospect soon appeared— a young paymaster. He hooked up with him and they left together.

Captain Worley didn't make many friends. He was an aloof and taciturn man, but he stayed in good with his paymasters. If this caused an eyebrow to be raised in others, as it did in young Lt. Burkhart, it would later when that paymaster was indicted for embezzlement. He would become only one in a line of paymasters who would have "difficulty" with that same charge.

Supplies were always short aboard the *Cyclops*. There wasn't enough food to go around for the men and, if rotten, it was still cooked. Barbary Coast bookkeeping was certainly expert at the art of chicken tracks. It would take the Navy quite a bit to later uncover disturbing implications of embezzlement. But was Worley a part of it or was it merely being done under his often inebriated nose? How many of the problems aboard the vessel were the direct result of Worley's bouts of drinking or indirectly as other officers and men took advantage of the situation?

This is the world to which, thanks to World War I, regular officers like Mr. Hodge and Mr. Page would find themselves. If either of them ever brought some disgruntled vignettes back home, they were no doubt shrugged off as interesting stories of life at sea. Senator Page might remind his young grandson that the Auxiliary was a rough place. The captain is the captain. Therefore young Page probably took Worley in stride. The crude old seadog was supreme, and that is how he had to accept it.

But the approach of World War I was bringing another and more volatile change to the Auxiliary Service. Before the United States entry, the nation had been torn over who was right in Europe, the Kaiser or the King. The average American really didn't know who was who on either side; nor comprehended the history of these European alliances and why the assassination in Serbia of an Austrian Archduke could start anything. However, the progressive Wilson administration wanted in on the British side. But the Monroe Doctrine laid down the United States' dogma about keeping Europe out of the Americas. Isolationists viewed any American involvement in "Europe's war" as hypocritical. This approach naturally was favored and accentuated by tens of thousands of pro-Germans.

World War I was not a war like World War II. There was no ideological agenda to purge races and conquer the world. No madman and party banners. It was an old fashioned war over rights and land. There had been no holocausts. There was no stigma upon the German people. Millions of Germans had immigrated and made up the backbone of Midwest farming.

In this case, America could afford to take sides. America had no real history of bad relations with Germany, but it had a long history of problems with Britain. Anglophobes were in large number in American politics and especially in the US Navy, the military branch most wary since it had to compete with the King's Union Jack. Why should America help Britain? Pro-Germanness was entrenched, and not at all disreputable. Many Americans, whether of German background or not, favored Germany over the British Empire. It was viewed as an industrious nation that could keep a dagger at the side of the all-powerful British Navy.

But the northeast of the United States, with its wealth and influence, and equally with its British heritage, favored the British. It also favored France, never forgetting Lafayette, though there was quite a paradox in combining the two since Lafayette and France aided the fledging America in its fight for independence from the British. The South, too, favored the British, for the heritage of the South was largely British, and

Britain had also unofficially favored the South in its war with the North in the late lamented US Civil War.

Although these areas were only a fraction of the United States, the pro-British had something in their favor: the bitterness of the war. The Germans had pioneered some very novel forms of "modern" warfare, which included huge zeppelins bombing cities. What a bizarre sight for a Victorian world, and for its elders who had been born to Dickens' London. We greet the refinements of technology today with a musing smile or shrug— attack by drones as an expected although unwelcomed advance in a SCI-FI world we've long prophesied in fiction. But World War I saw many new devices of death put into action for the first time.

Like the early 20th Century, like the *Cyclops* and the Auxiliary Service, World War I was a strange hybrid too. It was at the cusp of modern mechanized warfare and technological terror, but in mentality it was a European war as in days when aristocratic youths led their troops out in spring to sortie and all around engage in pitch battles, then retire for the winter. The mechanized potential was there for crushing blitzkrieg, but the old mentality locked WWI's soldiers in the dreaded trenches. Technology gave the armies gas and chemicals, but inexperience had not told them what the effects would be. It was a ghastly, mutant war, not really modern, not really the art or gallantry of Waterloo. It was bleak. Uninforms were bleak. Skies were daubed by the putrid color of gas warfare— yellow diluted with the breeze to a vapid, dead tope. Biplanes were the newest addition to war. They had no counterpart in anything before. Tanks were mechanized cavalry, but aircraft were horrid birds of prey, some designed with wings that mutely reflected bat wings. They were forever jousting overhead ack ack acking at an opponent.

Who indeed was right? The long debate, 3 years of it by 1917, had not answered it. Isolationists had huge support. And as much as factions favored sides, none favored them enough to go to war. But Germany had taken initiative. Its strategy called for the elimination of France first. This made Germany look like the aggressor, and a vigorous "information" campaign in America by the pro-British Wilson Administration made sure this is how Americans would view it.

The war became a "battle for democracy." The German Kaiser was vilified. The attitudes of social reformation that were sweeping the world were put to good use. Kaiser Wilhelm was made to look like the last remaining vestige of the old tyrannical despot. Home front photos showed your average "guy"— a newer term back then— holding a banner out his shop window: "Kick the Kaiser!" Cropped, the image was good for the War Service. But uncropped it showed how deeply Pro-Germanness was entrenched. The propaganda between 1914 and 1917 was more to motivate the country to help its old enemy of Britain as much as vilify a nation the United States had little contact with and no real reason to fight against.

Wilson's Committee on Public Information remained hard at work, but sadly Germany played a stupid hand. Despite the German Ambassador warning Americans not to take passage on the *Lusitania* before she sailed, many did. Off Ireland a U-boat would torpedo the ship. America was enraged. Soon it was behind the war enthusiastically. Wilson's concept of America's moral superiority ignited the nation and made any conscientious objector a traitor. When a renowned Columbia University professor, Henry W.L. Dana, objected to the war and Columbia's enthusiasm for it, he was sent packing. Another professor, Charles Beard, resigned in protest. Propaganda spared no triviality. Anybody sporting a German name was viewed as potentially disloyal. Even in cuisine, German staples became a no-no. Sauerkraut became "liberty cabbage"; hamburger "Salisbury steak." The war had been raging 3 years by the time the US entered it tardily in 1917. America took the British side. The Yanks were now coming "over there."

Propaganda would obviously not admit it, but what was left behind was still a divided nation; divided not only about being "other there" but about who was right. Propaganda was still too provincial to attack the true dangers of entering war late and for trumped-up reasons. Rather in this humorous and popular incarnation— accompanied by the good old Victrola— it merely drum-beated anti-Germanness.

With an Apology to "Hoch Der Kaiser"
Contributed by a disgusted Americanized German
(To be sung in Rag Time)

GOTT ALMIGHDY VILHELM

Behold der Great Kaiser tremendous und gruff,
Mit his furious mustaches pointed abuff;
To remind efry creature upon German sot,
Dot he is der Kaiser, py Chesus py Gott

He determined to rule, and he took a notion,
All people vot lif on his side off der earth;
To chase efry kicker right into der ocean,
Unt to make his enemies simply a dearth.

Oh he's a rethot potentate,
Dis mighdy man of great estate;
He does not pause a little bit,
To let us know he's all of it.

Now ven der Kaiser makes a speech,
He doesn't holler, shout or screech;
But, mit aspect shtern unt Shtubborn vill,
He tries to all der people thrill;
To set all lands in great commotion;
Unt rattle up der mighdy ocean.

I am der Mighdy Kaiser off you all,
Ven I open vide my mout you come unto my call.
Chehovah he discovered me unt set me right in motion,
Unt you who cannot see der point most chump into der ocean.

Vell did Kaiser rushed right into battle,
Mit his bristling mustaches unt cannons rattle;
A flock of mighdy big hot air balloons;
Chiant caterpillar enchines und pontoons,

An amazing swarm of Uhland lancers,
Unt other sorts off fancy prancers.

Now dot Kaiser he did soon find out,
Dot der vere udders who could do some shooting,
To put his soldiers in a rout,
Und send his cohort homevard scooting.

Dot mighdy mustache is now drooping,
For tings haf happened thick und fast;
Der var Gott to der rear is trooping,
Und vondering if his chob vill last.

Vell, after dis war dere comes Democracy,
To knock out Kings und Aristocracy;
To queer der chob of being Kaisers,
Und udder humbug curtain risers.

Bah! dis war is monkey business, a bumb-geschaft.
Dot rattles up der people, und makes dem all go daft.
Ven it iss over den der Kaiser he must go,
Und give to all der peoples a half vay decent show.

Funny, yes, with its pidgin German; but as a vanguard of action it was horribly naïve. It was very unlikely it was actually from an "Americanized" German. Equally improbable was the footnote that "The guy who got the above out of his system died the next day"— ostensibly indicating death in battle. It was aimed at the heartland. It tried to incite old feelings amongst German immigrants who had had a bad encounter with the German nobility.

Anti-German culture cartoons, however, were missing the mark by a mile. Pro-Germanness extended far beyond ethnic borders. Isolationists represented a broad spectrum of Americans who didn't think America had any business in Europe. Britain was such a world empire that is seemed ridiculous that America should help it. We could not be fighting for democracy with the Czar as our ally. He was the last autocrat left in this world. Even the Russian people were rebelling against him.

Pro-German sentiments had not been disloyal before the war. Now that the US was in the war, those sentiments had naturally not stopped. They were expressed more diplomatically. Those who had been openly Pro-German before war made it plain that they were always for America. They simply were not for Britain.

Yet Pro-Germanness was so feared by Wilsonian propaganda— a reflection no doubt of how they knew the war was trumped— that even this compromise was ardently condemned. The War Service published an article by Herbert Quick that rather arbitrarily and vociferously proscribes what now constituted a Pro-German. "A pro-German is a man who, by private or public utterances, stands in the way of a wholehearted prosecution of this war and the defeat of the German will to conquer . . . many individuals say they are for America, but none of them say they are against Germany. He who is for us is Against Germany. He who is not against Germany, tooth and nail, in this war is not for America. You can tell the pro-German by another test: If he is against France, or against Italy, or against Russia, he is pro-German . . . The enemy of Great Britain is pro-German. The enemy of Russia is pro-German and anti-democratic. The enemy of Italy is against America. The enemy of France is lost to every claim of patriotism . . . Do not let these pro-Germans poison the atmosphere in your locality by slandering our allies without challenge."

The problem with Wilsonian propaganda was that not only did its ardor reveal how deeply divided the nation was, it was aimed only at Anywhere USA— encouraging people in their "locality" to intimidate others who really couldn't do anything to hamper the war effort anyway. It wasn't aimed at the 15% who knew what Europe was like. They least of all were going to be taken in about the battle for democracy, not with Russia, Britain and Italy, all monarchies, as allies. And by not taking into account the foreign 15%, propaganda did not take into account a large part of those who could make a difference.

The greatest danger was within the Fleet and within the cruder Auxiliary Service with its mongrel background. Bigotry in the Auxiliary formed along the lines of old and bitter alliances. Turks paired off with Germans, both allies in World War I thanks to the Sultan's agreement with Berlin. Greeks would spy on Turks, their hated enemy, and French and Germans would clash. Paradoxically, these louts and mountebanks were more in tune, even firsthand, to Europe and its age old alliances. The overwhelming enthusiasm for the war in America, despite the average American's ignorance of what it was all about, would only breed contempt in the Auxiliary. The average American looked like a rube. Perhaps only in this would all the different factions below decks agree.

Subtlety became the key in dealing with the problems in the Fleet. Every ship's crew knew the dangers after the incident on the *Rochester*, in which a coal passer tried to betray the vessel. He was currently in prison in England awaiting his fate.

How would a crude old Barbary Coast seadog like George Worley, with one too many pints of grog in him, handle these problems? Certainly the contentions existed aboard the *Cyclops*, perhaps more than in other ships because of Worley's unique character and background. All were sure that Worley was pro-German and hated anti-Germans as much as he hated the regular Navy. Most of the old timers could recall he had changed his name from something German like Witzman, Wirpman, Weakman or Wieschman. Old timers, too, may have recalled the days when Worley openly lauded Germany.

Now it was hard to say. By this time, he had retreated into a world of shadows he knew well, that same world he had used to create Witchardt's brutal power and make it look different from his own. In this world Worley spoke by inference. He maintained aboard Ensign Hugo Schonof, who spoke with a notable German accent. Then there was the dreaded Ensign Stephen Konstovich. A brutal Quartermaster, Keller, did Worley's bidding. Worley was always fawned over by his loyal toady, the 'Turk.' Everybody knew the Turk. He had been aboard for 4 years. He was a Levantine named Cost George who had been born in Turkey, where his father still lived. This was a disturbing coincidence, yet another of the inferences aboard. Turkey, of course, was ally with Germany due to the Sultan's desire to grab back much of the Ottoman Empire he had lost.

Only one thing was certain aboard the ship, as certain at least as anything is in the world of odd shadows. Factions existed aboard the *Cyclops* which eradicated pro-Germans, and factions existed which harassed anti-Germans.

For example, one fireman, Schneidelberg by name, was thought so untrustworthy that he was removed from the engine gang by the Engineering Officer, Glenn Maguet, and brought topside to work where he could be watched more closely. Maguet was a rough and tumble Pennsylvania Irishman, and he didn't bother to slack his accent when he ordered the "Jerry" topside. His superior, fellow Irishman Sam Dowdy, had backed him up. If anything had caused Maguet caution it was that the cunning Austrian Konstovich was his next in command.

On the other hand, there was Walter McDaniel. He was a crass seaman able who took Quick's judgment to heart. He brought a .45 automatic aboard the *Cyclops* and tucked it in his berth "for use on the Germans in case the ship was taken." He was soon approached by other men, a group headed by Keller. They were indignant and said that they were told that he had turned them in. He said he had not, "but if things did not change, I will." Soon thereafter began petty persecutions of McDaniel. Finally, the ship's surgeon, Burt Asper, told him he was not well and convinced him to be transferred to the hospital on land. There McDaniel was surprised to find that the *Cyclops'* doctor had declared him insane. The hospital soon found him sane and released him.

There is a difference, of course, in the above two examples. McDaniel seems to have triggered a nerve that led to Captain Worley whereas Maguet and Dowdy acted on their own. Worley, the picayune seadog, who certainly hated Dowdy and knew in turn his Chief Engineer couldn't stand him, seems to have played no direct hand in the Schneidleberg affair. It was all quietly done. Schneidleberg (actually Herman Schmiedeberg) may actually not have been suspected of disloyalty but rather suspected of being Worley's snitch in the engineering force. The suspicion was a front for Maguet or Dowdy to get him transferred and at the same time to see if Worley would tip his hand. But Worley said nothing. Unbeknownst to them, however, he made sure Schmiedeberg remained aboard.

Yet to what extent had Worley been equally subtle in persecuting McDaniel? Burt Asper's hand in delivering McDaniel could infer that Worley had been behind it. Worley hated Asper. Asper also hated Worley. Worley hated Asper more. Like Hodge and Page, Burt Asper was a wartime arrival. But unlike Hodge and Page, Asper became proactive. As the medical officer, Asper had a certain immunity and unchallenged professional authority, especially when compared to Worley and his lower class accent of "yous" instead of "you." He would gladly spare a persecuted man just to spite his hated master. He was USN too and respectable Pennsylvania to boot, but this was just a thin veneer in Worley's eyes for a moon-howling drunk. Asper was quickly proving to be Worley's arch enemy aboard, and he was certainly the only man Worley feared.

It was hard to say whether the cruel old seadog had played a hand in persecuting McDaniel, but he was more than capable of concealing his shrewd will. From that world of shadows, he soon directed his will against his enemy Sam Dowdy. He would carefully conceal his biased hand from the crew when it came to Liberty, issuing Dowdy such strict orders that it basically didn't allow him to give Liberty to any Regular Navy man or draftee. The result was that Dowdy was becoming hated by the crew. As war loomed, more and more "Regulars" had been trickling aboard by assignment. Worley still hated the regular Navy. He wouldn't tolerate it in a radioman years before. He wouldn't tolerate it now that there were dozens and dozens of them. Dowdy had finally had enough of his encounters with his odd master. He transferred off, condemning Worley both in letter and to his next master, the former Lt. Burkhart now a Lt.

Commander and captain of the *Culgoa*, as a "drunk."

The extent to which the Fleet kept troubles to itself is seen in how even firsthand observers could not detect the tensions. William Wallace Swinyer, though not a great or academic writer, was allowed to travel with the fleet in 1917 just after war was declared. The result was his 1918 book, much in the mold of a Richard Halliburton travelogue— *A Squadron of the United States Navy: On a Friendly Cruise Around Latin America*. Swinyer shows he is aware of the large conglomerate of foreigners in the Navy, yet nothing but the Wilsonian propaganda's blunt antagonist/protagonist formula seems to register with him. Pro-German alone remains the concern. Swinyer even reproduces Herbert Quick's article in its entirety in his appendix. But he had little inkling of the extent to which Turks, Germany's allies, were throughout the fleet and could be used as a shield by pro-Germans. /

In July 1917, months after war was declared, Worley was on paper complaining to his superiors about how many of his trained Auxiliary men had been transferred and replaced by untrained USN inductees. On August 1, a muster was taken of the crew of the *Cyclops* by Bureau of Navigation. In it the remaining foreign crewmen of the Auxiliary Service were noted on a separate sheet. He was now down to only 28 men, a drop in the bucket compared to the crew of 225 plus. Of the names listed, 10 were from Turkey and 9 were from Greece, though a couple bore a Turkish name. Those listed as born in other locations come down to Greek or Turkish names, with rare exceptions. This list must reflect Worley's dwindling influence to keep key foreign crewmen aboard.[2]

It is not a coincidence that the Auxiliary men remaining represent Germany's allies. By no means could a Greek be relied on simply because of his name. Many were loyal to the abdicated King Constantine, brother-in-law to Kaiser Wilhelm, who had tried to keep Greece neutral but secretly in favor of Germany. The current schism in Greece can best be appreciat-

---

[2] Some of those listed as USNRF (United States Naval Reserve Force) had been Auxiliary men, so that Worley still had far more of his old crew than this suggests.

ed by the fact that Czar Nicholas, Germany's enemy, insisted Constantine, also his cousin, be kept on the throne. Constantine's royal cabinet had worked in favor of Wilhelm while his prime minister worked avidly for the allies.

Isolationists were right. This was Europe's war. Each nation involved had limited goals and conflicts of interest. Animosities for the most part were only decades old, and came and went, such as the Greek and Turkish wars. None of them had anything to do with that far and distant country of America and all the abstracts that Wilson's propaganda used to motivate a thoroughly uninvolved nation.

Turkey's involvement, for one, reflects the traditional mentality behind the war. Turkey wanted back land. Berlin wanted a sure route into Mesopotamia— Berlin-Constantinople-Bagdad. In a nutshell, this required the last vestige of the Holy Roman Empire— the Habsburgs in Austria-Hungary. Russia wasn't going to tolerate this. Russia had barely tolerated Turkey for centuries. They were the only two that had long term animosities. With Turkey's involvement came other factors. Britain and France had to go from former Turkish territory.

Turkey was then still the glorious Ottomans, successors every bit to the lands of the Eastern Roman Empire which they had finally conquered in 1453 when the walls of Constantinople, which had withstood the Gothic spears a thousand years before, fell at last to medieval cannon. But in spirit the Sultan claimed even more land, not just the land of the Romans but all that was bequeathed as the Caliphate from Mohammed— Arabia and all the Islamic lands east to all of North Africa west, including those parts that used to belong to the Western Roman Empire. The Ottomans, too, were quite a hybrid now. The army was little different than the days in which Darius the Persian, king of kings, could summon warriors from all nations of his empire in these same lands in order to fight that invading scoundrel Alexander the Great. The Sultan had Arabs, Egyptians, Armenians, Persians, Berbers, Greeks, Muslims, Hindu and Christians at his disposal. The army wore the bleak olive uniforms of the time, but officers had the red Fez, and the pageantry of the Ottoman court still saw the great twirled and bejeweled turbans of the days or *Arabian Nights* and Harun Al Rashid.

It was quite grand for the Sultan to sit in Constantinople and be Caliph of all Islam and appropriate and still use the title Caesar of Rome, but in substance the Ottomans were strapped. Since 1882 the Sultan had to suffer British occupation of Egypt, a prime holding of ancient Rome, then Islam's Caliphate, and then the Ottomans. The Khedive still ruled Egypt as the Sultan's nominal vassal, but he was also subservient to the British. It was a strange hybrid relationship too, fit for the world changing from empires to nations. The British Army remained, and the Khedive was largely a puppet waiting to break free and become a vassal again . . . though whose was not sure.

What an interesting hybrid the time was. Indeed, what an exotic time. The Sultan still claimed to be Caesar— the unbroken use of the title since Augustus in 27 BC. But the last Eastern Roman Emperor's niece married the first Czar. Thus for hundreds of years Russia insisted it was the successor to Rome, and the title Czar was merely their pronunciation of Caesar. The Russian imperial crown was a sphere, the sphere made popular by Roman emperors as signifying they ruled the world. In the Russian case it was cleaved in half, indicating the separation of the Western and Eastern Empires. Ever since Catherine the Great, Russia dreamt of taking back Constantinople, the great city of Christianity and restoring it as a summer capitol. Catherine was seen in portraiture striding the Black Sea, one foot in the Crimea, the other on Constantinople's infidel minarets of Islam. But then the Habsburg's too were the successors to Rome. They had been the Holy Roman Emperors, the successors to Charlemagne in the West. Since Napoleon did away with that in the early 19th century, they had to settle with being just Emperor of Austria-Hungary, but I'm sure they had hopes. It was the murder of a Habsburg that instigated World War I. But then again there was that upstart Prussian king, now the Kaiser— German pronunciation of

Caesar— that was Emperor of the united Germany.

With Germany besetting England, this was the Sultan's chance to rid the English from Egypt. The Sultan threw in his lot with the Kaiser. It seemed a wise choice. Alas, Ottoman glory was not up to it. Arab tribes rebelled in Arabia around Mecca, Janbo and Medina, now supplied by the British at Cairo and commanded by that enigmatic hybrid, T.E. Lawrence. By 1917, General Allenby was marching north through Palestine pushing the Turks back past Jerusalem and even to the entire sector capitol of Damascus. Lord Rothschild was already facilitating events that would lead to the Balfour Declaration which would pave the way for a homeland for the Jews back in Palestine. And there was the infamous Sykes-Picot agreement by which France and Britain would carve up the Ottoman Empire amongst themselves, each naively or completely indifferent to tribal borders and ethnic populations.

Geopolitically, The Great War was certainly an interesting war. It was not a battle for empire but a battle between empires. But the battles weren't happening within the empires. The head nations of these empires— Britain, France, Germany, Russia, Austria— were fighting head on. Since the Napoleonic wars Europe had not had to suffer such depredations. But there was no swift advance as in Napoleon's time. Only Turkey was suffering invasion of its empire. It was being whittled away by Britain. A morbid, gray war was dragging the brighter banners of the past, along with the Sultan's silk turban and jeweled scimitar, through the mud. The Sultan had made a mistake.

The British, with their typical reserve, marched on, their king cousin to most of the hopeful Caesars. Germany was now beleaguered; Austria was in chaos; Russia was starving; the Ottoman's were retreating. In a year, 4 Caesars would fall. The last strings to a fabulous and ancient past would be cut. The British and French would grab what they could and, to everybody's dismay, the Bolsheviks grabbed all of "Holy Russia."

One thing had been turning the tides of war and making all this possible now— the uncouth American republic. Had it not entered the war, Germany would have been able to hold its own on the Western Front after knocking Russia out of the war on the Eastern Front. Pro-Germans and Turks, especially those in the Auxiliary and in America, had the most reason to be upset. America was responsible for turning the tide and, in their way, pro-Germans were helping this, especially those in the Service by doing their duty. America even entering the war was ironic, for American companies had violated neutrality many times to supply Germany just for a buck.

Now beleaguered, Germany's greatest ally was money. It was the only weapon it could get remotely close to America. The fear had always been there. Herbert Quick had ended his rancorous article with: "The world has in the past been conquered by traitors— oftener than it was ever by arms. The Mexican people fought each other into slavery by Spain. Let us not be bought by German gold into slavery to Germany."

There was more fear now in 1918. War's grim reality had disillusioned the nation. The ardor of the propaganda was now coming back to haunt those who were enthusiastic. This now allowed many to see that moral superiority had only been Wilson's thinly veiled self-righteousness. How many had to die for this? Wilson's barking Committee on Public Information would lose its teeth if the war continued and gas casualties continued to rise.

Pro-Germanness could arise in another form— a peace movement. After all, Russia had made peace with Germany. Certainly this potential was seen, and it contradicted Wilson's attitude of no compromise with the Germans. Those presses that favored a compromise, as Russia had finally achieved before pulling out of the war, found their presses confiscated and their offices closed. The very fact such presses had been seized showed to what extent America was souring quickly of the war, and how a peace movement was feared.

This was America in 1918. Deeply divided, and the effects of war only positioning the disillusioned and the pro-German on the brim of vocal resurfacing.

How indeed would an eccentric, brutal oaf like George Worley, the Barbary Coast saloon keeper, handle all the changes the complexity of the war would require? We are given a clue by one other change the war brought. It added inductees— ignorant American farm boys ill-trained and without even proper uniforms. They thought they were entering the same glorious service of John Paul Jones, but they were rather plunged below decks into a microcosm of international turmoil. Their baptism of fire was dealing with nationalities they knew little about and then trying to redress the grievances with the old seadog. Worley hated them the most. He hated the regular Navy. He hated oversight, and he hated any young American who liked to follow the sea and who had noble ideals about it.

The result came after the *Cyclops'* first voyage into the war zone off France. The crude Barbary Coast seadog hadn't handled it well at all. He had been called before the mast for being boozed through the submarine lines. Because of the results of this embarrassing Board of Inquiry, the *Cyclops* was kept in American waters. This is ironic, for this set her on her last voyage. The Bureau of Navigation's intent was to keep her out of harm's way in the war zone, but the reviewing officers could not look beyond the charges of drunkenness to see the more dangerous implications of sabotage and treason aboard. This nearsightedness set the *Cyclops* into the deepest nest of German sympathy in the Americas, with a goal to pick up the hottest cargo there was.

The irony, and even more the gravity of the decision, cannot be appreciated without knowing a little of what South America was like at the time. World news, of course, concentrated on Europe. For a touch of the exotic, there was coverage of Allenby in Palestine and Lawrence in Arabia. But just as exotic, and for the Navy an even more important sideshow, was South America. Yet it was a show that played on largely behind the curtains. Spies were everywhere. The German Imperial Navy raiders had in the beginning of the war tried to keep the sea lanes open in order to access the natural bounties of the rich soil. But the British Navy had proved too powerful and Germany too stupid. One too many Brazilian ships had been accidently sunk by U-boats. Brazil broke off relations with Germany and seized dozens of German freighters in every major port. Supplies now had to be brokered clandestinely through other nations, but it was a long and labored process, and Germany was now after the disastrous Battle of Jutland largely suffocating at sea.

Brazil was a part of this strange hybrid world. It was a nation of old whitewashed port towns picking at fabled and deep jungles. Legends of lost El Dorado connected with raucous Latin cabanas. So far as anybody knew, lost Indian cities of gold weaved in twirling vines just a mile off the jungle roads to the inland cities. Percy Fawcett was sincerely searching for them, believing that they would reveal the fabulous past of human prehistory. In truth, undiscovered tribes were still in the heartland of the Amazon. But one thing was discovered about Brazil: its massive natural resources seemed limitless. It became a battle of intrigue by much more practical explorers.

Officially Sao Paolo, the capitol, had declared the nation belligerent to Germany. It hailed the Monroe Doctrine and declared it had to stick with North America. All Americans had to stick together. But in substance Brazil was a nest of pro-Germans. Spies were thus able to watch their enemies' fleets close at hand, and German companies, fronting other names, could broker supplies to Buenos Aires, Argentina, a neutral country, and from there through stages to the Fatherland. Nothing so far had come to a head. Brazil didn't saber rattle too much, and its huge German colonies didn't really do much to stir things up. Malaise was met with equal malaise. But potential was there. It just needed to be ignited.

The coal passer on the *Rochester* was a fool to try his stunt near an allied power. But South America was a land where entire cities could be swallowed by the jungle. And it did not take going that far to be accepted in South America. "Simpatico" was everywhere and was probably one of the first words any American sailor learned.

It is not a coincidence that W.W. Swinyer was suddenly allowed to travel with the South American squadron of the fleet and write his travelogue. Nor is it a coincidence that anti-German appendices were placed therein. It is a reflection of the trouble and the fear of what could happen here successfully and nowhere else.

The map below, provided by Swinyer, was egregiously captioned as "Nearly All Americas are Anti-German, Map Shows." In reality, the black areas which showed the nations that had

declared war on Germany were both British and American protectorates— Belize and Panama. The shaded nations which had severed open diplomatic relations were teaming with sympathizers. Only Brazil would declare war on "the central powers" in 1917. Peru and Uruguay, though shaded here, were indifferent allies. History would show to what extent Argentina could be easily turned pro-German officially, though here marked in white indicating neutral.

What Swinyer and his ilk were trying to prove, though perhaps not so deftly, was that South America was not a plush Tahiti with Simpatico natives waiting to embrace mutineers or traitors. It was a ploy designed to work on ignorant seamen perhaps, like the engineer aboard the *Rochester*, but what effect would it have with seasoned seamen like those old louts of the Naval Auxiliary? Swinyer didn't understand anything about the Auxiliary Service. He was given his cruise as a guest on the flagship, the cruiser *Pittsburgh*. He knew nothing of the careers of the "feather merchants" turned naval officers that were throughout its ranks.

Of the Navy, Swinyer declared: "Beyond question Uncle Sam's enlisted men do average up better than any equal number of persons picked en masse from any walk of civil life, the church not excepted. You will not find in the navy any man, inclusive of Asiatics, who did not take sufficient interest in the country to learn its language; nor any whose chief concern is to amass money for expenditure in a foreign land; neither those who refuse to become citizens and sneak around denouncing the country that shelters them. Again, there are no 'I won't work' freaks, anarchists or blatherskites in Uncle Sam's Navy..."

Reading between the lines, it is clear how the regular Navy had a large foreign base; it is also obvious that Swinyer saw how the opposite of what he praised was a temptation. This glowing picture of loyalty, gleaned largely from a flagship crew, also gives us a portrait of the Auxiliary Service that is a little more unflattering by comparison.

It is quite clear that Swinyer also detected problems in the regular Navy. This is underscored by the advice that he now gives for the good of the Navy. "It is necessary for the government and each citizen to take a vital interest in the sailors not just in wartime but in peace too. Do this so as to disabuse the lads' minds from the sordid idea that this interest is mercenary." Swinyer doesn't tell us what motivated the attitude in the men, but it must have been wide scale.

Caricature of what they in Montevideo considered a typical American sailor during Admiral Caperton's squadron's stay off Uruguay. Reproduced by W.W. Swinyer.

This in itself would not necessarily be dangerous unless, of course, there was an element around that could exploit it for other ends, as indeed there was. Revolution was sweeping Russia. Socialism was and had been feared for decades. But Swinyer wasn't surgical enough for this. He had only one drum to beat. German gold and pro-Germans were a threat, and all these fears underlie his comments.

How bad was it? This is hard to say. Swinyer's typewriter keys are always pecking on egg shells. This is seen in how he gives us the most puritan gloss of a sailor's life ashore in South America. "Surround the enlisted men with at least so many good influences as they are now assailed by those that are bad and the morale of the navy will become vastly better. When sailor lads go ashore, weary from a prolonged cruise, the very gates of Hell in every port are thrown wide open and the forces there just shout for the boys. Surely it is the manifest duty of every good citizen to 'stand by' then. Just cut out the thought that sailors will be sailors and conceive of the fact that sailors can be men."

A more candid example of the Navy, especially the South American squadron and in particular the *Pittsburgh*, comes from contrasting the roll call of that ship, which Swinyer reproduced as a tribute, with the events that went on therein. The names of Moss Whiteside, Barney Devoe, James Coker, and Oscar Stewart are *inter alia* listed. They would later be connected by one tragic event. The former 3 were tried and found guilty of beating to death, or contributing thereto, the latter for suspected homosexual tendencies. Whiteside was to receive 15 years for not stopping it, Devoe life, and Coker was to be hanged. Along with them over 50 of their shipmates would be sent back to the States for transfer, 50 men who didn't think their mates deserved such punishment; *all fifty*, each one, regular Navy from a real warship.

Mr. Kenneth Murchison, a sales engineer for W.R. Grace & Co., had many US Naval officers over for dinner in Bahia, Brazil, that Christmas 1917. The events aboard the *Pittsburgh* had been big news. More than one officer said they would "hate to come North" on whatever ship was assigned to bring the men back for punishment. Murchison got a very disturbing feeling from the conversation. Each man, including himself, had traveled extensively in South America. Each knew of hidden lagoons and murky river mouths where huge ships could be hidden, towns and villages where fleeing crew would be welcomed. He would not be surprised if a mutiny here was more possible than anywhere else, and that if seized by mutineers such a ship could be "navigated off the track of the usual trade routes."

As fate would have it, *Cyclops* was to be the ship that was to bring this contentious group and the condemned prisoners home from Rio. She was scheduled to leave Hampton Roads, Virginia, on January 8, 1918, two weeks away from Murchison's festive dinner conversation, for the voyage south.

What indeed was the *Cyclops* like at this time? It is necessary to backtrack to August 1917. We must join the Board of Inquiry in session, for in a very true sense the voyage off France in the summer of 1917 is the starting point of the final voyage off the plush coasts of South America in 1918. The testimony gives us a detailed image of what life was like aboard the *Cyclops* through the words of those involved. The personalities, the antagonists and protagonists, and the same events, will resurface and replay again and again. For years to come, references would become more numerous and direct us back to the events recorded in this Board of Inquiry. The fears, too, inspired by these records would haunt the Navy and color each new discovery the investigation would turn up.

With this in mind . . . we begin

AUXILIARY SERVICE, U.S. NAVY
U.S.S. CYCLOPS.

From: The Undersigned,
To: Secretary of the Navy:

SUBJECT: Request for Board of Investigation on board
U.S.S. CYCLOPS

Sir:

It is requested that a board of investigation be held on board the U.S.S. CYCLOPS for the purpose of making known to the Secretary of the Navy that George W. Worley, Lieutenant Commander, U.S.N.R.F., commanding the U.S. ship CYCLOPS is, in the opinion of all the men who signed these specifications, morally and proficiently unfit to command a fighting ship, or a crew of fighting men of the United States Navy.

1. It is specified that Capt. Worley did call an enlisted man of the U.S. Navy a name that no man can bear and be born of a woman.

2. It is specified that on July 17, 1917 at about 9:00 P.M. Capt. Worley did come on deck apparently under the influence of intoxicating liquor.

3. It is specified that in so doing Capt. Worley has endangered the lives of fighting men of the U.S. Navy and risked the loss of a U.S. ship.

4. It is specified that while the U.S.S. Cyclops was at sea and in emminent [sic] danger of enemy submarines that Captain Worley was unfit for duty and therefore unfit to command a fighting ship or a crew of fighting men of the U.S. Navy at sea.

(SIGNED)

W.F. Howard, HA 1c	W.H. Duke, Oiler
J.F. Puckhaber, Mach	L. Waff, Oiler
S.G. Dowdy, Oiler	John Callahan, M.M. 1c
D.D. Hale, D. Std.	W. Roy Herbert, Oiler
W.E. Kight, M.M. 1c	Carl E. Clauson, Oiler
Harry Sherrard, F2c	J. B. McCormick, F 3c
R. Kyle, F 2c	Roy B. Swoveland, Oiler
J.E. Smith, fire 3c	Juan Guillermo, Messn
Charles G. Graves, F1c	Andrea Salerno, F3c
Geo. A. Langren, Q.M.1c	J.M. Daly, F1c

To Secy. Navy –

SUBJECT: Request for Board of Investigation on board
                      U.S.S. Cyclops

Anthony Glowka, F3c	John Butler F3c
Laurence Merkel, F3c	Laurence F. Robinson, Fire. 2c
Fred L. Waddell, F2c	H. Otis Ramsey, F3c
W. D. Ward, Fire 3c	L. C. Day. F 2c
T. Carey, F 3c	W.H. West, F 2c
A. Poff, F, 3c	W. A. Pope, F 3c
Lowman, D. E., F 3c	T. A. Lawrence, F 3c
J. O. Hall, F 3c	O. F. Hotchkiss, F. 3c
L. Minch, F3c	M. J. Elliot, F 3c
T. V. Lee, F3c	G. W. Smith, Sea 2c.

2

NOW HEAR THIS

"He treats us like dogs when sitting on deck, and never has a pleasant word and does not treat us like we were human."
—Roy Swoveland

THE PALMY WEATHER OUTSIDE MADE it stuffy and hot for the semi-secret Board of Inquiry cramped within. The only view of the Roads outside the Mess porthole was an uninviting Navy gray skyline of derricks and masts from all the various supply and military ships berthed in their positions. It was a jungle of pointed spires crisscrossed with communication and support wires; a dismal ornamentation, looking more like cobwebs streaked on a neglected, burned-out forest. The bright blue sky was veiled beyond by the thin smoke curling up from the smokestacks of the idle vessels, as if it were the last smoldering dirty haze of just such a blaze. The mood of such an inquiry, of course, did not allow for a happier interpretation of the view.

Between the gray walls of the ship's Mess were squeezed dozens of men in their dress whites. The Dias before them was a long Mess table at which sat an officer in his dress whites, flanked by a recorder and an assistant. Formality seemed out of place in such a scullery. Commander William Whitted's elevated position was more like the sprig of herb stuck fastidiously into the molten slob of last voyage's rotten stew.

The witness chair looked like a footstool before the lordly Dias. It stood isolated yet in the midst of all in that purgatory before the audience. On here fidgeted a lone figure. Only his voice spoke to this austere backdrop. It had the attention of everybody present.

"I approached Captain Worley, sir, about the Mess. The fish we had for dinner had not even been cleaned and smelled bad. Captain Worley was lying on his bunk. He got up and put on his trousers. 'The whole God-damned lot of yous are only a lot of God-damned sons of bitches,' he said. I told him I resented being called by a name which no man born of a woman could stand. Captain Worley then insisted he had never called me or any man aboard— *ever*— a son of a bitch."

Quartermaster George Landgren, jaw clenched, tensed by indignation at the recollection, then testified that he asked for an apology.

All eyes were now on the accused, their salty master, Lt. Commander George W. Worley. He sat in a spindly chair under a porthole, stiff and taciturn, isolated in the position of his own defense counsel. Though to one side and also at the footstool of the Dais, he was still an intimidating presence— oafish size and bull neck counterbalanced the hawk nose and thug's deep-set eyes; they were actually shark's eyes, dull, glazed, carrying some menacing calculation but no vitality or swiftness. Bristle-like, thick hair was well in place but held a deep imprint from the brim of his removed hat.

The presiding officer, the clerkish Commander Whitted, didn't bother to look over. Grasped with official curiosity, he now leaned forward.

"What did he do then?"

Landgren's voice teetered with amazement: "He then called me a son of a bitch and confined me for two days!"

The atmosphere was too heavy for anyone to let even a restrained chuckle at Worley's notorious sarcastic humor. His denying it would mean little to the crew. No one could imitate his delivery. Everything about the confrontation was original Worley and not invented. However, knowing what we do now, should we not be gracious in our judgment and think it a great inconvenience for the captain to be disturbed while in his bunk? We might well sympathize and even laugh, though the audience daren't. At the moment of trying to awake from the frazzled half-sleep world induced by much more than medicinal amounts of drink, Worley was not to form.

It is a paltry accusation anyway. It is obvious that it could never get Worley removed from the command of his ship. Why then should such a solitary encounter find its way as one critical point amongst 3 far more dreadful allegations by 40 of the

George W. Worley

ship's company against their captain? Moreover, why did the cocky Landgren even take the chance? The allegation is craftily placed, this is evident. It is No. 1 on the list. But by removing the context it allows the accusation to stand out like a dangling tongue. Nebulous accusations always invite curiosity. This in itself makes the accusation the proverbial one-more-straw that would force the Navy to make George Worley undergo what he hated the most— oversight.

Poor Landgren couldn't aspire to this level of spite or duplicity. Nor could he be stirred by feelings of Navy honor and tradition. He was a former 'bad conduct' discharge on an earlier enlistment. But Landgren wasn't a dullard either. By now he must have realized that he had been manipulated into this unforgiving chair by someone far cleverer than himself; someone who knew the right moment to send him to his surly master at the wrong moment. He said his peace, though, as petty as it might be. He now sat there on the witness chair, hat in hand, still fidgeting.

The overhead fan lent only a simile of vitality in the room. The shadows of its lethargic blades monotonously drug themselves along the walls in their sluggish orbit. It spun slowly and not so surely; the squeak almost a misplaced giggle.

The tableau the moment conjures for us is not just that of a moment in time. This is the Janus Point of many voyages before and of that which will ultimately come and upon which this book will focus. I want this scene, frozen in time, to remain in the reader's mind. The tableau I describe is not one of literary license. It is painted by the decorum of the time. An ugly Mess hall aboard an equally ugly duckling of the fleet, cramped wall to wall with petitioners, was the scene before which played out a personal feud between two men.

The antagonist and the protagonist are certainly here, but in this case it is hard to choose which is better or worse. Certainly only one was visible in the crowded Mess. This was, of course, George Worley. The other is Burt Asper. The contrast couldn't be greater. The ship's surgeon had no prominent position. Moles don't. In a crowded room, he didn't even stand out except for the sweet pomade that mixed incongruously with the stale odor of breakfast. If there can be such a thing as an anti-Hero— not personally likable or physically impressive— then Asper is it. But if so, then Worley might be considered an anti-Villain. Compared to Asper he had the better personality, but power also allowed him to put into practice his brutal will. Asper, we shall see, was attempting to thwart that. . .but his cowardly, selfish nature doesn't inspire any admiration.

The Navy's perfunctory interest was well represented in William Whitted. Diminutive and bespectacled, he looked like a comic marionette that Worley could balance on one thigh if he so desired, though there was also that agility and mocking intelligence to him that marionettes and not their masters have.

The bloodlessness of the affair was in the gray and white colors and in nothing else— gray Navy walls, Spartan tables, stiff chairs, row after row of men in their dress whites waiting to testify; the ignobility in the residual odors of the Japanese cook's idea of digestibility.

The moment now came. The moment George Worley had been waiting for, to introduce what he was eager to introduce— his antagonist. This moment allowed him to reveal, however indirectly, his entire line of defense— that a plot existed against him inspired by that ferret of a ship's doctor. So now he motioned that he wished to cross-examine the skinny, young Quartermaster.

Aplomb is not a word to be applied to George Worley. Implacable perhaps, but aplomb implies a nobility or dignity which the old tavern keeper did not possess. But he attempted the game, and far better here than Whitted could appreciate. The pomp of courtly etiquette, however, was banished the moment he spoke.

"How long have yous been on this ship?" he asked Landgren.

"Thirteen months," replied the Quartermaster.

"Did you ever hear me curse anyone else?"

"No sir, I never did."

As crude as Worley was, he seemed remarkably careful. He neither denied nor admitted he cussed out Landgren. His line of questioning only qualified that if it had happened it had been a rare occurrence. Such subtlety was truly a rare thing for Worley.

The subtlety of his next question, however, carried a sharp aftertaste. His eyes fixed on the ship's surgeon, Burt Asper, in the audience. "Did you give sass to the Doctor before coming to me?"

"No sir, I did not." It was a quick, emphasized reply.

Captain Worley let the cat out of the bag. It was the only time he would mention the ship's doctor. Whether Landgren responded truthfully or not, it does not alter the implication. Worley openly invoked before the whole audience and a superior officer— Whitted was the Assistant Supervisor of all Naval Auxiliaries— his bitter feud with the ship's surgeon. Landgren may or may not have realized he had been a pawn, and now regretted it, but at the very least his firm reply acknowledged he understood the antagonism between the two and the lengths they went to use situations as pawns in their game of spiteful chess aboard.

It would have been impossible for Whitted not to have followed the implication, especially with Worley's contemptuous leer targeting Asper. But he too remained subtle. He preferred eye-witnesses. Judiciously, he asked: "Did anyone overhear the remarks between you and Captain Worley?"

"The Boatswain George."

The audience of officers and men gave a collective and silent sigh. The very name 'Boatswain George' sat ill with the men. Each man seemed to either let out a silent groan of doom or roll his eyes in contempt. For Landgren— cocky but without brains— to utter the name of the Captain's toady as if help was near-at-hand was as meaningful as a drowning man reaching for an anvil.

Landgren had been the 3rd witness to testify. Worley had exculpated himself rather well in the first 2 witness, Oilers Duke and Dowdy, and even set the stage by asking "Did any officer know that you signed this paper?" Dowdy had squirmed in the witness chair. He had reasons. He was the son of the Chief Engineer aboard of the same name. His dad had finally left the ship on August 1, condemning Worley as a drunk. But that's not what Worley was after. He had waited. Dowdy replied carefully. "None that I know of."

Naturally, Asper, as the ship's surgeon, had to have known about it and in his own indirect way approved of it or instigated it. It was an open scandal on the ship that when the petition wasn't being circulated by his Hospital Apprentice W. Howard it hung openly in the sickbay. Almost every man that would soon be called was asked the vital question— "Who got you to sign?" Invariably, the name was Howard.

It became so obvious there was a ringleader that a few witnesses later William Whitted openly tried to trap Willie E. Kight on the stand. He had confessed he didn't know the Hospital Apprentice's name. He declared that the apprentice only circulated the petition, "but it was written up by the crew." But Whitted's tone narrowed and he asked: "What other men?" This put Kight on the defensive. "Everyone that signed the paper." Whitted probed for a conspiracy or sea lawyer at work. He asked if they had had a meeting. "No sir, no meeting at all, just word passed along."

Kight, of course, could not have been correct. Forty men— as diverse as those who signed— could not come up with the petition like a continental congress and then sign it. Howard may have had the gumption to start the petition but not the direction. He was the legs indeed. He walked it about the ship. But Asper had to be brains behind it. If Landgren now felt manipulated, certainly Howard should have felt this more so. His name will be the most mentioned in the whole long ordeal of the Board of Inquiry. Yet he will never speak. He was the first to sign . . . and the first to be silenced. Asper had made sure to transfer him off the ship already.

Nevertheless, 40 men just don't join into a private vendetta unless there are other problems aboard. As testimony would soon convey, many had signed the petition for one or two reasons specified thereon, or for another reason they felt applied more to them, even if the allegation was not specified.

Captain Worley held his own with the early witnesses. But after Kight he was overwhelmed. After the typical first question of "why" did he sign, Kight rather summed up the problems best for all. "Captain Worley gets drunk and chases the crew around. He was drunk on the way to France, chased the officers from the port side to the starboard. In Newport, Rhode Island, he was drunk two times to my knowledge in 1916. I was running the motor boat. He was drunk in New York, on the trip that we made to go to France, when he came aboard. When he came over the gangway he chased us all off from the side of the ship and told the officer of the deck to keep the damn men away from the gangway. By the way, I consider Captain Worley not fit to handle a Navy ship with Navy men under Navy Regulations."

Kight's tone had been so certain that it took Whitted a bit to follow up on what was actually the most peculiar part of his whole statement.

A few questions later, he asked: "You stated that Captain Worley chased the officers from Port to Starboard. What officers?"

"Mr. Cain, Mr. Hodge and Mr. Wheeler."

"About what date?"

"Do not know date."

"Why do you think Captain Worley was intoxicated at that time?"

"I passed him on deck just before he reached the officers and I smelled liquor on him, on occasion stated above."

The occasion stated above was only one installment in a series that had begun in New York harbor before the voyage to France commenced. Lonnie Waff, Oiler, had been the first to introduce it. He, along with many others, had been around the gangway when their surly master staggered aboard and reeked of liquor. He testified how Worley ran them away from the gangway, and even from 5 feet away he could smell liquor on him.

"Who was with you?"

"I don't know who was with me, but quite a bunch."

It only went from bad to worse when each member of the 'bunch' was called. Worley no longer even marked their coming and going. This was obvious in how he only cross-examined a few, and his questioning showed rather disturbingly he wasn't paying attention or really had no defense.

This was first markedly seen in the testimony of Roy Swoveland. "I have seen Captain Worley drunk several times. He treats us like dogs when sitting on deck, and never has a pleasant word and does not treat us like we were human. We were kept aboard in France and should have had liberty several times, could not account for it, only that the Captain was drunk. That is all I can say, as I have been on the ship a short while." Under further questioning, Swoveland elaborated that the drunkenness was obvious. "About noon, when a man cannot walk down the deck straight, there must be something wrong with him and you could plainly smell liquor. There must be some cause." He had smelled liquor on him many other times, but added he couldn't swear he was drunk. But "he was drunk on several occasions: in France he was drunk, at St. Naziere."

Yet to all this and more, Worley only asked "Who do you go to for liberty?" and said nothing else.

Swoveland could not have been alone in his surprised reaction at how Worley incongruously introduced his cross-questioning. Swoveland had only touched on liberty in passing. Rather than being the actions of a stumbling old barkentine skipper, Worley was trying to introduce Sam Dowdy as another officer, like Asper, who was out to get him.

Swoveland answered correctly: "First Assistant or Chief Engineer"—Dowdy.

Captain Worley let it drop for now.

With each new witness it was becoming painfully clear: Worley was imbibing way too much. The certainty with which Carl Clausen testified to Worley's drunkenness left no doubt. But yet again in response to the testimony that he was effectively stewed to the gills, Worley only asked him "Have I ever abused you?"

Surprised, Clausen only responded: "No."

This did not stop his taciturn master. "Have yous seen me abuse anyone else?"

"No, sir."

Worley was clearly not paying attention.

The testimony of so many men had effectively taken the hearing along a different tack than that which had opened it with Landgren. Worley was primed to defend along only one course of action— Asper. When it came to matters outside of that antagonism, Worley seemed completely unprepared and thoroughly unskilled. And too many men, either witnesses in groups or as individuals, were testifying as to their encounters with their salty captain's drunken behavior at sea.

When Robert Kyle, Fireman 2nd class, declared that he had been deprived of a liberty in France because he had come back from a previous liberty with a small dog, he revealed the petty and vindictive types of punishment meted out on the *Cyclops.* Furthermore, he too insisted that Worley had been drunk at another time, this time far more recent than others had claimed. "A week ago Sunday," he began, "I was sitting on the poop deck outside the galley and the Captain came along and he told me to get up and I got up and stood to attention and he seemed like he was intoxicated. One time before I stood to attention and he told me to sit down, that I didn't have to stand to attention. He started to put me in the brig for that a week ago Sunday."

Whitted was less officious by now and just bland. "How can you tell?"

"Why," replied Kyle, "I can tell when a man is drunk, something seemed wrong. There was something wrong with him."

Captain Worley, he continued to testify, then staggered into the galley and started to chew out the Commissary Steward and the Japanese cook. "'This galley is lousy, lousier than it's been for ten years!'"

When Whitted motioned if he wanted to cross-question Kyle, Worley merely shook his head.

If Whitted showed any significant reaction it was disappointment. Instead of continuing, he called a break for lunch.

It was indeed a fortuitous break for George Worley. He had made little effort to counter-attack, and in those moments when he tried he slipped up and revealed to what extent he anticipated other problems aboard which were not specified in the petition and in which Asper could not have had a hand. In short, he had made a poor showing and furthermore he revealed that there was much more dirty laundry aboard his ship that wanted airing. But the crew, too, did not make the best showing. The men sounded disrespectful, petty or expecting at times, and this rankled Whitted.

After lunch, when the proceedings once again took up, with the officious nod of Commander Whitted, it was clear that Worley had had a long chat with himself. He now seemed more primed to fight. He would present a condescending air to show the men were simply raw recruits unaware of Navy procedure. Thus when J.B. McCormack testified that he was not "satisfied with the ship at all" and "sometimes I would be sitting along the deck and the Captain would come along and would run us away" Captain Worley steered his course up to him, sure in his manner like he was talking to a little boy.

"Didn't you have orders not to set on deck in any dirty clothes?" asked Worley.

"Yes sir," replied the young McCormack.

"Who gave you those orders?"

"Mr. Robinson, First Officer."

"Were you clean when I chased you away?" asked Worley.

"Yes, sir," replied McCormack. Then he added: "Some may have been dirty, but you chased us all away." There was no doubt that incredulous teeter to his voice that almost brought laughter.

Worley fumbled. "You were leaning up against the paint, were you not?"

"No sir, I was sitting on the deck."

Worley's attack fizzled not only this time but against each man to follow. Soon he was back to his incongruous responses. J.A. Smith's testimony confirmed how the meals weren't fit to eat half the time. To this Worley demanded "Who got you to sign this paper?" After Fireman 1st C.G. Graves said Captain Worley was "standing propped in a doorway and appeared drunk" Worley rather challenged another issue not raised in the petition. He asked, as he had with Swoveland and another earlier witness, Harry Sherrard, why hadn't Graves come to him for liberty instead of the Chief Engineer. Graves' replied: "I understood we got it from the Chief Engineer."

Seaman Graves, however, had said that a seaman Daly had been a co-witness to one of Worley's drunken episodes. He was now called and declared boldly that there was "no system of running things in the Engineering Department." He'd "put in eight years" in the Navy and there simply was no system on the *Cyclops*. "In different instances when the Engineer's force is on the deck sometime they will be sitting down and Captain

Worley will pass by and the men get up to salute and he says never mind. On other times he makes you get up and do it."

Daly, obviously a seasoned mariner, then offered another reason why he signed the petition, and this opened a can of worms that dominated the rest of the day's proceedings. There was indeed a liberty issue. There was a strange partiality that he believed Worley showed in granting liberty while in France: Auxiliary men— from whose rag-tangle ranks Worley had been drawn— got liberties but Regular Navy men, like Daly, did not.

Whitted was still taking notes over the serious implications when Worley addressed Daly. Another incongruous challenge caused Whitted to look up with mild bewilderment.

"Did the Chief ever come down to inspect your food?"

—Certainly this hadn't come up in Daly's testimony. But his quick answer revealed it too was a problem. "Some of the men went up to the Chief Engineer in regard to the food."

T.A. Lawrence added that, curiously, rations were short on the ship. Lawrence was the Messman, and he said there simply wasn't enough food to go around, one reason perhaps why fish known to be rotten was still fed to the men.

Man after man testified to 'drunk in New York, drunk the way over, chasing from the gangplank in New York, not letting us off in France.' Fireman L. Finch was a pitbull about it. "The following words I say is fact. Captain Worley wasn't treating us fairly and I saw him intoxicated coming up to the bridge here." Injury was added to insult by every man to follow. A slough of men were called in quick order, each having the same complaint: liberty . . . and none of it. The questions amounted to no more than 2 or 3 and then they were dismissed. Anthony Glowka added a comical touch by stating in his crude Jersey accent: "We didn't get liberty. When we was in New York all dressed up ready to go on liberty, Captain Worley came out on deck and ran us back down again. The Auxiliary men were granted two or three days liberty but the regular Navy men only granted 5 hours." T.V. Lee added another morsel: at Hampton Roads the Auxiliary Navy men got liberty every night, but the Regular Navy only every 3 days.

Worley hadn't stirred as the men were rushed upon the witness chair and then down again. By having clarified that the Chief Engineer, Sam Dowdy, was responsible, he must have felt that he had saved himself.

But Worley could not wholeheartedly blame his Chief. M.J. Elliot confirmed in testimony that the command ship *Seattle* signaled all vessels to permit liberty one night, but none such was granted aboard the *Cyclops*. Sam Dowdy cannot be held accountable for this. He had neither the position nor the hearty bravery to buck a fleet order. The message would have been picked up on the bridge by the Officer of the Deck and given to Worley who forever perched nearby in his emergency cabin.

Captain Worley had few cards to play. But now an officer was called. This was different— and Lieutenant E. F. Robinson, a dull man given to sighs, rolls of the eye, and minimizing, placed a saving spin on much of the day's accusations regarding the food. "There were no more than the usual amount of complaints aboard ship. There may have been two or three times and we straightened them out. When the food was bad we cooked more for them."

Yet when Whitted asked who makes out the liberty list, Robinson couldn't help but implicate his master. "The Chief Engineer and the First Officer, by direction of the Captain."

Robinson's next answers on liberty were ambiguous. He said there had been no discrimination. Then "as far as he knew" they all had their turn, all those who requested liberty, that is, but never clarifying if the men were told they had to request it first. Robinson insisted it was granted every afternoon to "anyone who requested to go and Paris liberty was restricted to 48 hours."

As Robinson's testimony continued, he minimized his Master's drinking. He admitted that Worley was indeed under the influence when coming aboard in New York, but hastened to add he was not drunk. He was indeed under the influence at sea, but "never intoxicated." Nor did his drinking ever interfere with Robinson's work. What his long testimony amounted to was that he never saw his captain slip up at sea. Since no man ever complained to him about Worley being drunk, he never thought the drinking was much of anything.

Worley had been very satisfied by his Executive Officer's testimony. He was the first witness that he bothered to cross-examine in a while.

It was now 4:30 p.m.

Mercifully, the first day's session came to a close. Whitted adjourned, gathered his notes and, after the room cleared, left out the door with his assistant. Escorted by Captain Worley, of course, they strolled along the deck and departed at the infamous gangplank.

DOUBLE GROG — AUGUST 6, 1917

The heat of August was tempered by the fresh wind skipping over Chesapeake Bay. At 10:30 a.m. there was no need yet for the overhead fan. The crowded Mess Room was ventilated only by the portholes. In wafted the fresh salty harbor air. Tar and brine took the staleness out of the heavy atmosphere, but there was still a trace of last voyage's rotten fish.

All the preliminaries were over. Commander Whitted was now comfortable at his long table. The first day he had been hard to read. Except for trying to discover whether the men had had a meeting, he had remained officiously bland. But now he mussed with his papers and called a surprise witness.

Lieutenant W. A. Hamilton was not a man who had signed the petition. He was one of Whitted's finds. Hamilton had sent a letter in to HQ requesting a transfer from the vessel and this had come to Whitted's attention. Whitted was doing nothing but silently reading the letter. The stillness in the room was louder than anything. Finally, Whitted set the letter aside, and carefully posed his question.

"You have requested to be transferred to some other station, stating as a reason the Commanding Officer has been under the influence of alcohol on several occasions of late, and in your opinion jeopardizing the ship and all concerned, and making existing conditions very uncertain. Please state particulars."

"My statement," replied the young lieutenant, "is based on the Commanding Officer, Captain Worley, being under the influence of liquor before leaving New York. Another instance, when the lifeboat was coming back to the ship, after rescuing three men overboard, from a destroyer. . ." Hamilton described in detail the problems. Basically, the left hand didn't know what the right hand was doing. Robinson ordered the men to hold the ropes taut but Worley, at the stern, told the men holding the rope to fall back. The "consequence was, both falls were let go, and the sea was running made it a very hard matter to get the boat alongside and get the boat hooked on again." It was only 9:30 in the morning. "In my opinion he was under the influence of alcohol, he so fairly reprimanded the Chief Engineer [Dowdy] in public for not putting oil on the water, when the Chief Engineer knew nothing about oil being wanted on the water, and by his actions he got all the men in that vicinity very excited."

"Was Captain Worley's actions that of an excited man or of a drunken man?"

"No," replied Hamilton quickly, "it was not in my opinion of an excited man, but due to the influence of a drunken man."

The above incident happened on June 15, and when asked to state any other times, he too mentioned the earlier date of June 12 in New York when all the men were chased from the gangplank.

Hamilton's testimony only got worse, for it implicated Worley on all counts. The liberty discrimination was raised. So small was the number of men of the Engineer's Force who were granted liberty, Hamilton could name them. "Waff, L. -- Dowdy, S.-- Duke, W. -- Bailey, L.-- Lamb, A. — all reserve men."

"How were these men selected and no Navy men?"

"I asked the Chief Engineer [Samuel Dowdy Sr.] how many would be allowed to go, and he said only four or five would be allowed. I asked him about the Navy crew and he said he could get no satisfaction from the Captain. I asked him if I would make out the list, or would he, and he said that he would. This was about a 48 hour liberty. This was the only one going to Paris."

(Sam Dowdy Jr. no doubt got to go because his dad was the Chief Engineer, and Duke was his buddy.)

"Who makes out the liberty list for the engineers?"

"I make out the list myself, and turn it over to the Chief Engineer, and he gets his permission from the Captain."

"Are there any other complaints to make against Captain Worley?"

"Yes. On the last trip to Guantanamo, entering Hampton Roads, Captain Worley was in my opinion under the influence of alcohol, as he fell out of the door on the starboard side from the quarterdeck on going to the bridge. He ordered his First Officer, Mr. Shaw, off the bridge shortly after arriving on the bridge."

"What other officers were present at this time?"

"I saw no other officers as I was looking out the port."

"What other officers were present when Captain Worley reprimanded the Chief Engineer as stated above?"

"Mr. Sjolander and Mr. Smith I think."

"What date does the log show the ship entering Hampton Roads on the incident stated above?"

"March 22, 1917," replied Hamilton quickly.

Whitted was a complete mask of his feelings while he in-gested the information. Worley, too, kept to his stony expression. When Whitted motioned if he wanted to cross-examine Hamilton, he offered no more than a negligible shake of his head.

Naturally, the other officers had to be called. Roy T. Smith, was a small guy, monotone and unexciting in appearance as he was close-lipped in his answers. Whitted asked him straight out if he had seen Worley "under the influence." A dull "No" was his answer. To the next 3 questions, his answers were just "no sir," and then "No sir, I heard nothing." These questions sur-rounded whether he was by the lifeboat when they were picking up the men that had gone overboard. "I was sick in my bunk." And he claimed he was not on the ship on the voyage from Guantanamo to New York.

Worley didn't bother to step forward to cross-examine, but merely asked from his chair. "Did you ever see me excitable or drunk?"

To which the brave Smith replied: "No sir."

Smith was quickly dismissed.

The questioning of the Chief Boatswain's Mate, Cost George, was finally at hand. We don't know if Whitted knew he was Worley's personal on-board toady. But the questioning was hardly grueling. Whitted asked very little, although George was the key witness to Landgren's confrontation with Worley over the "foul" fish. But by today it was clear that booze, inconsistent discipline and bigoted liberty were the bigger issues. George, a stocky, grayish imp with dark eyes and hair, spoke in a slight Turkish accent. He admitted he heard the conversation between Landgren and Worley. Then when asked to "state what was said?" he replied: "I and Landgren went to the Captain complaining about the food; Landgren talked to the Captain and said he had nothing to eat. The Captain said to see the Commissary Steward, and if he hasn't got anything, to hell with it. This was all he said."

"Did you hear," asked Whitted clearly, "Captain Worley call the crew or the Quartermaster any insulting names?"

"No sir."

Captain Worley was particularly pleased at the moment and leaned forward. "How long have yous been with me?"

"Over four years," replied Cost George manner-of-factly.

"Did you ever hear me call the men bad names?"

"No sir."

"Any other complaints to make?"

"No sir," replied George definitely.

Worley clearly felt confident with George, as he had in cross-examining Landgren at the beginning. It was the only time he really remained on topic.

Whitted: "Mr. Cost, you are excused."[3]

A passel of seamen were rushed through, being asked only a few questions, the first invariably "Why?" Each answered he signed because the liberty or because they saw the Captain stagger on the voyage to France. The only humor was added by G.W. Smith, Seaman Second, when he answered Whitted's routine "Why?" with "In New York we were all waiting for liberty and the Captain was pretty full, and would not grant us liberty."

It is interesting that of all witnesses to be recalled, it would be Lt. E.F. Robinson, the officer whose testimony had tempered so much of the first day's acrimony against Worley. Perhaps he seemed reliable to Whitted for the very reason he could frankly admit Worley drank but was still capable of his duty. More than this, however, Robinson was significant because he had been a participant in the men overboard incident of June 15, 1917. The largely unschooled drafters of the petition had accused Worley of a serious charge— dereliction of duty— but in their ignorance they basically also limited it to the encounter with trying to rescue men over-the-side. Whitted wasn't going to probe for more examples. It is to this incident that he immediately came back. Robinson confirmed he was in the lifeboat at the time. He also avoided any judgment of Worley's behavior because "I do not know how conditions were on deck." Whitted then perfunctorily asked if Captain Worley "endangered" or "jeopardized" the hoisting of the boat. Robinson, remaining cautious, only replied that, given the "existing conditions I think the boat was hoisted in a seaman-like manner."

It only got better for Worley. Whitted asked a couple quick questions next. Was there anything strange about Worley's behavior when Robinson finally got on deck? Robinson ambiguously and tersely replied "not to my knowledge;" and, second, was G.W. Smith, one of the aggrieved signers, granted the same liberty as the other men on deck, and was there any special prejudice shown him? "Yes, same as any other man that was not first class in their work and cleanliness and conduct."

---

[3] Cost George was his actual name, but few ever got it straight.

William Whitted seemed pleasantly relieved. Despite the damning testimony, Whitted seemed to be looking for an easy way out today. In a number of ways he was becoming Worley's own defense counsel.

The next witness therefore was crucial, and his testimony, as cautious as it was, should have raised red flags. The witness was the ship's Second Officer, Clarence Roosevelt Hodge. So far every officer still attached to the *Cyclops* had either subtly exonerated Worley or wriggled out of any contention. None had signed the petition, of course. They were called as witnesses to some of the events listed. Hodge was a compromise. He would speak the truth, but not offer it.

When asked by Whitted whether he "noticed" Worley under the influence of liquor on the trip to France, Hodge replied "Yes." When told to "state when" Hodge was specific, stating that it was on the 20th of June about 1:30 p.m. "I saw the Captain on the bridge and noticed from his actions that he was apparently under the influence of liquor."

"Were there any other officers present at the time?" asked Whitted.

Hodge replied: "I believe Mr. Robinson was on the bridge at the time."

Amazingly, although Hodge was one of those officers mentioned by Kight as having been chased by the surly seadog when drunk, Whitted didn't pursue it with him. All he asked Hodge next was: "Are there any other cases that you know of?"

Hodge's reply let the carrot dangle: "Not while in New York."

Yet Whitted didn't pursue it. He had given Hodge the opportunity and he didn't take it. He was dismissed. Does guilt lie with Hodge for not taking it, or does irresponsibility lie with Whitted for not pushing the point?

Putting the dates together, the testimony shows that Worley was drunk while boarding the *Cyclops* at New York around the 12th of June before departing for France. He was also apparently under the influence on the 15th when they had to rescue men overboard from a destroyer; on the 17th, the day most attested to by witnesses, and now on the 20th. This was obviously not some New York binge. Worley was getting his liquor aboard ship.

This was a bad opening for the main event. The next witness was none other than Burt J. Asper, the ship's surgeon. We must remember that it had been his assistant, Howard, who had started the petition and circulated it amongst the crew and when not doing this had it openly hanging in the sickbay for any to come and read and sign. *Forty men* aboard the *Cyclops* had signed because of Howard, and Howard could not have done this without the cover of the ship's medical man and the immunity that he carried. All that Worley was now enduring was because of Asper. Everybody knew this. . .and everybody waited to see what would happen next. This was the main event.

When his name was called, what did Worley do? It is not recorded, of course, but we can well imagine that the salty master restrained himself. Asper had not signed the petition naturally. But being the medical man, being that the petition hung openly in sickbay, and being that Worley had implied he had baited Landgren, Whitted could not exactly ignore calling him "independently." Asper took the stand, swore the oath and sat down.

Whitted was careful to frame his questions. "Have you observed Captain Worley being under the influence of liquor while on board ship?"

Asper went for the jugular right off. "Yes," he said, no doubt with professional gusto.

"State when and circumstances," intoned Whitted.

"On June 9th, I reported on board and at dinner time (12 noon) noted that Captain Worley was under the influence of intoxicants. I reported on board the ship at about 9:00 a.m. and know that Captain Worley went ashore soon thereafter."

Drinking as soon as he got to shore?

Whitted: "Do you know of any other occasions on board ship that Captain Worley was under the influence of liquor?"

I know that Captain Worley used, to my knowledge, irregularly, liquor for several days out of New York."

"Was he able to perform his duties properly during this time?"

—A hot and loaded question!

Asper was careful and professional. His reply was perfect: "I am unable to state."

"How was the food going over to France, was it good or bad?"

"In my judgment the food was good. On one occasion there was a complaint at the noonday meal, the fish was discovered to be bad, and the crew was supplied with other food to take the place of the fish. The preparation of the food could have been better."

Despite his bland approach to his duties, Whitted most certainly had caught Worley's inference the first day when he asked Landgren about if he had given "sass" to the doctor first, for Whitted now asks: "Did you have any trouble with the men regarding the food on the way to France?"

Asper's response was stunning: "On one occasion where a complaint had been made regarding the fish, Landgren, Quartermaster, was disrespectful in manner and rather insubordinate and disciplinary action was taken. This is the same occasion as reported in proceedings before."

Both Whitted and Worley should have been surprised, but Worley less so. He had already learned what a mole Asper was. Asper's testimony was, in fact, a terrible slip-up. Worley had asked Landgren if he had "given sass to the doctor" before coming to him. This implicitly fingered Asper as the antagonist in the whole affair. Asper must have been taken aback by that on the previous trial day and now, rather clumsily, tried to show how neutral he was in the whole affair. Yet it was a terrible mistake. Cost George did not testify that Landgren had been insubordinate; and Asper certainly had not been a witness to the event.

The truth of that whole sordid moment was as Worley had suspected. *Landgren* had upset *Asper* prior to seeing him. The spiteful, conniving Asper thus had baited an angry Landgren to go to the drunken captain. The end result was satisfying for Asper: Worley got peeved and Landgren spent 2 days in the brig.

But now Worley didn't show well either. Instead of catching Asper and elaborating, he asked: "Who was on deck at all times, going and coming from France?"

Asper was shrewd enough to make a show about how incongruous the question was. It was abrupt and certainly a change of subject. He looked back and forth between Whitted and the burly seadog before answering manner-of-factly to Whitted: "Captain Worley."

Worley: "What were my orders regarding lights on board?"

Asper's eyes were uneasy at another sudden change of topic. "No lights must be visible anywhere," he answered naturally.

Worley nodded approvingly and leaned back in his chair.

Whitted had not stirred except to scribble a couple of short notes. He beckoned Worley to continue, but, receiving a deferring look, realized that Worley was finished with Asper.

Asper's expression openly enquired of Whitted if it was over.

Whitted merely nodded in a confirming way.

"Thank you," replied Asper. He got up, tucked his hat under his arm and walked out the door. Professional . . . and trite.

The remaining group of men in the audience must have been astounded. Although they may have hoped for more professional indictment of their hated master, they were left marooned . . . until an unexpected savior came. The next witness would in his clumsy innocence redeem Asper's obvious failure. Next called was Boatswain Ensign J.J. Cain.

The young officer was clearly nervous and not used to the oppressive atmosphere of an inquiry aboard ship. His reply to Whitted's mandatory question whether he had seen Worley under the influence on the voyage was a complete avoidance. "At sea he was always on the bridge and on the job."

Tired after the long morning, Commander Whitted got sharply to the point: "Did he appear to be drinking on the trip to France?"

"Yes," finally admitted Cain.

"Can you state any particular instances?"

"On one occasion," began the boyish-faced Ensign, "I saw liquor in his room; this was about one-half way across going over."

That wasn't exactly an on-topic answer to the question, and Whitted's response reflects that he meant actual instances of drinking. "Was Captain Worley in his room at the time?"

"No," Cain replied. Then he stumbled out: "The liquor was in a quart bottle" —a rather nice bit of gratuitous information.

Fully cognizant of the statement's implications, Whitted nevertheless avoided it and rather came back to the lifeboat issue. "Were you on deck when the men were picked up by the lifeboat June 15th?"

"I was Officer of the Deck and was relieved by the Captain and sent aft to assist in the lowering of the boat."

"Did Captain Worley handle the ship and hoist the boat in a seaman-like manner?"

"Yes, sir, he did."

"Was he under the influence of liquor at this time?"

Cain responded: "Yes, sir, I think he was."

Captain Worley once again showed he wasn't entirely following the testimony and, in this case, he showed delayed reaction. He rather should have said nothing and let Whitted continue to gloss over Cain's earlier observation of the bottle. But the old seadog interrupted in a narrow tone. "How came you to be in my room when you saw the liquor?"

—A good question which Whitted had not yet asked . . . but he nevertheless must have been as surprised as Cain by Worley's sudden shift to the subject.

"Quartermaster Daniels called me in the room."

"What business had he in there?" almost demanded Worley.

"I think he was cleaning the room out."

There was an awkward moment in the Mess. Then, with no further questions, Cain was finally dismissed.

It was remarkable that Whitted did not pursue it further. The very reason Daniels called Cain into the Captain's room indicates that the Captain's condition had been noticed by a number of men on board, whether they had signed or not. The "source" had now been located, and Daniels was calling attention to it.

C.R. Daniels, though he had not signed, was now called to corroborate.

Whitted was direct. "Do you clean Captain Worley's room?"

"I cleaned his room on the way across and back again," admitted Daniels.

"Did you show Mr. Cain a bottle of whiskey?"

"I showed Mr. Cain a bottle of whiskey but could not state whether it contained liquor or not."

"Why did you show it to Mr. Cain?"

Daniel's reply was remarkable: "I had no certain reasons to call his attention to it."

Even Whitted could not remain officious at such a lame answer. "Was there any label on the bottle?"

"I could not say if there was or not. I did not pay any attention."

"Was it empty?"

"I could not say. There was a cork in the bottle. I could not say if it contained liquor or coffee of what." [4]

So basically what Daniels was saying is that he saw a bottle in the Captain's room. He didn't know if it had liquor, what label it had, if it was empty, half empty or full. He called it to the attention of Ensign Cain, but did not know why he called it to his attention.

There was no point continuing. When challenged, Daniels asserted what he had said was "the truth, the whole truth and nothing but the truth." He was dismissed.

Whitted expressed the desire that a few others should be called to testify for the afternoon session. He felt them to be key witnesses. However, he was now informed that W.F. How-

---

[4] Not really necessary. When Worley growled out his question to Cain he admitted there was liquor in it. "How came you to be in my room when you saw the liquor?"

ard, the Hospital Apprentice so central to the whole petition, was now conveniently serving in the Naval Hospital, Norfolk, Virginia, and so was, surprisingly, the Commissary Steward, W.D. Hale. Juan Guillermo, the messman, and J.F. Puckhaber, a machinist, had both been discharged from the Service.

With nothing else to do, Whitted gathered his notes and cued Worley with a look, asking him if he would like to call his witnesses at this time. Worley said that he would not call any witnesses. He would make his statements later.

Well then, it was settled. Whitted pulled out his watch by the fob and checked the time: 1:45. p.m.

Thus, given the anticlimax of it all, they rose awkwardly. Whitted pronounced the inquiry over. He picked up his notes and the minutes taken by the clerk, and would let Worley know when it was his time to respond. He would be given command privilege to respond to the charges and testimony privately at the headquarters in Norfolk, or in writing. All those in the room now knew it was over. Short of being removed from command, they would have no idea of the outcome of Worley's private defense.

It was indeed time for Worley to defend himself. But what would be his approach? How would he defend himself on the liberty issue? The drinking problem was testified to more than any other offence. Indeed, many things not touched directly upon were still tied in to the charges of his drinking— abuse, inconsistency with discipline— and there seemed to be no doubt Worley *was* a drinker.

The Naval Auxiliary Service was in for a surprise from the salty captain's upcoming defense.

3

U.S. NAVAL RESERVE FORCE

SEX ON THE BRAIN

"Permit me to say at the outset that the charges are the
result of a plot on the part of certain officers and men
on board the Cyclops, which has for its sole purpose
my removal as the commanding officer of this ship."
—George W. Worley

"SEX, SEX, SEX; THAT IS all Dr. Asper talked about. I desire to say
that on June 10th Dr. Asper reported on board the ship before
my leaving for the Sub-Treasury to get payroll money. When I
returned, Dr. Asper came to my room shortly thereafter and
started a conversation about 'women falling for him.' I told
him he had better be careful how he talked around Clubs and
on shore in that manner as he might get hurt, and he took offence and left my room . . ."

George Worley perused what he had written. His expression
must have been subtly touched by his excellent sense of sar-
casm. He had obtained a copy of the minutes of the B of I and
had spent, quite uncustomarily, all day August 9, 1917, in his
aft cabin typing his detailed response.

He slipped in another piece of *Cyclops* letterhead stationary
and continued. "This subject of women seemed to be on his
brain all the time," the keys pecked out none too surely under

his clumsy fingers, "as he would continue to talk to all of the men and officers on the ship in the same manner until some of the officers on the ship were unable to stand it any longer, and Second Officer Hodge, also Third Officer Kane,[5] complained to me that they were unable to rest on account of the loud conversations regarding women engaged in between Dr. Asper, Dowdy,[6] Kainnard, Robinson, and others. I, myself, heard the conversation at different times, and on one occasion I took my meal below and this subject appeared to be the whole conversation at the table. I informed all of the officers, including Dr. Asper, that this must be stopped and immediately issued a written order to that effect. Dr. Asper took umbrage and great offense, and from that day he was constantly with Hospital Apprentice Howard, either on the 'afterbit' or in the doctor's room. It is my honest opinion that Dr. Asper and Howard are the sponsors for the whole matter, also including the engineers."

A bit crude. Perhaps Whitted, like the rest of us, found it amusing. Yet we really shouldn't. Although Worley was now pages into his defense, his first page had been a bit alarming. In the second paragraph, he had declared: "Permit me to say at the outset that the charges are the result of a plot on the part of certain officers and men on board the *Cyclops*, which has for its sole purpose my removal as the commanding officer of this ship."

Though such a statement was one that was obviously meant to be carefully worded, it came out very unskillfully. To start off with the claim of a plot is a serious matter, but it was one that Worley either believed or an excuse he thought he could get away with. It controlled his entire defense thereafter, a total of 9 typed pages when he was finally finished. He perused each page, probably several times while typing and after removing the page from the typewriter. He must have been satisfied with the course he had charted.

---

5 Taken from his written defense. He means J.J. Cain.
6 Chief Engineer Samuel Dowdy. He is not to be confused with his son, one of the petitioners, Samuel Dowdy, oiler.

Dark and uncharted waters may be hazardous for the mariner, but they are also waters in which fabulous beasties and any imaginable monster can be said to dwell. Wisely, Worley did not chart his course clearly. Only undercurrents of a plot, perhaps more than one but none of them very definite, continue.

For the accusations of drunkenness, he admitted (after his conspiracy paragraph) that it "is manifestly impossible" for him to respond with any detail to all of the witnesses' statements; instead he chose an interesting defense: "I shall, however, touch briefly on a few of the salient features in connection with these charges."

To Worley, this meant placing his own spin on the testimony. "Nowhere does it appear that any of these witnesses saw me take a drop of liquor. Several of the witnesses testified that they detected the odor of liquor, but the testimony is quite amusing when you consider that the odor was detected at a distance of approximately five feet. A reading of the record in this case will disclose evidence as follows."

The seadog now extracted some supportive lines, such as 'No, Sir, I could not swear to it as I did not see him take a drink'; 'It is rumored around the ship'; 'I was around the gangway when he returned on board and smelled it'; 'About five feet'; 'I smelled liquor only, but did not say he was drunk'; 'I signed it because I was asked to and on the spur of the moment'; 'Captain treated me like a dog my first trip at sea.'

The recital was capped off with: "Invariably all witnesses testified that the signature to the paper was secured by Hospital Apprentice Howard."

Worley's wisest strategic move was in how he used the Liberty issue to his advantage. Much of the testimony had been devoted to it, especially on the second day, though it was not an allegation that was found in the petition. For Worley, this was their "ulterior motive." The allegations of drunkenness were only trumped up charges. That's why, inferred Worley, the Liberty issue wasn't on the petition. He extracted a line here, a sentence there, from select testimony, as he had above, to underscore his reasoning— "'Kyle why did you sign this paper?' Answer: 'I signed it because I was deprived of my liberty in France. Any further complaint? No sir.'"

"I respectfully submit," Worley then declared, "that the motive for all of the testimony of the men was the result of my not allowing them shore leave and enforcing discipline, as shown by their own evidence."

When did Worley uncover this petty motive for such a bold conspiracy? His defense does not clue us in. Most likely, however, it wasn't from "a perusal of the testimony," as he had declared in written defense. He did not go before a Board of Inquiry without some form of defense already planned. Rather, from his own conduct at the B of I he anticipated the subject of biased Liberty coming up. This gives us some insight into why he and nobody else introduced the Liberty issue incongruously. He forced the issue out in the open, or at least gave the appearance he is responsible, in order that he might build to this moment. Now he declared it to have always been the reason, implicitly suggesting it was such a paltry excuse the men had to come up with something far more damning on the petition in order to get their way.

He now capped off the main body of his defense by repeating: "I respectfully call your attention to the fact that a majority of the witnesses who testified were all solicited to sign the paper setting forth certain charges, and that the person who secured their signatures was invariably Howard, Hospital Apprentice." This sandwiched his recital of the complaints between two very strategic statements. It all began with Howard, and it ended with Howard . . . and that ultimately meant Asper.

Drinking was obviously a serious charge, and so far Worley had skirted the issue by implicitly blaming Howard and the Liberty plot, and by saying no one ever saw him take a drink. It was rather weak, especially since smelling liquor on a man while 5 feet away implies the opposite of what Worley was trying to guide Whitted into believing. Frankly, it meant Worley was stinko with drink, so that it was possible in open air to smell him that far away.

77

Officers, too, none of whom had signed the petition, of course, had admitted Worley was under the influence. Now he addressed that, invoking his loyal Lt. Robinson, quoting him declaring 'I have never seen Captain Worley unable to perform his duties. . .' And so Worley diligently went through the testimony, showing that Robinson only had a slight impression of him being under the influence.

All well and good, from Worley's point of view anyway, but Whitted had proven himself diligent enough to have acted upon Lt Hamilton's letter. Worley could not overlook that. He typed away, explaining that this was a part of the plot. He blamed Chief Engineer Samuel Dowdy. Dowdy lost his argument with Worley about his orders that the men were not to be allowed to leave ship in civilian clothes. According to Worley, that night Dowdy handed him a letter requesting transfer and then sent the letter "which is now in the possession of the Supervisor, facts charging me with being drunk. . ." Continuing with this scenario, Worley typed next: "The next day the First Assistant, Mr. Hamilton, followed with a similar letter. And immediately thereafter there appeared the 'Round Robin' "— Worley's expression for the plot.

One must ask, however, which plot? The first one invoked by Worley was "certain officers and men" and it clearly hinged on Howard and therewith implicitly upon Asper and Worley's mocking of his libidinous bar-howling. But now Dowdy is credited as starting it, an officer who seemed to have faithfully followed his master's bigoted orders until he was sick of it.

An excuse had to be given. He boldly uses the shore leave excuse again:

Lieutenant Hamilton and Chief Engineer Dowdy both had it in for me because of my refusal to allow them shore leave immediately after anchoring, because of the fact that their families, friends and relatives lived in Norfolk and desired to leave the ship and see them without regard to the safety of the ship.

The episode with the cocky Landgren had been a minor thing over which Worley no doubt felt sure he had defended himself well. He only lightly touched on it and reminded Whitted that "Boatswain's Mate George's testimony shows that I did not call the crew any insulting names."

However, Worley was so conspiracy bound that this disturbingly remained his continuing explanation. He names more men, blaming them for signing because he had refused to let them have shore leave. This became his excuse even when it came to Hodge and Cain. Their testimony was "due to the fact that I did not allow them to have shore leave while in France whenever they wished it. Of course, had I met their wishes the ship would have been forsaken most of the time, thereby endangering the ship."

Pretty gutsy, one might just say at this moment, pretty gutsy indeed for so many men to independently concoct or support the idea that their captain had been under the influence of drinking just because some did not get a shore leave. In reality, Worley only clumsily revealed his animosity toward the officers in question, especially Hodge. He, like other officers, had not testified negatively against Worley at all. He had merely answered "Yes" when asked about Worley's drinking and then gave a date. Lt. Robinson, Worley's defender, had said as much too. Yet Worley specifically adds Hodge to the plot when it would have been wiser to simply ignore his entire testimony. Cain, too, whose name Worley strangely spells interchangeably as Kane/Kain, could also have been glossed over. The young Ensign had tried to avoid any controversy to begin with but then stumbled out the damning information about the bottle. That obviously is what really had Worley's back to the wall. It was evidence.

Foolishly, Worley did the same thing with Asper. He devoted much space to him, showing us undeniably the hatred he had for his satyr-dandy ship's surgeon, Asper USN. It is evident in his careful wording and in his humor that his typewriter's ink was dipped in blood. Yet, in truth, Asper had said very little. Indeed, like Hodge's or Robinson's testimony, it wasn't really damning. He had said "Yes" about Worley drinking. In addition, Asper had back-peddled and had gotten Worley's neck out of the Landgren encounter, though not very believably. Worley could even use Asper positively, but only briefly. "Even Dr. Asper testified that I was on deck at all times going and coming from France."

Yet of all the officers mentioned, Worley's long response, his explicit statements and his cutting humor tell us he knew Asper was behind it all. From beginning to end, no matter how many subplots Worley unintentionally or simply unskillfully weaved in, it was all Asper. It was merely for his sarcastic rebuff about Asper's beagle magnetism with women. For all the others it was Liberty.

Second only to Asper was Cain in the seadog's contempt list. It forced him to deal with the bottle. He devotes more space to that bottle than he did even to Asper.

Boatswain Kain testified that he found liquor in my room, and that his presence there was due to his being called by Quartermaster Daniels.

The testimony of Quartermaster Daniels on page 44 shows that he showed Mr. Kain a bottle but did not state whether it contained liquor or not. He further testified that it did not contain any label, and it might have contained coffee or some other liquid substance."

I desire to state that this bottle contained medicine that I have used for many years and I most emphatically deny that the bottle contained ardent spirits.

Replying to Quartermaster Daniel's and Mr. Hamilton's testimony of my 'stumbling,' giving the cause of it as alcohol, I beg to state is utterly absurd, and easily explained. I am never surefooted during the hot summer months, due to a former disease of beri-beri, contracted in 1899, on my voyage from Norfolk to Manila, lasting 152 days, in the square-rigged ship St. Mark. On arrival at Manila, I was three months in the first Reserve Hospital before being able to walk without the assistance of a cane. This disease comes back to me in warm climates and unless I take iodine of potash, peruna or sarsaparilla at once, I begin to stumble badly. Therefore I always keep some of the medicine aboard. Iodine is a harsh medicine to take unless mixed with a tablespoonful of Sherry or Port Wine, and that was the mixture the Quartermaster Daniels showed to Boatswain Kain. The bottle is still in the same place in my room on the bridge. On leaving port I usually provide myself with a small supply of Peruna or Sarsaparilla, together with a bottle of port or sherry, which is taken only for medicinal purposes.

I have seen continuous service as ship master for twenty-two years and eight months, and in the Auxiliary Service seventeen years. I have been eight years on the Cyclops. And this is the first time that I have been subjected to the embarrassment of an investigation of this character. It is needless for me to say that any case can be proven by selected witnesses more especially when actuated by malice. I believe I have shown from a hurried analysis of the testimony a motive on the part of the officers for testifying as they did. That it is due largely to my seeing that orders were carried out in accordance with instructions. There is nothing I have done that I would not do over again.

In conclusion I beg to state that instead of being hard on the boys, I treat them like a father. Rather than see them walking around on the iron decks barefooted, and barely clothed, I gave them underwear, shoes and oil skins, as there was no regulation clothing to be had before leaving for France. I even advanced them money out of my own pocket to let them have a few cents to spend when going on liberty in France, and only got it back on our return to the States, after their accounts came on board.

Referring to my ordering them away from the gangway, I can only say that in no well regulated ship the crew is allowed to hang around and obstruct the passageway.

George Worley's defense was really no defense at all. It was a compilation of accusations and counter accusations meant to cause Whitted to interpret all the testimony in his favor. When all was said and done, Worley merely relied upon his "perusal" of the testimony.

Yet a perusal of his defense is far more damning to his position. As unsurely as he typed, so equally unsurely does he exculpate himself from the charges. He admitted the men didn't have proper clothing, but he also admitted that he and Chief Engineer Dowdy clashed over not allowing any man to leave the ship in civies. His orders therefore excluded most of the men except his seasoned Auxiliary men from leaving ship, and that was certainly made clear to him by Dowdy. His orders thus allowed him to hide his bias against Navy men and inductees by forbidding Liberty unless in uniform. It was not Dowdy who was keeping the men from Liberty; it was Worley. Even Robinson, who had been Worley's best witness, confirmed Worley oversaw all Liberties. So much for Worley's fatherly claims.

In fact, Worley doesn't even come off as well-informed about his own crew. He can't spell J.J. Cain's name properly, and he doesn't seem to be aware that Samuel Dowdy, oiler, is Sam Dowdy's son. Accentuating that relationship would be perfect for his repeated defense of a plot. Young Sam had even been one of the first to sign the petition. But Worley never makes reference to it.

Instead he excoriates Landgren again needlessly, telling Whitted he had been kicked out on a "bad conduct" discharge from a previous enlistment. The contemptible Howard was a "former deserter" on a previous enlistment, but had signed up again on the outbreak of war.

"Mostly all the other signers of the 'round robin' I believe were coaxed by older 'sea lawyers' and mischief makers as the majority of signers are mere boys just from the country and have no idea of ship life, rules or discipline. Most I think will make good men."

Graciousness is always a good way to end, but it was merely for show. His defense has already told us everything. He needlessly revealed his underlying animosity for certain officers and men, and failed to successfully weave together all the plots into one, or desires us to believe all these plots were wholly independent.

"I do not believe that the evidence in this case," he concluded, "is sufficient to send a stray dog to the pound much less sufficient to request the removal of a commanding officer who has been in the Auxiliary Service for seventeen years, on testimony of such a flimsy character."

Captain Worley must have felt confident with his 9 pages of explanations and counter accusations, accusations to which none of those accused could ever reply. By rank and custom, he had the final word. He got the paperwork off that very day to Naval Auxiliary Headquarters in Norfolk. How long did Whitted peruse it? Probably not much. That very August day he too typed a letter to his superior, Captain Arthur Orenham.

Whitted essentially whitewashed Worley. He dismissed the accusation that Worley cussed-out Landgren and that he was unfit for duty; but he did accept that he was under the influence of alcohol on several occasions. When Whitted conceded that "there was some discrimination used by Chief Engineer S. Dowdy, (now detached) in selecting the liberty party to go to Paris from the *Cyclops* in that no regular navy men were included in it" he didn't bother to advance beyond that to implicate Worley as the one who supervised Dowdy and refused to let the men leave in civies. Worley was bigoted against regular Navy men, and Whitted was about the only one who didn't detect that.

A captain who claims there is a plot to get rid of him, especially one who has been drinking to excess, should have been a concern to Whitted and Orenham and not the recipient of a whitewash. Orenham, however, didn't bother to give Whitted's findings or Worley's defense much review. He addressed a formal letter to his superiors in Washington D.C. at the Bureau of Navigation on the following day of Whitted's letter, August 10, 1917, in which he asserted: "It is evident that these charges were not inspired by a sense of duty, nor from a fear for the safety of the ship due to the intemperate habits of the Captain, but rather by a spirit of revenge. Most of the signers felt aggrieved by the refusal of the Captain to grant them leave, to which they considered themselves entitled. . ." He added: "Most of the signers of the complaint do not appear to appreciate the seriousness of their act. They simply followed some leader without much thought of the possible consequences."

In his next paragraph he had to admit that "apparently, from the testimony" Worley "drank intoxicating liquor on the ship's passage to France, and, was at times, under its influence, but there is no evidence that he was, at any time, incompetent to perform his duties . . ." Thus Orenham could admit Worley was indeed, well, drunk at times, without believing it affected his performance. What would happen if Worley were stone drunk on the next voyage and something major should happen? No sense of future caution influenced Orenham. He finished his letter with an adamant declaration of character: "Captain Worley has been in the auxiliary service since 1900 with the exception of a few months. His standing and reputation are of the best, and he is considered one of the most efficient and competent Captains of the Auxiliary Service."

Clearly the basic records Orenham had before him were mere abbreviations of an officer's career. They could not have contained details. Those "few months" Orenham refers to were actually in 1908, following the infamous beheading of the First Mate of the *Abarenda*, which we must delve into further in a later chapter of this volume. Here it is best to remind the reader that Worley had left the Service in a huff after being tried at Norfolk in connection with the macabre incident. Worley was acquitted of negligence but upset he was ever tried. He went to Canada briefly but then came back into the Service.

In like manner now, Navy men began to hear how Worley regarded his latest Board of Inquiry. He considered himself the recipient of "shabby treatment." If *status quo* is all that followed the hearing, then Worley could only deduce that he was cleared by the fact he remained in command of the *Cyclops*. This was clearly not enough to comb his ruffled tail feathers. It left him in a terrible limbo wondering if the axe was still hovering over his head. Had he received praise or even an unofficial pat on the back from Whitted, it seems unlikely he would have continued to claim "shabby treatment," and there seems no doubt that those were his own words.

But if Worley felt the axe was still hovering over him, it is hard to explain his continuing behavior. He didn't change at all. On the contrary, things continued to get worse aboard ship.

In December 1918 the *Cyclops* was sent on a short voyage to Halifax, Nova Scotia, for disaster relief. For some inexplicable reason, Worley wanted to anchor off the coast. Yet his bad navigating seems responsible for the fact he couldn't find his desired location right off. He sent the *Cyclops* in circles trying to find a place to anchor. Since there was no bottom the anchor would reach, he resumed his course again. He then ordered "dark ship," but he himself remained in violation of "lights out." W.J. Jeffers was standing gun watch on the quarterdeck by Worley's aft cabin. Uncharacteristically, Worley was spending time in there this night rather than in his emergency cabin on the bridge. Jeffers could see his lights shining through the porthole. He knocked on the door and entered.

"Sir, your lights can be seen."

Worley basically grunted and paid no attention. Shortly afterward Jeffers returned and reminded him. "He told me to get out and shut my mouth, and in a few minutes he flashed his lights three times, and then he told me to go turn in my bunk, but I would not do it. When we docked in Halifax he put me a prisoner at large and then gave me five days bread and water, when we got under way to the fleet he put me in the brig but gave me my meals from the fleet to Norfolk, Virginia."

W.J. Jeffers had been stationed aboard the *Cyclops* from August 20, 1917, to January 2, 1918, and as such he gives us some insight into Worley's behavior on his first significant voyage after the embarrassing Board of Inquiry. "While we were in the fleet at Port Jefferson, the Captain and Doctor were drunk most of the time. He would not give us liberty that went on aboard at Norfolk, but the men who served in the Auxiliary with him were granted liberty at any time."

The effect of the whitewash Worley received from Orenham and Whitted is keenly testified to here, for Jeffers came aboard only a couple of weeks after the Board of Inquiry and yet testifies to the exact same abuses the 'Round Robin' had brought against their drunken captain during the earlier voyage to France. Dowdy cannot be blamed. He was long gone.

However, Jeffers continues with more disturbing information. His encounter of that night brought him eventually face to face with Asper.

I was on the boat deck taking a water breaker to the head and slipped up and hurt my shoulder, not enough to go to the hospital but the doctor said I was too wise. He told to stand by to go to hospital. When he sent me he wrote on my health record "This man is playing for a bad conduct discharge." He told me he wished I would die before I got to the hospital. . .I was transferred to the hospital January 2, 1918.

Burt J. Asper

. . .Shortly before the *Cyclops* would sail on her last voyage.

Asper's actions are hard to interpret. If we knew nothing of the B of I we could assume he was defending Worley by getting off ship a witness who had seen him engaging in suspicious behavior. But that obviously cannot be. From what we know, rather we could say he was saving Jeffers from future persecution. Jeffers must have talked about the encounter. How else would Asper know? Shipmates aboard knew he had been put in the brig for nothing.

But if that is Asper's motive, why try and destroy Jeffers' reputation? He also did that with McDaniel. He delivered him from persecution but then wrote down he was insane.

Perhaps the answer lies in Asper's character. He not only liked to dabble in psychology, it was in a vague way what he enjoyed. He had graduated from University of Maryland's

School of Medicine in 1911 with honor and as a "Gold Medal Man." Neuropsychiatric disease was his specialty— not exactly a broad practice back then. He served as resident staff in two hospitals, but never achieved his own practice. He returned to University of Maryland to teach. War seemed a welcome prospect for his flagging career. He joined the Navy almost immediately. The *Cyclops* was his only assignment. At 28 he looked much older than his years. To some of the crew he was just as big a drunk as Worley. At present he had no real future in medicine.

Having touched a bit on Asper it is probably best to touch on the other officers before continuing. Hodge, for one. Aside from having a very distinctive middle name like Roosevelt, he was regular Navy. He had joined in 1910 and did duty on the USS *Constellation*, the Navy's tall ship used for training, then on the big stuff, like the battleships *Massachusetts* and *New Hampshire*. Then, at last, the lowly, stained collier *Cyclops*. It is little surprising that Worley didn't care for him.

Then there was Ensign John James Cain. His record is so sparse that it only lists the cruiser *Cincinnati* as his previous assignment. He worked his way up the ranks slowly; he had joined in 1910 and was now an Ensign. This may be explained by the fact the *Cincinnati* spent 6 years in Asia, with the legendary US Asiatic Fleet, which spent much of its time between the Philippines and China in order to keep the trade open. Though he did not become a "China Sailor," as they would be immortalized in *Sand Pebbles*, Cain had spent much of his career here so far. Coal duty with Worley was obviously quite ignoble compared to the exotic Orient and the China Station.

Louis J. Fingleton, from Massachusetts, was a lieutenant, though there wasn't much reason why. He was purely a supply man. He had been stationed on the collier *Vulcan* and then the freighter *Carib* which had been drafted by the Navy during the war. His limited career, beginning only on May 29, 1917, is a reflection of his Auxiliary background which was not recorded by the Navy.

The same can be said for Stephen Konstovich. His Navy

87

record shows very little. But he had, in fact, been with the Navy Auxiliary since 1910, when he had started as a coal passer on the USS *Vestal*. He viewed life from the inverted crescent that was his perpetual frown. He had been the third-in-line behind Sam Dowdy in the Engineering Force; now with Dowdy gone and Maguet as Chief Engineer, he was second in command. A crucial position for the pro-German ensign.

Glenn Maquet was as Irish as his name (pronounced McQuett) and from Pennsylvania. He had been an Auxiliarman for years, having been on *Cyclops'* sister ships *Nereus* and *Orion*, then stationed ashore at Norfolk Navy Yard. From there in June he was assigned to the *Cyclops*. Dowdy was certain of Maguet's loyalty, but both had learned how pro-German elements festered on the ship under the aegis of the captain. Dowdy had taught Maguet a certain amount of caution.

Konstovich would not be alone amidst those suspected of being German born. Worley had made sure to have assigned aboard Ensign Hugo Schonof. He came on the *Cyclops* the very day after the embarrassing Board of Inquiry, August 7, 1917. He had no other assignment in the records but the *Cyclops*, his career in the Auxiliary being much more vague and hard to trace.

Pay Clerk was an interesting rank amongst the Warranted officers. An enlisted man with enough time behind him in the Navy could rise up to petty officer and from there to Pay Clerk as an officer. Worley liked his Pay Clerks. Two had had embezzlement problems and a third was very praiseworthy of him. Hugh Morris was to be his Pay Clerk this time. His date of service began only on August 23, 1917, just after the Board of Inquiry. He had no Auxiliary background. He was educated at St. Ann's in New York, then became an accountant at the American Bank Note Company. He resigned and took an enlistment as a Warrant Officer.

Poor C.J. Holmes, Boatswain, had had a hectic Naval career. He had been assigned to many coastal ships, interned freighters, and converted minesweepers, all since April 1917. *Cyclops* was the largest and most important ship he had been assigned to, but it wasn't certain how long he'd last here. He hadn't had a long cruise yet.

Roy Smith, Ensign, who had proven loyal to Captain Worley at the Board of Inquiry, would remain aboard. He was an old Auxiliary man himself. He was formally enrolled on November 10, 1916, but had 10 years 7 months prior service as Seaman, Coxswain and Ass. Master-at-Arms. He had served on nothing but colliers, the *Proteus, Hector, Jason,* and *Cyclops.*

Elmer Green, Machinist, was another veteran of the Auxiliary. He had joined June 15, 1915, but was known to have had 4 years prior service, all of supply ships, *Hector, Solar, Proteus.*

There is such little known about a couple that they can be lumped together. Ensign Joe Mulvey entered in August just after the B of I, and the *Cyclops* was his first assignment. Boatswain Curtis Montgomery, of Banville, Kentucky, entered October 9, 1917.

A couple more will be mentioned later— Ensign Carroll Page, Senator Page's grandson, and the new Executive Officer and crack navigator, Harvey Forbes.

Last but not least we are back to the ship's libidinous psychoanalyst, Burt Asper. Naturally being a doctor his rank had jumped quicker than the others. He entered as a Lieutenant jg on April 12, 1917, and now was already a full Lieutenant.

Of all these officers, he was the only one who could challenge Worley's Barbary Coast ways. Nevertheless, it was quite precipitous. He had not been on the *Cyclops* long until he saw the need that Worley should go. The petition must have been circulating and hanging in his sickbay for a while. Thus about a month into the voyage he saw fit to attempt to remove a longstanding captain from his command. Worley was, truly, that bad. But Asper should have gone to his superiors to complain. Instead he tries an underhanded way. What do his weasely actions indicate? Was he as egotistical as Worley paints, or just naïve?

The unschooled attempt to rid the Navy of George Worley rather reflects badly on Asper. He hadn't banked on Roy Smith and a number of the officers being old Auxiliary hands. He essentially didn't understand what the Auxiliary had even been about. Nor had he sized himself up in comparison to Worley's career. Worley had been in the Auxiliary since 1900, and Asper had merely joined ship before she sailed for France in June. *Cyclops* arrived back in late July.

With most of the men who had signed the petition still aboard on the trip to Halifax, the ship must have been a nest of contention. The new incident with Jeffers would only make it worse. But Asper deals with it again in his underhanded way. Was that Asper's motive? Was it merely to keep another incident from stirring up the latent contention? Or was it more personal, selfish? After his poor showing, he may not have wanted to go through any kind of B of I again. Yet the men might still have seen him as their only hope. The only way for Asper to avoid being bugged to help yet again might be to get off any source of contention, such as Jeffers, and let it get around that he wasn't their friend.

Outside of Worley, Asper was the only one able to get a man off the ship. He certainly made sure that Howard, the cat's-paw in the whole Board of Inquiry affair, had been conveniently shipped off the *Cyclops* before the Inquiry. Howard was the only one, logically, who when cross-examined could completely and openly implicate Asper.

It is, however, quite unlikely that Asper was worried about a B of I being initiated by some more menial Landgren-like complaining. But Jeffers' experience was different. The last B of I showed how Worley implied other problems were aboard, especially the violations of "lights out." Along with many other men and officers, Asper was certain Worley was aggressively pro-German. The signal light incident with Jeffers could potentially stir up a hornet's nest. The surgeon doesn't seem to have wanted any part of it, but he had not lost his loathing for his sodden master. He got Jeffers off the ship, coarsely protecting himself and the *status quo* in the bargain by making sure his word ashore at the hospital was no good.

With this episode, only one of others that will be dealt with later, we can see how the atmosphere aboard ship must have been stifling. The men were at the mercy of a spiteful chess game. From the testimony we know that Asper baited crewmen who offended him. Certainly Worley knew that or he wouldn't have implied that Asper had manipulated Landgren after having received "sass" from him.

If anything had changed aboard, it was that the atmosphere was worse. The B of I had altered nothing. There was a sense of helplessness on the part of the crew. Since Worley remained and remained as surly as always, the crew could only interpret this one way. The Navy was behind him 100 percent. There was no redressing their grievances anymore.

In truth, the Navy had merely been lackadaisical. For this, Asper in particular should have been grateful. Had Whitted or Orenham given the minutes much consideration it wouldn't have been hard to see that Asper and Worley were bitter enemies. If they had been behind Worley 100 percent, they would have gotten rid of Asper. It's easier to replace a ship's surgeon than it is a ship's captain, especially one with knowledge of specialized cargoes and crucial fueling duties. But they didn't. Whitted and Orenham glossed over it all. This left Worley exonerated, but they also left the *Cyclops* unchanged and the problems aboard unaddressed.

Asper may have had another reason to maintain the *status quo*. The *Cyclops* had docked back at Norfolk in late December. Almost immediately word spread that Worley was selling his house, retiring and moving to San Francisco. This was true. Worley wasted no time. Civilians were already visiting him aboard. Even before Jeffers was transferred on January 2, just a week after the *Cyclops* had returned, he had seen the civilians and inquired. It was certain. Worley was selling out.

The issues aboard would thereby soon be dealt with. Worley was leaving the Navy. Considering this was wartime, this is indeed surprising. But as far as any man aboard was concerned, especially Asper, there was no point in pursuing any of the problems anymore. They would all be solved shortly by George Worley's sudden, very sudden departure.

4

BOUNTY AND BREADFRUIT

"In the course of our conversation regarding this vessel and commanding officer, who I had formerly known, Dowdy made a number of statements as to the wishes of Commander Worley that Germany would win the war, being especially bitter against the English. Commander Worley was to be investigated, which I understand was recently done, after which he was very bitter in regards his so-called ill treatment by the government."
—Lt. Cmdr. Frank T. Burkhart

THE GENERATION OF A HUNDRED years ago must have had a greater sense of modernity than we do, for all around them were the stark contrasts of old and new, of phasing out and often cumbersome incorporating, both together accentuating the changes their generation was undergoing. Norfolk town was positioned to be the perfect example of this hybrid world. Over 300 years collided, mixed, and argued in Norfolk. Thundering breakers still reminded one of ancient and swarthy deeds along this coast. Somewhere nearby sandy dunes and sea oats concealed Blackbeard's treasure. Masts had crammed Hampton Roads like a solid forest of trade between Norfolk and Newport News. Now huge steamers idled under purring curls of dirty smoke. The aggravating drone of a heavy mosquito reminded people of the other end of the spectrum. Flight itself was dis-

covered nearby. Over the horizon of the outlying farms biplanes now buzzed along. Downtown and the docks looked little different than 50 years before. Cobblestones still bore the
scratches of Union and Confederate cannon wheels. Brightly
painted steamer cars, however, now putted along behind those
obnoxious horns. Skyline was a tasteful mixture of large brick
office buildings, a theatre, old colonial churches, gabled residential streets dating to the civil war, warehouses, spires, and
stately columned libraries. But old and new were linked by
something more than odd juxtaposition. Wires were everywhere. Poles sported electric wires, telephone wires, telegraph.
Main street looked like a shredded kite overhead. Wires were
not just the skeleton of the modern world of communications.
They were its body and soul.

Visually, it must have been extraordinary— cobblestones
and power poles, parasols and air raid sirens, horse-drawn cavalry and bright civilian automobiles done up in gaudy colors,
chrome, and carriage tops. Streets peopled by Edwardian dignity. With parasol in hand, American women in long dresses
strolled underneath the ugly communication wires. Men were
formal, with bowlers, starched white collars, and peering
through little round spectacles. Soldiers were in olive drab
uniforms and high gaiters; bizarre alien bug-like gas masks
now a part of their kit.

Your average boy's first novel was *Treasure Island*. On the
other end of the spectrum, both of age and literature, adults
wistfully discussed the possibilities of what H.G. Wells had
written in *War of the Worlds*. Navy men swaggered in their
blue uniforms and jauntily tilted white caps. Officers performed their formal functions in their bicorn hats, bulging
gold epaulets and swords at their side. . .and perhaps *The Time
Machine* awaiting their reading pleasure in their ship's library
below.

Modernism is seen most in the ebullience we associate with
each spring and the warm memories we have of winter firesides and tradition. This was the Spring of the modern world,
still anchored to Victorian and Georgian firesides.

"Yankee Know How" went part and parcel with it. Americans were always into gadgets, conveniences and fads. They have more often praised ingenuity and industry than intelligence. The great American boom was about to hit. Catering to this became the mother of invention rather than necessity. The Republic always favored the embodiment of ideals along ancient Roman and Greek concepts. This, too, was the winter fireside of its warm traditions. Roman goddesses now naturally wore Gibson hairdos in order to declare established order and paradoxically to sanctify the latest trend. An enthroned Gibson goddess of Justice, holding proud the scales of equity, was the motto for Sear-Roebuck's pre-fab homes: "Honor built modern homes." One could get anything from a Sears catalog. For $1,257.00 the two story beginner charm house was yours. Sear's competitor Sterling Homes boasted it could build their homes in 11 days, not including "SASH," which must have been the new vogue acronym for "Saturday's Sundays, Holidays excluded." Their Windmere floor plan was a favorite. It had basement, two stories, with a windowed attic. All the homes had porches, of course. What American middleclass home did not have a porch?

The "Roaring Twenties" would give us an exhilarating taste of what was only now incubating in 1918. Free from the war, the average American would reach for the boundless life. Pre-fab homes, automobiles, pan-American highways— California-New York in a week.

It was the world of no limits because there was the mindset of no limits. When first a dream pops into our heads we always dazzle ourselves with its limitless potential. After all, optimists feed on trifles. This was the era of first dreams. Flight caused us to dream of space. Engineering caused us to be both shocked and intrigued by *Metropolis*. Huge telescopes suggested there were canals on Mars. Flight made us certain we could get there. But theory like dreams is easy. Logistics is difficult. This era hadn't yet considered the logistics of all this. It was still in that euphoric world of extrapolation.

The Great War was the problem. Logistically, it told us how

Sterling out-boasted Sears, declaring that its Windmere House could be built in 11 days not counting SASH.

we could ruin it all. It was causing a damper on what modernity could do. That nasty Kaiser! The marvels of the world at our fingertips were soiled by train stations full of men in drab uniforms who didn't want to go off to war. Why should we do this? We never did it before. America had only had wars to defend itself and protect its interests. What did all those European royal cousins and their squabbles have to do with us? Trainloads were now returning wounded, awaited by ranks and ranks of women in long Edwardian dresses and white aprons with red crosses on them. Amputations. Gas poisoning. When was this going to end? This nasty war because of this pompous Kaiser! Society was desperately awaiting peace.

This world was making George Worley more and more a thing of the past. Within this world he had to keep silent about his political sympathies. His old tyrannical ways had even come under scrutiny. He was already obsolete, but now he was also becoming something strangely foreign as he ambled through these "anywhere USA" colonial streets to visit the frozen docks of January 1918.

Inspecting the minimal repairs that the Navy saw fit to give the *Cyclops* only irked him more. They didn't seem to understand that the ship's engines desperately needed overhaul. How many times had he mentioned the engine problems? He mentioned it while off France, before Halifax, and even in his written defense. On page 8 he had justified not letting the men have Liberty because "lots of repairs had to be made to the main engines."

To Worley, the Navy just didn't understand much at all. They didn't understand about Asper in spite of the fact he basically threw the libidinous sawbones on a silver plate and painted him as a petty conspirator. His nemesis remained aboard. Ironically, Burt Asper didn't ask for a transfer. Instead he got stuck with him. This simply confirmed for Worley that Asper knew he was a deadbeat. If he was so good, he would have been a successful doctor on land. The fact he was a ship's doctor meant he was a loser. And Worley knew why. He was a booze hound. He was stewed one too many times while in port and then howling with those beagles that he boasted went for his crooning magnetism. Worley's sarcastic humor blinded him to his own hypocrisy.

The Auxiliary days must have already seemed like glory days to George Worley. He had done well then. He had done so well that there was no pre-fab home for him. He had a brick home on Pennsylvania Avenue in Colonial Place. It was the type of home that such upstarts as the Windmere plan was based on. It wasn't wide. Most houses downtown aren't in Norfolk. It's a town with a notorious past of narrow lots. But it was very nice for him, his wife and little girl Ginny, who was named after their State of Virginia. It had a 7 window attic, 4 large front upstairs windows, and wonderful white painted wood porch to offset the wonderful American brick, and a basement with large windows. It wasn't unique. It was one of at least 3 identical floor plans on that side of the street, but it was one of the nice plans.

It must have proved surprising for the Worleys' neighbors to see a 'for sale' sign reflect the sun off the bright blanket of snow. Norfolk is a Navy town. Wives mingle while their husbands are out to sea and naturally gossip to them when they return. His wife Selma, the one whom all the neighbors knew, told them that George said it was time to retire and go back to San Francisco, back home. They must have been surprised indeed. Why not wait? No, even though early January and that George was leaving soon for a long voyage, he wanted the house up for sale. It must have seemed odd to the neighbors, especially in light of the Board of Inquiry. After all, this was war. How could an experienced captain retire during war? But there were hints of ill health. Selma told them George needed surgery. There would be a long recuperation. When sold, Selma could rent, she said, until he returned. They would also sell their car and furniture. Then when he returned, they would take the train to San Francisco.

George Worley's resolve was strange, and perhaps few in the Navy grapevine bought into it. Those from his past knew he couldn't storm out of the Navy now like he had the Auxiliary when he had been called before the mast in 1908. There was no coming back that easily, and, of course, there was the war. It wouldn't look good. But to many it still didn't look good. It looked like an intolerant man in a temper fit.

For the average citizen there may not have been much of a difference between Auxiliary and the Navy, but within the ranks there was an enormous difference. Worley had been a Captain in the Auxiliary. When he was enrolled in the Naval Reserve he lost a bar and a half and became a Lt. Commander. He willfully submitted to this. Maybe he had been surprised by it. Maybe the changes were hard. He now had to salute some of those who once had to salute him. But he had not waited for war and automatic enrollment in April 1918. He had submitted his enlistment on February 21, 1917, months before the war. Perhaps few knew this. Perhaps even fewer knew he hadn't been accepted right away, even after 17 years in the Auxiliary. He was accepted only after war came and automatic enrollment started.

But all knew he was a qualified commander in the Naval Reserve in wartime. Just what was this illness?

People in Norfolk had a right to know. George Worley had

been vociferously in favor of Germany. He had walked around and visited shops with the captains of the German freighters that were interned. After one-too-many he had even gotten in verbal brawls over who was right in the war. Now that the war was declared it wasn't enough that he only self-consciously waved off the question "How are your German friends?" with "I don't associate with those people anymore." Worley was leaving the Navy and he only "needed surgery." What is this? It was never qualified.

A few friends remained. All of them had German names.

George remained aloof. He came and went from his home in his car. Sometimes he was coming and going from the icy docks. Other times he was merely gone for a while. Then the car would pull up the narrow street and George would park it by the porch and slip inside.

A lazy Sunday would find him nestled in his parlor sneering at the thought of his ship's surgeon. "Sex fiend," he once snorted, only quickly to be chastised by his wife's voice from the next room.

"Language!"

It is hard to say whether Selma had been surprised by the decision to sell the house. She was fiercely protective of their reputation, and probably would say nothing, even to a close friend. But it certainly made no sense that George should remain in the Navy for one last voyage when they were selling out.

Well, this is of course dependent on believing the front that Selma and George put up. You see, George had a couple of female friends. This was no secret to other Navy men. This wasn't the case of a lonely sailor with a gal in Mandalay. Both women lived in Norfolk. Both were also prostitutes. It is possible that Selma found out. Thus there was a split-up and hurried selling of the house. This would also explain why George still decided to remain in the Navy and not retire right away. Maybe he really didn't intend to retire at all. But there had to be an excuse why they were suddenly selling.

When his next assignment came, it was perfect. He was to

pick up a very important cargo of manganese ore. It would be a long voyage. It wouldn't be in the war zone, and for this voyage the *Cyclops* would not even be directly in the Naval Service. She was chartered by the United States and Brazil Steamship Co. The object: head to Rio de Janeiro and pick up 10,000 tons of the stuff for the US. On the way there the *Cyclops* would do double duty and refuel Admiral William Caperton's ships off South America.

Knowledge of manganese ore is obviously not on anybody's high priority list. Manganese is but a trace mineral in our own bodies, but very vital. Without it thousands of chemical reactions do not work. Likewise manganese ore was critical for armaments production. The utensils of war were not made of manganese, but in a small way it was indispensable. Without it all those cannon, tanks, guns, ships, bombs, and missiles would quickly rust. Nations and armies could smith cannons and tanks, but how long would the new steel cavalries and navies last without it?

In World War I manganese was quite the rage. Its ability to delay rusting and protect iron was only discovered in 1912. That made it the new thing in industry and warfare. Its ability to prolong armaments life also made it doubly important for nations and armies on a budget. Rust protection meant extending the life of the equipment. On top of this, manganese was an easy metal to oxidize. This made the process of manganese phosphating of armaments easier. It was for the world of engineering as exciting a discovery as a new spice had been on far distant islands in the 18th century. Needless to say all sides in the war wanted manganese.

It was, in fact, better than breadfruit. There was nothing subjective about its use. Slaves didn't have to like it. Its use was assured and it was guaranteed by applied science. But like in the days of the spice trade, there was no stockpile in Europe or America. It came from exotic places. It grew plenty in Brazil. Fortunately, this little metal rock didn't mean much to them, just as breadfruit meant little to Tahiti. Yet this didn't make it easy. Long voyages are the most dangerous. Brazil was the only South American nation to say to hell with Germany, true. But this also made it an island amidst officially neutral nations seething with German agents and coasts clutching secret lagoons and hiding places for German raiders and subs.

Until America entered the war, allied ships carrying the stuff were in danger of U-boats. When America entered the war it could wisely transport it safely enough since American ships could hug the coast and remain far from the war zone. U-boats could rarely get so far from Germany as to stalk the American east coast for any duration. From these or a Canadian port manganese would then be shipped by convoy protection to Britain and France.

But surface raiders and spies remained a problem. Raiders could hide in the various sequestered lagoons of South America. Given a tip off by German spies, they could lay in wait for the vessel.

For obvious reasons, shipping had to remain completely secret. The problem was, how to do this? Manganese was heavy, much heavier than coal. For the safety of the ship it took days to load. Spies in Rio certainly would know what the cargo was just by looking at the loading lighters and the direction they came from. It also wasn't hard to buy dockside knowledge. Therefore spies had more than enough time to send telegraphs to port towns on the north of Brazil or in Venezuela to alert a roosting raider.

But dockside lingo couldn't predict an ETA, nor even impart a course. Only Worley and top officers would know that. Though the *Cyclops* was under civilian charter, the paperwork would be handled by the US consulate in Rio. Only the highest there would know the destination port and ETA.

By assigning George Worley to ship manganese the Navy was indeed making a gesture of faith in his sailorly skills. But was it redemption or just ignorance? One cannot say that it was because of a false sense of security that the *Cyclops* was given the duty, but if the Navy had one it was only because of Captain Arthur Orenham's glowing appraisal that no deeper probe was initiated into George Worley's behavior and that no red flags were subsequently raised.

As it stood now in the first week of January, George Worley probably had no reason to return to America and no desire to miss this voyage. Unusual things, to say the least, transpired, that suggest this.

There was a surprise at the Worley house. Little Ginny was terribly sick. Selma was beside herself and became finally convinced that it was scarlet fever. George Worley now had his excuse to avoid his last voyage. If he finally wanted out of the Navy, out of his final voyage, he undeniably had the excuse. But he had no intentions of avoiding the voyage to South America. Selma pled with her implacable husband that they must call a doctor, but George dissuaded her. If there is even a breath of scarlet fever mentioned he feared he might be personally quarantined.

Selma understood his commitment to duty and relented, returning to the bedside, feeding broth into Ginny and changing the cool rags on her forehead.

As heartless as the old seadog might have seemed, he knew every backwater and stagnant disease a tramp steamer could contract. He may have invoked his knowledge of topical and exotic diseases and thereby assured her this was not scarlet fever. Perhaps he told Selma more. We can never know. But she knew that George had to make this voyage.

He was justified in only a couple of days. The fever broke, and it seemed Ginny would be all right. Selma slept soundly for the first time in days, and the old seadog was left alone to sit in the darkened parlor, caress the cork on his bottle, and plan his voyage.

The Roads informed him the *Cyclops* was icebound. That didn't matter. He intended to leave January 8 no matter what.

5

HELL SHIP

"He had a fund of tales, mostly humorous, but he was quite erratic at times. Without the slightest pause between words, his mood would change to that a very opinionated man— a self-proclaimed genius who thought he had never arrived but should have. It was while in these moods that he'd take out his rage on some unknowing officer."

—Conrad A. Nervig

A VERY BLEAK JANUARY 8, 1918, finally came. Hampton Roads was a blurry image, as defined as images seen through a stained glass window. Snow flurries skipped over the shelf ice in Chesapeake Bay; in the far distance the departing Navy ships were almost obscured as if they were little models in a shaken glass snowball.

Soft gray plumes of smoke began to rise from the *Cyclops'* tall smokestacks and stain the gloomy overcast like diluted ink in milk. The great vessel was coming to life anticipating the arrival of the one and only master she had ever known.

Waiting upon deck was Conrad Nervig, a young Ensign who had been transferred to the South American squadron of the Fleet and was shipping out on the vessel. With hands in his heavy overcoat pockets, he stood by the gangplank, the notorious gangplank, his shoulders huddled together in the cold, damp weather. Through the misty puffs of his own breath his eyes never left off the approaching sea captain. In an ominous way he too was emerging from the flurries. They played about before him on the dock, but wisely seemed to part and scamper away, seized by a sudden impulse of caution the nearer he huffed and puffed. The brute's face was red from the cold, and his breath all from his nose, like an angry bull. Ice crystals sparkled off his buttoned overcoat. His bristle-like hair, frayed under the brim of a Lieutenant Commander's hat, was laced with droplets. His footing was sure on the wet dock, and he walked as if taking a stroll in the park, advancing briskly with a poke and an uplifted flourish of his fancy mahogany cane— a curious sight in such a rough place as Hampton Roads. The seadog seemed to fit in so well with the scroungey dock rats despite his clean long overcoat and walking cane. What a tableau to behold: a loutish Navy figurehead eloped from the prow of some old New England whaler.

Some innate sense told Nervig who was coming. Turning but a fraction to the Officer of the Deck, Ensign J.J. Cain, his unenthusiastic reaction confirmed to Nervig that the notorious Captain Worley was approaching his command. Cain's eyes were frozen upon the crusty apparition, and barely any frosty breath emerged as he ever-so slightly and mournfully sighed.

The young, shivering Ensign didn't need to render a caption for the scene that greeted Nervig. His answer lay in the seamen who stood nearby. They broke ranks and walked away, each and sundry barely uttering even a grumble. It was perhaps just a collective moan, more visible than hearable. Little did Nervig know that this was the gangplank from which Worley had chased so many in New York.

By this time Captain Worley was halfway up the gangplank, poking his cane out and then sticking it back into the gradient with each mounting step. With each step his breath puffed with dragon-like bursts. As he mounted the deck he didn't bother to shift the cane in order to salute properly; rather, in response to Cain's perfunctory salute he touched his cap's bill with its silver handle.

Nervig's first impression of the sea captain was that of a "nice man." Anybody around Cain, however, would fare better by comparison, except for Asper, in Worley's eyes, so that Nervig was no doubt the object of Worley's friendly interest. Polite introductions gave the seadog a way to ignore Cain and concentrate on the guest. But even more important than being

someone unconnected with the past controversies, it was the cut of Nervig's jib. He was 29, and though a Naval Reservist he had come up the ranks the hard way. He was no snot-nosed young Mr. Cain, with cheeks too rosy, voice too quavering, and mouth too unschooled. Nervig had a bit of a swarthy face, long, even gaunt, and a thin, suave mustache. He didn't seem too Navy, and he wasn't crusty Auxiliary. He was, as he would find out, a perfect compromise for his culturally stunted master. And, though Nervig couldn't appreciate it then, he also had a Germanic name.

The captain walked away to his bridge, breaking off the introductions as gruffly as he had come aboard and as casually as he had saluted.

The deck of the *Cyclops* did not inspire the piping and pageantry as warships do. There wasn't really a sign of war about or of anything elegant that goes with a warship. All the gearworks of the main deck— winches, motors, boxes, vents— were in mimic suspension like a frozen army covered with caps of snow. The tall derricks crowded together like naked trees in winter drippings. Inverted spires of ice wept from the cold steel. The great girders were dusted with the night's snow.

Through this forlorn jungle the captain slogged to the bridge. It could be seen as a cabin might appear through stands of ugly tree trunks. It was an artless box set high on steel girders. It stretched from starboard to port and straddled the narrow bow. Worley stomped up the stairs, then along an open platform underneath and then disappeared upward along another flight of stairs into that uninviting tower.

"Commander Worley was a gruff, eccentric salt of the old school, given to carrying a cane, but possessing few other cultural attainments. He was a very indifferent seaman and a poor, overly cautious navigator. Unfriendly and taciturn, he was generally disliked by both officers and men."

A picture can certainly make one speak, but Cain did not impart this information to Nervig, nor would he. I make a point of saying this here, for Nervig's summary is purely observational. It is not from informed opinion. It begins with this moment— the only time he ever saw Worley in full form with walking cane— and the synopsis that followed of his character although it is entirely accurate it remains largely detached. There is never any real indication that the officers and men told him much of anything. Nervig never learned of "beri-beri" and the captain's "need" to carry a cane in summer months. It was to him merely an affectation that starkly contrasted with his crusty appearance and behavior.

For our purpose it is good that Nervig remained locked in a bubble of silence. His narrative in *The Cyclops Mystery* shows us he is a good observer, but the contentions that stifled open communication aboard the ship spared his observations from ever being tainted by past bias. He is therefore only capable of giving us brief snapshots, those significant dots. Yet with the massive amount of paperwork on Worley and the *Cyclops*, this is enough for us to draw the connecting lines and create a reliable outline for the voyage south.

By late morning the snow was still gently falling in playful flurries. The last of the men and supplies were aboard. *Cyclops* was heavily loaded down to her plimsol line with coal and other miscellany for the fleet. Last aboard was the mail, bags and bags of it headed to Admiral Caperton's squadron off South America.

Down in his cabin Nervig felt the ship vibrate. The engines were churning the great screws. Engine room coal and oil tainted the warm air inside, but it was much better than the gloomy sight outside the porthole. Everything was blurred by the sheet of ice on the glass. Some of the docks were several stories tall, with huge coal chutes angled out by which the colliers were loaded. But it was all one distorted blur like an image in a funhouse mirror. The stories of piers and crossbeams angled like S, the snowcapped chutes curled like a gross, yawning tongue; and there was no way to clear the ice off the porthole to enjoy a normal view of flurries sprinkling down over the hibernation of Norfolk town's colonial skyline. He continued unpacking. He took his wife's picture from his suitcase and considered it happily before he set it carefully on a small writing desk.

Outside the porthole the warped docks and warehouses should be slipping away smoothly as the *Cyclops* slowly glided out. But there was terrible crunching. There was breaking and shattering. No sooner had the porthole shuddered violently, sending the blurry image dancing.

Cyclops had been icebound. Worley had been prepared for that. It was as if he was at the helm himself right now, angrily backing up, pushing forward, breaking up every bit of ice to get the *Cyclops* out into the channel.

Young Carroll Page now knocked on Nervig's cabin's half open door and told him, rather redundantly, they were off. He was a plump-face Ensign, but 24 years old, but he looked much older than his years. He was also a breath of the Navy. His tailored blues fit perfectly, and his hat's black glossy bill was regulation just above his eyes. Yet there was an ease about his manner.

As a passenger, Nervig had no assigned duties, but Page would tell him of the Mess hours and seating in the wardroom. Obviously, Page needn't elaborate about events aboard. So far Nervig only had impressions. Even if Nervig would make the usual offhand comment deferring to the dining arrangements  being "Captain's orders," Mr. Page would only respond that Captain Worley seldom takes his meals in the wardroom. Page, of course, knew of the sex conversations, which Worley in his written defense probably exaggerated with his sarcastic innuendos. But true enough, we know Worley seldom ever ate with his officers. And, though there is nothing for us but Nervig's later comments on the conditions of the wardroom, Worley probably never ate with the officers again after the embarrassing Board of Inquiry.

Page was circumspect enough, of course, to say nothing too compromising the first time meeting Nervig. But there is no question the two hit it off right away. Page's convivial manner was enchanting, and his humor was contagious. He was also pragmatic, thick skinned, and someone who could laugh at himself. He was Senator Carroll Page's grandson, but there was no hint of the affluent Vermonter. His grandfather had been self-made in hide dealing, and brought the boldness of the self-made to the Senate. In many respects young Carroll had those boisterous qualities, but he did not have the need to direct them to making a living immediately. Young Carroll more than anyone in the family was reaping the rewards of success and could drift a bit. As his grandson he had been educated at some nice prep schools, including one military academy and the National Cathedral School in Washington DC. Yet he wouldn't graduate any of them. This earned him the jocular nickname "Flunko." For his enthusiasm for his schemes, he would also earn the nickname "Boom." In his biography at University of Vermont, where he would graduate, his gregarious, sarcastic character was evident:

> This young man has been very highly educated, having attended three institutions of higher learning in his short prep school career. In spite of this fact, however just as soon as tests come around, Boom flunks out of College, so he tells us. These statements are highly contradictory to the irrevocable fact that he is still with us and in our class. Boom has had wild and, as yet, unrealized ideals of going to some other college, but it looks now as if he is going to be with us at graduation. Boom has a very philanthropic disposition and has been known to be a spendthrift if the occasion required. His ambition in College has been limited to raising a mustache that resembles a cross between the Kaiser's and a hair-lip. In the serious vein, we find Boom a very likable fellow, with some mighty good stuff. He does make a little "boom" occasionally, but he is not all noise, by any means. He has many good ideas, and is not afraid to lend courage to his convictions. He has a happy faculty for making friends who stand by him, and is liked wherever he goes.

Probably the war was a welcome call for "Boom," at least the exciting prospects it offered. He had intended, at least at graduation, to enter the family business of banking and hide dealing, but for one of his character that would be boring. Now he was on the high seas to exotic lands. Worley was probably something very interesting to him, and with his idle ambitions the duty aboard the *Cyclops* was greeted as one passing but highly entertaining step on his road to adventure.

After he scooted off to other duties, Nervig thoughtfully retreated back into his room and continued to unpack, stopping only to look out the porthole at the warped contours of grays and nothing else. The *Cyclops* was steaming in the Roads now, heading for the bay. Breathy mist fogged the porthole glass as he craned his neck to see the sea. They were making a sure speed through the ice channel. The broken ice layer skipped and bounced along the gray hull, causing thuds, echoes, and breaking to bits like glass.

In his cabin Nervig could not know why the *Cyclops* hit so much ice. Only those on the bridge were aware. After crashing his way out, Captain Worley had taken the notion to cut across the ice shelf to make the channel. It meant little to him that a ship was already rightfully in the channel and heading out.

The bridge was Worley's personal kingdom. It also fit his character— elevated, straddling the ship, the superimposition of disproportion. This rectangular box held the bridge, radio room and Worley's emergency cabin. A couple of portholes overlooked the main deck, a few were grouped in the center where the bridge overlooked the bow. The whole riveted mass of artless engineering was approachable only by a flight of metal stairs that led up into the bottom like the bridge was really just a massive crow's nest.

Mr. Robinson was long gone. There was yet again a new Executive Officer aboard, Mr. Harvey Forbes. The sight of the *Cyclops* coming to the channel in such a fashion sent his shoes tapping hurriedly up the ladder to the bridge.

Coming down carefully was the Second Officer. Mr. Hodge was a tall, lean figure, even in his long heavy saddle overcoat. Right now his arms were huddled by his side and hands buried in his coat's deep pockets. His face, long and alabaster, made him look older, but his maturity lay more in his restraint and circumspection, a winking eye, or finger to the side of his nose. He always seemed relaxed, in fact, but his eyes were lively and irascible. His voice was natural, as if bidding good day to a frequent acquaintance.

"Best not."

Forbes was a shorter man, compact and lively, and thus with close-set facial features he was sharper and more demonstrative in his responses. There was no rudeness in his quickness; there was passion and sometimes brashness. Forbes had stopped suddenly and eyed the junior officer sharply.

Stopping from his descent, and turning, Hodge said: "It implies the captain isn't handling things properly. Best take it slow." Hodge now reburied his chin in his bundling scarf and set his intents to turn and keep descending.

But Forbes was bold and certain. Forbes knew of only one way to navigate— from point A to Point B. Worley was smashing through the ice field.

"Best not," advised Hodge again at seeing Forbes ready to sprint up. He said nothing else and continued down the wet metal steps.

Forbes was not going to heed the warning. But he waited a moment. He watched Hodge safely maneuver the "bike path" along the main deck. This elevated catwalk ran the length of the ship to the afterdeck. When the heavy weather caused the *Cyclops* to shift seas, the men could still walk along the path, hold the rope railing and be relatively safe. It was just one piece of ugly gray matter on a deck cluttered with gray machinery, winch motors, boom bases, oiling hatches, hold hatches and vents— the outer workings of an intricate but disorganized clock— that were always clutched in the lattice work shadows of the 24 towering coal derricks.

There should be no doubts that Hodge was not going to get too involved in anything that might upset his captain. Worley didn't like him. Aside from Worley hating young officers, he disliked seasoned officers, like Hodge, who smacked too much of the real Navy, oversight, and tradition. As we know, Hodge had testified very conservatively at the Board of Inquiry. Yet Worley made a personal retaliation against Hodge's reputation.

Forbes was new, very new to anything Worley. He should have heeded any advice he could get, for First Officers had not fared well under Worley's command. On the voyage between Cuba, Mr. Shaw had been ordered off the bridge brusquely when Worley had seen fit, to the point it had disgusted other officers. Shaw was lucky to transfer before the voyage to France. Then Mr. Robinson had taken his duties, but only for that voyage. It was now up to Forbes.

Just seeing Forbes on the steps must have told Hodge everything about his new Exec's personality. And indeed it was incisive. Forbes scurried up the ladder and there disappeared into the great bridge.

Within the bridge there stood the bundled ranks of men in their long, thick coats, some with hands in pockets, others holding with gloved hands their binoculars; but all were watching just two things: Captain Worley and a US warship coming into the main channel from a cross channel in the blanket of ice.

"She's the Survey, sir," said Lt. Mulvey, a hay colored officer with frost-bitten cheeks. "She's Atlantic outbound for patrol."

Worley stood before a chosen porthole, one hand clutching a wooden railing bolted on the wall beneath it, the other holding his binoculars against his chest. He had been watching her like an indifferent hawk but a hawk nonetheless. He would not acknowledge. There would be the proverbial awkward silence that was broken only by Forbes entering the bridge. Mulvey would carefully speak up again. He had good reason. *Cyclops* was to windward, having the right of way, but *Survey* was ahead. *Cyclops* also cut across the shelf and would soon be merging with the main channel, where *Survey* had been rightfully sailing.

"Sir, she'll be merging with the main channel soon."

Worley sighed. "Well, son, if we hit her we were too close."

But Harvey Forbes adds a new dynamic to Worley's otherwise predictable behavior.

The results of the confrontation we do not know from within the bridge. We only know from our outward vantage, which had many witnesses. The *Cyclops* came into the channel and almost clipped the *Survey*'s stern, pitching and rolling from the *Survey*'s churning wake. The great screws went dead for a second. Then they churned in reverse. At the same moment that the *Cyclops*' propellers chopped the sea behind her to hold her back, the *Survey*'s propellers kicked the ocean into froth as she galloped ahead.

The *Survey* blew a nasty burst on her horn, which Worley ordered the *Cyclops* to return.

The actions brought the men topside. Many were still hanging about the rails watching the *Survey* when Nervig stepped out the aft deck, now bundled in his heavy coat. The others did not remain long. None wanted to be found huddled by the rails. All could imagine what mood Captain Worley was in. "Some beginning" was the standard quip.

It was a hazardous and long walk along the "bike path." The shadow of the tall derricks overhead crisscrossed over the snow covered deck and machinery. Each row flanked the tiny catwalk, stowed stiff and straight as if frozen soldiers at attention. Some were crusted on top by thick caps of snow, and sometimes a large clump fell and pelted Nervig.

Wiping his face, he got the last view of the *Survey* disappearing into the thin distant fog ahead. From her churning wake it was clear she wished to remain clear of the *Cyclops*.

From the *Survey*, Worley's *Cyclops* too must have looked like a small dark toy amidst a blanket of white ice. She was now certainly a lone island of life. The fog began coasting over her amidships, wrapping around her and concealing her from any point of reference. Lazy waves of fog swept the stern castle. The bow, too, was piercing a thick wall of it. Alone in the midst of the fog, Nervig felt strangely isolated on board this very unfriendly ship.

As he stepped by the foot of the metal stairs leading up to the foc's'le, the bridge came into view high overhead, like a misty dark block on tiny stilts. The bridge door clanked shut. Footsteps mounted another rung of metal stairs upward to the open flying bridge. There was a fretful groan facing duty. Mr. Cain, it seems, would be blamed.

The *Cyclops'* journey to becoming a hell ship was preceded by a tormenting prelude. Anticipation can be a dreadful terror. That inner question 'Who will be the next victim?' is a terrible preamble to each morning's rising. So far, the question had haunted two mornings. This, the second day out, the officers' wardroom had been a particularly gloomy place. The mealtime angst had been set in motion by the dread that Worley might, just might, call an officer forward and accuse, berate and all around dress him down for some trivial matter.

Some had to worry more than others. There were prime targets. Mr. Cain, for one. Hodge was another. It was clear that Harvey Forbes and the night school navigator were not going to get along. So far, however, he only took out his animosity on young Mr. Cain, constantly hounding the boy on issues until he couldn't make any decisions. By the second day out the lad was a pathetic package of nerves.

The recent trip to Halifax had made it clear the B of I hadn't changed Worley. And this present trip was a *long* trip *far* from the Navy's eye. And this, you may be sure of, is what caused the greatest amount of apprehension in the officers and men. Something as bold as a Board of Inquiry had not curtailed his manner or behavior whatsoever.

During the deep gloom of the wardroom's evening clandestine chats, Worley's frequent victim, Mr. J.J. Cain, could hardly repress a shiver when his irritable master's behavior for the day was discussed. He had good reason, for after the late night "coffee and smoke" meetings Cain would have to take the Dog Watch. This was the dullest duty imaginable. From midnight to 4 a.m. he was alone on the flying bridge, the pinnacle of vigilance and power on the ship. The duty required Mr. Cain to stroll the teak and scan the horizon forever looking for U-Boat conning towers, or any ship or anything remotely interesting. From a flight of internal stairs, the captain could merely walk up from his cabin and stand with the wind to his back and command the ship from here. This had set Mr. Cain on edge more than anything.

Vengeance finally came on the 5th day out. Worley blew his

top at Forbes. Nervig said it was over "some trivial matter regarding ship's work." In any case, he ordered him to his room under arrest— a much more ignoble fate than even Mr. Shaw had suffered. The rampage wasn't going to stop there. But Burt Asper wasn't finished yet with the game of chess between he and his hated master. He made a bold move. We don't know what hand J.J. Cain had played in the events that led up to Worley's rage, if any, but Dr. Asper knew that if any vengeance was due young Mr. Cain it would come tonight on the Dog Watch. He now had him committed to the Dispensary.

Alone out of the officers on board, Nervig seemed interested in just what had happened. When he entered the wardroom, he finally had something to look forward to. Yet he was surprised at how naturally the event had been taken. Concerning Forbes there was little surprise in the officers' reactions. "From all accounts," wrote Nervig, "this seemed to be a routine matter on ships commanded by Worley." As for young Ensign Cain, well, this is another matter. He writes with some pique about Cain being in good health, but that it "was the general opinion in the wardroom that this was done to save Mr. Cain from being a victim of the Commanding Officer's unreasoning temper. I do not recall that the doctor made any comment nor that he was in any way questioned regarding the matter; his acts and motives were taken for granted."

Indeed they were, and with good reason considering all the bad blood from the trip off France. But Nervig was wrong about an Exec. Officer under arrest being a "routine matter." Mr. Shaw had only been demeaned. Robinson had become dull and self-protective. Things were clearly getting worse, but were the officers accepting it stoically or just distrustful of each other to the extent that they would not openly and candidly discuss the events? Worley kept snitches aboard— like Cost George— and then there were handpicked officers like Hugo Schonof and Stephen Konstovich. Their presence in the wardroom would almost certainly inspire caution.

Nervig would soon learn for himself and make the obvious deduction. Worley hated young officers. Nevertheless, his utter lack of informed opinion remains amazing. We cannot completely attribute it to the fact he was a passenger and therefore did not mix much with the others except at mealtime. He was quickly forming a solid friendship with Carroll Page. Private conversations would be safe enough. Yet it seems Mr. Page, too, must have been told very little.

Did Asper's neutrality end with Cain or had it already ended with Forbes incarceration? Worley's rampage could have been such that Asper was forced to the Good Samaritan move. An executive officer being placed under house arrest over a "trivial" matter is cause for concern. Our dear ship's surgeon knew well that Worley hated young officers. Thus by his actions he was spiting his master by delivering an officer from undeserved punishment. However, Asper wasn't gearing up to be anybody's champion. This was a chess move. He was forcing Worley to appoint a replacement for the Dog Watch.

His surly captain now played a fitting move. He could have replaced Cain with any officer of his crew. The close-lipped Mr. Smith was still aboard, a man who saw fit to be unfit when asked sensitive questions about his master's ability at duty. He could have placed Hugo Schonof there, but it seems Schonof was one of the reasons the officers' wardroom was often silent. Worley had his own eyes and ears. He wanted his toadies to be elsewhere. Worley did his homework, though. He had looked at Nervig's jacket. He was destined to be the Watch Officer on the *Glacier*. This made him a logical fit.

But more than this, Worley detested most of his officers and had lumped them, even for the most innocuous answers at the Board of Inquiry, into the "Round Robin." Nervig was qualified because he was *only* a passenger. He was qualified because he wasn't a toady whose eyes and ears were needed elsewhere. He had a German name, and Worley certainly seemed to favor Germans. The seadog knew he could not risk another Board of Inquiry despite the whitewash. Nervig was no doubt Worley's chess move. Instead of putting into place some other officer and thereby giving Asper another chance at disqualifying a man, Worley chose Nervig. If he degraded Nervig, so what?

Asper could do nothing. Nervig was a passenger. He was leaving anyway. Worley was no fool about his surgeon. He knew Asper was waiting for another incident now. If he put but one more officer in the sickbay, there would be an inquiry. Worley could not afford to play into that.

Unquestionably ignorant of the vengeful game of chess aboard, Nervig jumped at the occasion. He now had something to do. He looked forward to the "balmy tropical nights under a full moon" and the "pleasant escape" they would provide from "the gloomy atmosphere of the wardroom."

Nervig finished his evening entry in his daily letters to his wife. He signed off for the night and folded again the paper. He put off his blue tunic and threw it down by his crisp white one outlaid for duty tonight. He turned off the light over his desk. He needed to rest a while anyway. Duty called in a few hours. Mr. Cain's Dog Watch.

6

U.S. NAVAL RESERVE FORCE

DOG WATCH

"Commander Worley never had much use for American
boys aboard the ship."

—Lt. Cmdr. McKay, USS *Celebes*

IT WAS A PALMY TROPICAL night, the night of the 5th day out.
The *Cyclops* steamed peacefully through the clear and calm
waters of the Caribbean. There were few sounds from her
decks. Moon glow danced on the gentle ocean ripples, but it
cut sinister shadows through the lattice of derricks on the
deck. The moon made enough light to turn the tropic night
from black to indigo, and the stars were pearlescent rather
than stark against this surreal color.

Mr. Nervig barely had time to appreciate the tropic soli-
tude. He was just at his station when he heard someone coming up the stairs. Almost dead center in the flying bridge there
was a railing on 2 sides of a dark black square hole. It looked
like a neat geometric ink blotch in the center of the teak deck.
This was the stairwell, the only way up and down. On a night
like this, with the silky white veil of bloodless light from the
moon, the hole stood out as the only distinct shape.

It is from this hole that the steps were clear to make out, but there was no tapping from the heel of a shoe. There was the single tap of a cane. Curious, Nervig stepped over and looked down. It was the captain. A fretful pause seized him. "What have I done?" he asked himself quickly. It was the tropics now and Nervig was sure orders were given for whites to be worn. His whites were a bit stiff, but he was dressed prim and proper with his hat's bill a glossy, clean black. He made sure to come to a stiff, formal salute. But as the captain stepped upon the flying bridge Nervig was taken aback. His eyes blinked in surprise. The captain was wearing his long woolen underwear. On his head he was crowned with a black derby hat. With each step, he stuck the tip of his fancy cane into the teak, and this is what had made the tapping sound. He wore no shoes, but gingerly walked upon his bare feet.

"Good morning, Captain," Nervig said.

"I frantically searched my memory for something I had done wrong or had neglected to do. He neither apologized for his attire, nor even so much as mentioned it, and my salute and 'Good Morning, Captain,' could not have been more correct or military. His affability soon relieved my anxiety, as I realized this was no official call, but a purely social one."

The seadog now leaned on the railing and motioned Nervig to come alongside. Captain Worley, the mean old "bucko" seadog, was so friendly and engaging Nervig completely relaxed on his forearms and listened to his captain's fond recollections. He chuckled at his stories and Worley laughed heartier in return. At more than one time, Nervig followed the old seadog's longing gaze at the stars. "This visit lasted some two hours, and as we leaned against the forward bridge rail, he regaled me with stories of his home and numerous incidents of his long life at sea. He had a fund of tales, mostly humorous."

At 2 a.m. Captain Worley bid farewell and descended down the black square to his emergency cabin. It had been a strange interlude in an otherwise dull night.

Nervig's *The Cyclops Mystery* proves quite frustrating at such junctures as this, and even a little parochial. It is under-

The flying bridge was atop the bridge.

standable that he was not going to ask why his skipper was dressed the way he was— at least why he walked around wearing a derby hat. But it's another thing altogether to write later about what one observes and then display only complete ennui at trying to account for such encounters. He doesn't even express wonder at what could have motivated his captain's dress. Worley's behavior was obviously outside the norm for any commanding officer. Yet there is no intent on Nervig's part to include others in his narrative and try and flesh out the problem. No conversations with Page speaking of the encounter. No indications Nervig inquired at all. No understanding that if word of such bizarre behavior reached Asper how he might have rejoiced at having yet another morsel to use against Worley if their feud should come to a head again. A lack of officers confiding in a stranger like Nervig is one thing, but the lack of initiative on Nervig's part is remarkable given the moment he describes for us.

Rather we only know that Nervig looked forward to the visits, for "These nocturnal visits became a regular routine, and I rather enjoyed them. His uniform, if it could be so called, never varied from what he had worn on the first occasion. I have often wondered to what I owed these nightly visits— his fondness for me or his sleeplessness."

The answer to Nervig's question lay elsewhere. It lay in the fact he was not some shirt tail officer. It lay in the fact he was a passenger. But most of all it lay in liquor. It is doubtful that Nervig could have remained parochial throughout the whole encounter had he known of Captain Worley's heavy drinking. A little digging would have uncovered a connection, but again Nervig remains both a closed conduit to us from the officers and crew.

Despite enjoying the visits, Nervig learned to take caution. Worley remained pleasant enough, but "he was quite erratic at times. Without the slightest pause between words, his mood would change to that a very opinionated man— a self-proclaimed genius who thought he had never arrived but should have. It was while in these moods that he'd take out his rage on some unknowing officer. Although he treats me very well— he seemed to like me—why?— I don't know. It was a part of his makeup."

It is only inadvertently that Nervig gives us a hint of how life continued aboard the ship. From the above we know that Worley's wrath against other officers continued. Mood swings and bitter memories played a hand in the current problems and, apparently, they happened during Nervig's Dog Watch or soon after otherwise Nervig would not have been able to see the cause and effect. It is obvious that it is at this time of night that his master drank the heaviest.

From the Board of Inquiry we know how much he drank and how inconsistent he was in discipline. Yet none of the accounts so far had come from an officer who strode the flying bridge at night. Although we may stand amazed at Nervig's lack of perception and curiosity, his encounters give us a close up of how truly odd Worley became after his sleepless hours in his cabin with his unmarked bottle.

Moreover, we have a clue as to what might have sent Mr. Cain over the edge. It is doubtful Worley bedecked himself just for Nervig. If that's the case, we can anticipate why Cain of all officers was protected by Asper. Perhaps Worley visited Cain dressed in like manner. Perhaps Cain's foot, which sadly often parked in his mouth, got lodged there right away with some unintentional off-color comment. Worley's outfit would only have commenced in the tropics, thus the night before Nervig took over. As such, Cain might have been taken aback when Worley stood there like some vaudeville performer waiting to break out in a soft shoe and dance. It need not be much of a comment. Brutal disciplinary moments had always been inspired by something trivial. Supposing this to be true, now with Cain in the sickbay we know that the conniving doctor was aware of Worley's quirky nighttime ensemble.

Thus from the 5th day out the picture we have is of a "bucko," brutal skipper during the day, a perfectly healthy young officer taken off the Dog Watch and confined to sickbay, the Executive confined to his own quarters, a wardroom full of gloomy officers at night, a disgruntled crew, and none of them feeling there was any redress of the problems aboard considering the former whitewash. To top this off it is contrasted by Nervig's encounters with the master in the dead of night, while the master looks like he's ready to tap dance a bawdy burlesque number in his long johns, derby hat, and fancy cane. And the most surprising thing is Worley doesn't seem to give a figue.

This is all just a lead in to an event that could be a tinderbox. Now only a day or so from Bahia, the first scheduled stop on the coast of Brazil, the *Cyclops* would be "crossing the line"— in other words, crossing the equator going south. Here one is in Neptune's Realm. They're neither in the northern hemisphere nor the southern. King Neptune alone presides here. His Majesty commands the day's events. The result is a ribald, hazing ritual in which all those who never crossed the line before must be initiated by those who have. All this is done at the command of a sailor in the guise of King Neptune, and carried out by his Royal Court of mischievous imps. Those who have crossed the equator before are the "shellbacks." They implement the day's initiation to the "pollywogs." It is a tradition for many navies, including the US Navy, and one still practiced today. It is a brutal event at times, obscene occasionally, and goes back to neoclassical days in the 18th century.

The raucous events of the day fit Worley's sense of humor, so it is unlikely that it did not occur. Yet the contentious voyage off France and the resulting Board of Inquiry must have made this an unusual, to say the least, crossing of the line. Most of the men who had signed the petition were still aboard. Many had been inductees. This meant they would all be undergoing the ceremony. Dozens, perhaps even most of the crew, would be undergoing the initiation, making it a daylong event.

Officers do not control the event, but shellbacks do. This means that old Auxiliary hands and a few old regular Navy hands aboard would be in control. This unquestionably put some of Worley's quartermasters in an influential position if not in charge— the "Hun" Keller, 'Weaselthal' (Wiesenthal), the suspicious Schneidleberg whom Worley had kept aboard, and perhaps even the seasoned toady, the Turk, and several of his countrymen.

King Neptune rises from the fo'c'sle, and his Royal Court is entirely of the men. Officers watch, and those never before who have crossed— usually some shave tail ensign, must participate. Executive officers would be dismissed after berating and being allowed to pay a fine, especially if the enlisted men needed money for a communal fund. A whopping "ten bucks" was demanded by King Neptune or, since they were on their way to Brazil, an extortionate 1 million reis of Brazilian money, which was about the same thing. But there would be no such mercy for the ranks of enlisted men.

The event was carefully prepared. Davy Jones, high scribe to his Royal Majesty, would appear on the deck the day before out of nowhere. The shellback playing him would be almost

The voyage of the Cyclops *south to Rio de Janeiro.*

unrecognizable in some old Navy uniform, perhaps even a tricorn hat on his head and wearing a frazzled beard of untwined rope. His sole duty this day is to place the written notice that crossing the line would occur. It might be formal and pompous or, more likely, tongue-in-cheek. William Swinyer records when they crossed the line on the way to Brazil that Davey Jones posted the following: "We will break out a hot time in the old realm tomorrow; especially for each one of you officers and men who have not blown hitherto hitherbefore."

Then he would disappear below. Here, secluded away, the shellbacks were preparing the implements to be used. Since it varies, I will list those that Swinyer saw used in his June 1917 crossing of the line ceremony, since it must have been identical to those in general use on all Navy ships.

> . . .Razors and shears, each two feet long, combs with teeth of six penny nails; gigantic lather brushes; bucksaws, rasps, tongs, etc., for dental and surgical use. Finally there were the 2 quart squirt guns and the never-to-be-forgotten medicines, that were to be used by the Imperial Medical staff. These medicines were of a startling variety, as may well be imagined, and they certainly did make a hit. First there was a red hot emetic to be shot between the teeth, and this was to be followed by a nauseous paste for ramming into each man's muzzle by the dirtiest hands that ever were seen. Last, but by no means least, were the barrels of an admixture called gugu, for smearing all over victims by resounding slaps of heavy brushes. Yes, the gugu was an admixture, consisting of sand, graphite, vaseline, and other greases. It was no joke to be covered by this stuff, whether it was done to a sailor in spotless dress white uniform, or after he had been forcibly stripped and then daubed.

Swinyer did not consider the "medicines" to be that bad because they were covered by a deep rich coating of melted chocolate made by the doctor. However, Swinyer shipped out on the flagship *Pittsburgh*, which had a doctor, a dentist, a brass band, everything— a far cry from the coal stained Auxiliary *Cyclops* and its spiteful surgeon and vindictive captain, both united only in their taste for the bottle. What would Asper have made for the disgruntled crew? He would certainly have seen the old Auxiliary hands and even German officers— Schonof and Konstovich— behind the day's ceremony. And behind them was Worley. On top of this there were the shortages aboard the ship. If the shortages were not just of basic foodstuffs, like main course fish, we can well imagine barrels of chocolate were not to be had.

Nevertheless, the ceremony would have gone according to certain tried and true ritual. The next morning a huge tank filled with water would have "magically" appeared overnight on the fo'c'sle. Swinyer tells us that barber chairs on swivels were set before it so that those put therein could be shaved and then the chairs leaned back and the men would slide into the tank for dunking.

The ceremony began with the royal procession. King Neptune, done up so much that the man was unrecognizable, would emerge with his court. His hair, beard and mustache were all of untwined rope. On his head he wore the golden diadem, his body draped in a long divine tunic— perhaps green— and he naturally carried a long trident thanks to the machine shop. Walking next to him was the Queen, the consort, with long untwined rope for hair but otherwise clean shaven. Perhaps his face was made up with paint in lieu of makeup. No doubt one of the better looking shellbacks was chosen for this role. But there was no denying it was a man, not just because there were no women in the Navy but because though he wore a long gown it was quite transparent . . . and the Queen wore nothing else underneath. No wonder some Queens wanted full makeup. Neptune, of course, had no such transparent gown. He was regal, though frazzled, befitting the King of the Deep.

Along with their majesties strode Davey Jones in some old uniform, probably barefooted. Numerous courtiers were done up differently; dentist had thick specs indicating he was near blind; courtiers a tall top hat; those going to instruct and punish the men with shellacking wore a professor's hat; skull and crossbones marked the medical man, and numerous shellbacks— the lambasters— were done up with bandanas and painted faces and looked quite scurvy. God forbid that any of them would dare to wear long johns and a derby!

It was quite a pageant as their majesties stroll to the foc's'le and mounted the dais. As soon as Neptune and his semi-nude consort ascended, the Royal Navigator ascends the bridge and takes control. With Worley's attitude, this must have been an interesting moment. As long as King Neptune presided, the Royal Navigator, in military uniform and a frazzled rope beard, mustache and wig, was in control. Then pollywogs were brought forth by Neptune's imps to kowtow before him. Officers were brought before him in their dress whites and berated for cowardice and then allowed a fine.

The vision we have is nothing without the sounds. Huge cheers would ring forth. "Have I no rights?" would protest an officer. "None!" would reply the King. A man who had a beard would be condemned for impersonating an officer. "Off!" Neptune would order. Then he was shaved.

One after the other the pollywogs were thrown into a barber chair to suffer under "Painful Parker," the diabolical dentist who administered the medicines with the help of chuckling imps. The men would yell and cheer loudly when a junior officer, in this case Carroll Page, was forced to "kiss the baby." The baby was usually some big sailor done up in britches and already painted with the shiny graphite mixture. Page would walk away with black, shiny lips. The men would cheer again. It was a raucous event that got to its loudest with the dunking. Swinyer records:

> As a grand finale the hapless victims were rushed, hauled and pulled through a menacing array of dentists, surgeons and lambasters to the dope fiend doctors. Then swish! They got it between the teeth with a two quart squirt gun. After which their mouths were jammed full of the nauseous mass of junk. Lastly they were shaven and shorn, smeared from top to toe and then hurled violently backward into the tank. . .Finally at the end of the ordeal, every man scurried away to either wash or destroy paint covered clothes.

It was unquestionably a fun event, but how was it tailored, even subtly, by Worley through his network of toadies? Swinyer tells us that the men while being drug through the tank by their heels weren't allowed to come up for a breath, and if they did their heads were repeatedly beaten with stuffed clubs. It doesn't take shotgun guessing to draw a tense picture of the day's events aboard the *Cyclops*. Many of the "Round Robin" would suffer. Some of those who had signed were old hands, like Daly and Kight. Did they warn the pollywogs about what was coming? Unlike the usual mardi gras fun of crossing the line, there would be far more hidden retributions here and even much more anxiety in the men who might have felt they were targeted for special payback. Asper could be of no help here. Despite what he did for McDaniel, Jeffers, and Cain, he seemed to care little about the men he delivered from Worley's wrath.

But it was a day off. It should have allowed a lot of steam to be blown off to release the pressure. If that is the case, the contention returned within a day. Forbes had been released for a few days now. He no doubt enjoyed the day's events. But he would soon challenge the captain again.

7

OFF PERNAMBUCO

"Captain Worley was an awful crank, and he would frequently drive members of the crew around the ship at the point of a gun. It was a disgraceful sight for a commanding officer to act in this manner."

—Yeoman Paul Roberts

ALTHOUGH NERVIG GIVES US NO insight into the unavoidable ritual of entering Neptune's Realm, he does take up the narrative with what would have to be the next major road marker for the voyage— South America. It came about on the Dog Watch on the 12th day out of Norfolk. A dark, long silhouette about 20 miles distant slowly rose over the entire horizon and languished in the moonlight on the indigo surface.

The seadog didn't care for it, though his hen-on-ice navigating was solely responsible. His response was just as haphazard. He bent into the intercom on the flying bridge and ordered the helm over. The *Cyclops* turned slowly and headed back out to sea. There was really no destination. Worley was simply avoiding an entire continent.

By this time Forbes greeted such events with cynical mirth. He immediately recognized the coastline as Pernambuco, Brazil. Pernambuco is the entire forehead of Brazil and the whole

South American continent. It's a big promontory and Forbes knew only one navigator couldn't miss it. Seeing the *Cyclops* was merely chugging out to sea, he set the courses to bring the ship neatly into Bahia, the first port of call.

Somehow Worley got wind of this. The old sea captain could sense changes even though he couldn't read directions. Without letting Forbes know it, he changed the course again. The upshot of this was not only did they miss Bahia altogether, the *Cyclops* was set on a suicide course with the coast. "Three more hours of darkness streaming on that course," Nervig reckoned, "would have had her aground." Forbes found out, changed the heading again, and confronted Worley about why he had monkeyed with the course. Worley was indignant. The result was not good for Forbes. Though Forbes had saved the ship, "Worley exploded and had Forbes immediately placed under arrest and confined to quarters" yet again.

The only thing to break the tension aboard, which must have been considerable with the Executive Officer in stir yet again, was reaching Bahia. Its emerald bay greeted them with deep moody colors over which was daubed the limpet reflections of the brighter green of the surrounding palm trees and lush hillside. The skies would suddenly flicker with neon streaks of magnificent red, orange, teal, blue and green as exotic, bright parrots or toucans darted from a tree and glided about. Whitewashed homes and buildings terraced up from the shore and their gray reflections wiggled in the edge of the bay like an impressionist painting. None were so high that they stood out incongruously from the palm trees beckoning in the wind.

Bahia is the oldest city of the Americas. Like Norfolk, it was an amazing hybrid. But in this case the modern world did not mix with 17th century colonialism but with conquistadores and princely navigators, and this gave this old port a link with the fabulous past of the Amazon and the legends that lured so many to seek the fountain of youth or lost El Dorado. The architecture still reflected the limited engineering skill of the earliest settlers— there were no spires despite the fact that from off the bay one could count 30 churches. Domes and copulas took their place. Only 2 roads for cars led up the hills from the bay. Elevators could be seen, even from the deck of the *Cyclops* as she lumbered in, carry people to the next level of the street.

The docks were sprawling— stucco arches, great tarry beams— crisscrossed in a lattice of cranes loading freighters. Fruit and coffee crates were being loaded onto ships, the produce of the plantations that surrounded the city. Battlewagons rode further out at anchor, an ugly gray reminder of the war. They were blotches on the otherwise gelatinous reflections of the buildings, palms and verdant cliffs. Another reminder of war was the line of freighters, quarantined, shoulder to shoulder. They were German merchantmen interned by Brazil when it turned belligerent against Germany. They sat in single file, rusting, neglected, tugging at their anchor chains in the hot sun.

Only one major American warship was there, and this was the cruiser *Raleigh*, one of those Roman galleons that had distinguished herself in Manila Bay in the Spanish-American war 20 years before. Her beautiful white and mustard livery was gone. She was gray now and old, seconded to the backwaters of the war. *Cyclops* was to coal her so she could help patrol the South Atlantic for U-boats and raiders.

This Worley set to do right away. He was going to get the work over with before he even considered a Liberty. It was hard work, but for the first time the men got to contrast their work with something very satisfying— the rugged and tantalizing beauty of Brazil all around them. Bahia sets on a huge bay, almost an inland sea. The town takes up only a little of the overall shore line. Thus the ships were 2 gray dots on placid, sparkling green glass with an unobstructed view of an almost mythic landscape.

As always the clamshells started their work. Dropping from cables, they bit into the coal and scooped it up and swung it over to the *Raleigh*. At last the *Raleigh*'s band struck up tunes from the stern. Some classic American tunes no doubt took a back seat to a few lively South American ones.

By the afternoon both ships were stained with black dust. The boats were now stowed, the derricks saluted fore and aft, stiff and regimented and the clamshells withdrew on their cables, lowered and locked into place. But now it happened. In starting up, the *Cyclops* came back into the *Raleigh* and banged her amidships. Terrible shudders went through both vessels. Officers came rolling out of the *Raleigh*'s bridge like oranges out of a crate. Men on both ships grabbed the rails and looked down the hulls. *Cyclops* idled and coasted. The aim was to drift apart and then churn the green into an aqua cauliflower with the great screws. Rather the *Cyclops* came back into the *Raleigh* and thudded against her. Starting the massive propellers now, the vessel ungainly parted and moved from the *Raleigh*. The *Cyclops'* men were embarrassed. They rushed down the rails looking to see if *Raleigh* was dented. There seemed little damage, but it didn't stop *Raleigh*'s men from mouthing epithets.

Nervig would blame Worley's poor navigating— a sure sign Forbes was indeed still in the brig. But there was little navigating to do in parting from the venerable *Raleigh*. Rather the *Cyclops'* bridge crew was reflecting the disorder that the captain had been long instilling in the grim ship.

The *Cyclops* chugged on slowly until finally casting anchor on the edge of the school of other ships of the fleet. She set down cable in peaceful waters, slightly isolated but prominent, like a kid in the corner with the dunce hat. There she secured for the night, rippled by the dancing reflections of the lighted skyline of Bahia.

Now pondering from the bridge in the after currents of such an event, Nervig realized how boring the Dog Watch was in harbor. There was really nothing to watch at anchor with the fleet. He checked his watch, anticipating impatiently a launch from the *Port Huron*. She was to come along and pick up the mail. Two men stood watch by the gangway, under a dim cone of light from the aft bulkhead.

Although Bahia was a short stay, there was indeed a limited

Cyclops *at anchor.*

Liberty. To what the men owed this remarkable occurrence is unknown. Perhaps it was to relieve the tension aboard from the disgrace of having fouled a veteran warship like the *Raleigh*. News of this had naturally gone through the ship, eliciting disdainful chuckles from some and snorts from the others. But then it had also gone through the port, provoking the same responses. Worley was not one to be gracious. But perhaps he didn't care, or even thought it amusing, if some of his men got in fights with the *Raleigh*'s men and had to return and be tended by their beloved ship's surgeon who didn't like to work or be inconvenienced in port. They rode the elevators to the highlife level of the old city and visited the hot spots. They crammed the Palace Hotel to send telegrams to family.

The main bulk of Admiral Capteron's fleet was at Rio, the *Cyclops*' next and final destination. She spent only a full day in Bahia. Already now on the 24th she rolled and wallowed and took the swells like an elegant though embarrassed whale. Her twin stacks belched black smoke as she raised as much steam as possible to escape the collective scowl of the fleet for the more charitable isolation of the open sea.

If Worley wasn't on the warpath because of the incident with the *Raleigh*, he would soon be rancid over another problem. He had long complained about his engines and had gotten nowhere. Now it happened. *Cyclops* blew a gasket!

It was a rare moment when Captain Worley actually read something over his dinner, and even rarer when he took dinner in his much larger aft cabin's sitting room. He indulged in the single page report by Glenn Maguet, who stood there hat tucked under his upper arm, waiting with more Navy-like poise than Worley was used to seeing on the *Cyclops*.

The report read:

At 4:50 p.m. January 27, 1918, the H.P. starboard engine was disabled, evidently caused by the breaking of one of the follower ring stud bolts which in turn caused the breaking of the follower ring, and the bursting of the cylinder and cylinder head, also the H.P. piston rod. So far, it is determined that the responsibility is with engineering officer Lt. (j.g) L.J. Fingleton who did not stop engines nor report noise.

The ship's force is now doing the work necessary to compound the engine.

/s/ G.E. Maguet

Worley could afford to look up with tolerant superiority. Maguet may have looked Navy, but he didn't understand the Navy as well as his crusty skipper. Blaming Fingleton meant little. The Navy would have to follow this up with a Board of Inquiry.

Maguet may have cringed at that word. That would have caused Worley to halt.

"You know what one of those is, don't you, son?"

But there was little reason for Worley to anticipate any ill aftereffects for himself. He was finally getting what he wanted.

The Navy was forced into looking into his engine troubles on an official level. The B of I would concentrate on Fingleton and the crew on duty. Worley could hear no engines on the bridge. He was safe from any fallout. He sent a message appended to Maguet's requesting a Board of Inquiry.

That night the *Cyclops* creaked and groaned steadily along. Her silhouette was dark as ink against the setting moon's glowing orb. A watchman strode the flying bridge, dark and lazy, the indolence of routine. Soon at Midnight it would be Nervig. Considering the way in which they narrowly avoided the rocks near Bahia, a dark humor dominated the ship when it came to Rio de Janeiro. All were sure they would make landfall, but would they get a Liberty? Rio was to be a long stay. Surely, they would all get a taste of "Simpatico."

Rio de Janeiro was an incredibly grander sight than Bahia. Sweeping palm-lined boulevards, cabanas, and temptation greeted the ship. *Cyclops'* arrival was not a big event. When Caperton's squadron had entered back in July 1917, it had been a national affair. Caperton was not only the commander of the South American squadron, he was special envoy from Washington. The city turned out in all its gaiety, as only Rio can. The Brazilian band played "Marching Through Georgia" and newspaper articles declared the nation's loyalty to North America and Brazil's praise of the Monroe Doctrine. Banners were strung over thoroughfares. Marching bands were preparing for the huge 4th of July spectacular— parades and festivals in which Caperton's men would march and the Navy band would lead.

South American press had covered the spectacle closely and, of course, US Diplomatic personnel were everywhere. Navy launches carried the Consul General of Brazil, Alfred Gottschalk, to the flagship *Pittsburgh*. The official moment was recorded in photos. They stood regally on the warship's aft deck. Gottschalk sported a tall top hat, long coat, spats, thick cravat and every other token that marked a haughty diplomat of Wilsonian progressiveness. With him were other dignitaries, stiff collars, tight suits and straw hats. Caperton was in tight dress whites. Light bulbs burst noisily, and plumes of smoke gasped as the men stood for a moment in time. Dinner would be on the quarterdeck, of course.

Now in February 1918 things had calmed down. Motor cars did not line the boulevards for the *Cyclops*. But plenty of carriages drawn by mules— horse were scarce in Rio— ambled along and there were a number of "vendors" there to offer services to the men. Little did they know *Cyclops'* master; Rio was not going to be a Liberty town.

Rio meant one glorious thing for Nervig. He was free! Orders came right away and he was detached that very day. The gig cut a smooth V wake away from the *Cyclops* on to its journey to the dock and to the *Glacier*. Nervig's final wave from the gig was answered by Page, who was now just a small white dot in the shadow of the *Cyclops'* giant derricks.

The great ship's screws turned, propelling her forward and spitting up the sea behind her. There was no warning at all. The movement sent the men scrambling by the rail to lift the gangplank.

For days Nervig got to see the old collier just like this. After first recoaling the flagship *Pittsburgh*, mercifully without incident, the *Cyclops* anchored here and there, recoaling, resupplying, refueling the fleet. Days of disemboweling her valuable cargo saw no man leave the ship, no Liberty granted in town. At last the *Cyclops*, riding high and empty, was able to take her place at the dock. Her most important purpose had come. Manganese.

8

DANGEROUS CARGO

"Vessel will supply equipment on board, except ore buckets,
and load and discharge continuously, working days and
nights if required by charterer's agents, to accomplish this."
—Admiral William Caperton

THE *CYCLOPS* TIED TO THE docks on February 8, and Worley intended to start loading the precious cargo the next day. By
contract the ship was controlled by the shippers, The United
States & Brazil Steamship Company, while it was being prepared for her new special cargo. The Cory Brothers were their
subsidiary that took care of the loading. Their stevedores were
soon swarming aboard. The holds had to be cleaned up in order to ship manganese. The dunnage, the wood insulation for
the holds, also had to be prepared. The *Cyclops* had plenty of
lumber already for that purpose. The ship's machinists and
carpenters were hard at work. Worley had been given special
instructions on how to load manganese and was even given the
authority to "load and discharge continuously, working days
and nights if required . . ." With that the Navy actually took the
burden of being the tyrant off Worley's back and placed it on
the agents. The special orders also restricted loading more
than 2500 tons of manganese a day, so that as one hold was be-

ing loaded the others were still being prepared.

During these days of preparation, how many men "in the way" were granted Liberty in Rio? It seems very little. Never knowing how many might be needed, the seadog kept the men close.

With Conrad Nervig's grateful departure from the *Cyclops* we are left without a voice aboard the ship, but eyes still surrounded the great vessel in port. She was the center of tragic scuttlebutt. Experience had taught Nervig to believe it. As the story goes, Worley had set the men to entirely clean up the ship. Amidst the jumble of her decks, the Engineer's Force stumbled along at their duties. They scraped and polished. They even hung off the sides on rope-held scaffolding or stood in lifeboats, scraping the ship's hull below the water line. The tragedy happened now. The *Cyclops'* great screws turned over, churning the murky water into a violent rust colored cauliflower. A man was back in a small launch by the stern and was drawn back, knocked overboard and drowned.

Nervig offers no explanation for this incident other than "This negligence, I feel, can be laid squarely at the feet of the Commanding Officer, who by his irrational methods of command had so thoroughly demoralized and disorganized the officers and men of the *Cyclops.*"

However, it requires more explanation than that. In a roundabout way it probably started with the blown gasket. Maguet had blamed Fingleton for it. It's hard to imagine why he was down there. Technically, Konstovich was next after Maguet, but apparently Fingleton, though not truly qualified, had been given the post. In any case, Fingleton couldn't even tell if something was amiss. Caperton had assigned 3 officers to come aboard as the Board of Inquiry. The only reason that Worley would turn over his engines while at anchor would be for the Board of Inquiry. He was, once again, pitching his problems. They, too, no doubt wanted to listen. This only explains the screws chopping the sea while the *Cyclops* rode at anchor; it does not excuse the complete disorganization that must have led to not even knowing where the men were off the ship and to not warning them to get aboard.

Nothing could stop the loading— not even the engines or a man floating in the harbor. Work concentrated in the holds. They were dark open pits echoing with hammering, sawing, thuds and clanging resonance, and men hollering at each other. They swept and mopped the bottom and sides while the skeleton of the dunnage took form in the hands of the ship's carpenters. Then the flanks were built and angled on the sides. This would prevent the shifting of the cargo. This also kept the manganese oxide from ever touching the metal holds of the ship. Worley was quite attentive to this. He would stand on the lip of the holds and hawk-like watch while the men scurried about like ants beneath him.

As work progressed, E.G. Fontes, the sales rep. for Morro de Minho, came aboard. He was a little, stocky guy, prim and proper in a tight suit and tight stiff collar that constricted his neck. His black hair was slicked and combed down, with a part in the middle. The ends of his black mustache were greased to perfect, upturned peaks. He was taken below. From the open door to the hold, he could see its underbelly. The heavy beam and crossbeam frame of the dunnage stood 8 feet above the floor. Over this was being hammered heavy timbers to make a platform covering the entire bottom of the hold. Amidst the thunderous echo of ship's carpenters, plank by plank the final pieces of the dunnage were hammered onto the supporting frame, each shutting out the last rays of light.

The Brazilian beamed in satisfaction. "Excellente," he had approved.

Worley concurred. He then escorted him aft to the gangway. He made sure that the Original Cory was doing the loading and not some "leather monkey."

Fontes chuckled at the captain's crude jest. His toothy smile was fit for a diplomat. He assured him he would especially take care of it, and reminded "senhor capitan" that Morro di Minos had close relationship with the Brazilian Coaling Company (Cory Brothers). Fontes' smile now directed Worley across Rio bay, pointing out the stockyard there on Ilha de Ferreiras.

The lighters were already being loaded. Tomorrow it would begin.

The sunrise was spectacular. The amber rays streaked over Rio harbor like the crown of Helios and painted one side of Sugar Loaf Mountain in early morning gold. As the sun continued to rise, the mountain slowly pulled in its shadow, which moved like a great sundial arm over all in its path. Traffic, slow but steady, churned the harbor. Ships belched smoke and departed; others slowly ambled in under whispering curls.

True to form the lighters from Ilha de Ferrairas were already forming a link of steady traffic to the *Cyclops*. Manuel Pereira, a skinny Latin in a not so fashionable suit, stood on the dock at the bottom of the gangplank happily and eagerly gesturing to the men on watch. Pereira, who looked every bit the wrinkled official, came aboard. There with Worley he pointed off. At the end of his long extended arm his finger followed the advance of the lead lighter.

Seated on its bow in a wicker nightclub throne, with somewhat seedy majesty, was an ebullient Latin. His crown was a grand straw hat; his royal jewels a shiny orb in his earlobe. A monkey crawled about this smiling man's arm and shoulders. A woman dancer, still dressed from last night's festivities, raven hair pulled tight and held by flamboyant combs, danced about him. Troubadours stood about playing their instruments and men happily sang along and laughed at anything in their joy. A colorful parrot squawked, inciting the monkey to scream. Amidst all this the Original Cory continued to smile, look very macho and act like the toreador for loading coal. To those on the docks he was a king on parade. He threw backhanded waves to acquaintances, smiled grandly, and seemed an eager professional ready to lead men. It was all-in-all a triumphant entry for a king of the dockworks.

Pereira turned back and put his hands on his hips. He beamed proudly up at the captain. His expression was the exclamation point of the morning's orchestrated perfection, his perfection!

When work got started, it was quick and professional. Of all the stevedores that flooded on board, only the Original Cory remained in charge as things got underway. He leaned over Hold No. 1 commandingly directing (though unnecessarily) the first bucket in. His hand stopped waving it on as the great metal scoop hovered right above the dunnage. Then he signaled 'let it spill.' It was a flamboyant flourish. His hand swooped like a swallow. The heavy manganese tumbled onto the wood platform, deafening all topside.

Below decks, the sound was horrendous. Pereira and Worley stood by the open bulkhead door leading into No. 1 hold. The dark space below the platform echoed with the manganese pelting and thudding on the top. Then the giant bucket squeaked while it teetered and was withdrawn. The pile of manganese covered the center of the platform. What few slivers of light had snuck through now snipped out. The braces creaked and settled into place.

As the sound of the bucket rising faded, there was hollering. It was from Original Cory, evidently satisfied the dunnage was secure.

Each day the *Cyclops* settled deeper into the murky harbor. Each day about 2500 tons of the manganese was evenly spread out in the holds. Worley was anxious to get it over with and go. He had already estimated leaving Rio on the 14th, then he set it to the 15th. With a cargo of 10,800 tons it took all of 5 days to load. He now planned on leaving Saturday the 16th of February at 9 a.m.

Today, Thursday the 14th, a different type of cargo was being loaded aboard. A Navy launch clunked alongside the dock. Armed shore patrol was escorting 5 men off the boat, all in leg and arm shackles. Their destination was the gangplank of the *Cyclops*. It was poor timing for all. Along the dock from shore a group of sailors, all carrying kit bags, was heading toward the *Cyclops*. They were a quiet enough group when passing the dock shack where Pereira was conversing with some men, but when they saw the prisoners the straggling line of sailors communicated like the pulses in a single nerve. The leaders turned and passed the word and eventually the last man in the group knew what was up ahead. The passengers, fellow shipmates of the men now in chains, had arrived.

The men on the *Cyclops* must not have been happy. There were at least 50 men on the dock in addition to the prisoners. With the tension aboard the ship, this did not bode well. This meant 50 men unfamiliar with Captain Worley's manner and the feud aboard between he and Asper. We know well the results off France when so many uninitiated crewmen were aboard the *Cyclops* for the first time. In addition to that potential problem, these were 50 men the *Cyclops* didn't need. They were 50 real USN men from a warship, the kind Worley hated. Where would they put them?

The *Cyclops'* busy men had slowly left off work to watch, with mixed apprehension and distaste, the line of sailors approaching. The mixed feelings were caused by the jovial and friendly shouts between the sailors and the 5 prisoners. Clearly some of the men were former shipmates, and the fact they were now convicts meant little to some of the rougher looking sailors shipping aboard. No doubt hoping to avoid a burst of camaraderie, the shore patrol held up the prisoners until the passenger-sailors boarded.

Yet hollers of friendship continued to resound up the gangplank until the last man reported in. At the top of the gangplank Hodge and Page checked each sailor off and verified his name. Each in turn threw their kitbags over their shoulders and ushered back in a steady line to the door of the aft deck bulkhead.

During this muster, Forbes strode up to the railing of the flying bridge. He saw the men and shook his head in reluctant acceptance. He knew his release was contingent on these "bilge rats." There would be too much ahead to leave him in stir.

After the last of the seamen able disappeared into the aft bulkhead door, Captain Worley strode down the starboard aft deck stairs and joined Hodge and Page. It is very likely that

Asper was made to stand behind his shoulder in order to see his new patients. All others stood poised to greet or, more proper perhaps, confront the convicts. The 5 shackled seamen, in company of their shore patrol keepers, were now almost at the head of the gangplank.

No man aboard could be ignorant of the fact that murder was involved. All eyes watched the first convict presented. He stood defiantly, legs apart and hands folded before groin.

The yeoman in charge of the shore patrol mounted, saluted, walked past his two guards, and then saluted Worley and presented papers. "Per orders from Admiral Caperton, sir."

Worley did not salute. He really didn't give recognition to the yeoman. He waved aside the paperwork, indicating Page. He was far more interested in the third prisoner. At no other time had Worley appeared less a Navy captain and the old sea-dog than now.

The yeoman dutifully handed the papers to Mr. Page and stood aside. Page meanwhile unfolded them.

The first two men Worley also brushed aside. Page had announced their names and that they were headed for stateside for 2 years in prison for being AWOL. That was small potatoes to Worley.

It was with the approach of the next convict— that defiant third man— that Worley smiled with grim satisfaction. The seaman approached. Page read: "Whiteside, Moss, petty officer, for not stopping and participating in a drunken party, 15 years in prison."

Shore patrol took him in arms and led him aft in company of *Cyclops*' own armed detachment.

The next man appeared. His chains rattled to a stop and he looked at Worley as mean and as smug as he could.

Page read: "Devoe, Barney, Fireman second. Complicity in the murder of Oscar Stewart, Fireman Third; USS Pittsburgh; 50 to 99 years."

Worley jerked his head over his shoulder, dismissing Devoe and his keepers aft.

The next prisoner stood apart from the others in many

ways. His stance before the seadog was with an air of bitter challenge and not defiance. He was a white, pale man, made so from the term of his imprisonment and trial. His eyes were dark, mean, with heavy lines underneath. A livid scar was on his right arm and a bruised tattoo of a dancing girl on this left. He wasn't big, but he was firm, stringy and strong.

Page's eyes left of their own uneasy study of the man and clumsily scanned the paperwork to regain his place. "Coker, James, Fireman First, for the murder of Oscar Stewart, Fireman Third." He paused impressively. "Death by hanging."

Worley was delighted. With another jerk of his head he directed the shore patrol and prisoner aft. Coker remained defiant, sneering contemptuously over his shoulder as he was hauled back.

Just as Worley and Hodge took a step to vacate the way for the men to finish securing No. 4 Hatch, an officer mounted the gangplank. Worley stopped. The officer stepped forward and saluted. He was Lieutenant Albert Winkle reporting aboard.

It had no effect on Worley. The man had merely boarded at the right time to catch the Master in a semi-awaiting position. Indeed, the old seadog was ready to take his stride to leave until Page, rustling through the paperwork, clarified he was shipping aboard from the *Glacier.*

The officer whom Nervig had replaced.

9

DISTINGUISHED PASSENGER

"His chief fault lay in his being a newspaper man and secondarily Consul General. This, together with a disagreeable personality, caused Americans and other foreigners to dislike him intensely."
—secret dispatch, Secret Service agent Hil, Rio.

DAWN WARMED RIO, ITS SHIPS and buildings, as the dull embers of a fireplace might glow over a quiet room's furniture. The sun's rays sliced through the city. The golden rods of morning created deep and impressive shadows in the lee of buildings and dockside equipment. The *Cyclops'* shadow was a distorted ink blotch, dark and bottomless; it menacingly grasped the dock and warehouses.

Approaching this abyss was a limousine. A grand personage of sorts must have been safely concealed in the back, judging by the appearance of the chauffeur in the open front seat. He was formally dressed, with a jaunty little tilt to his otherwise formal hat. The dignity of the personage he carried at present reclined under the elegance of a beautiful burgundy rag top.

Its headlights swept the cold, uninviting hull of the *Cyclops* as it turned and disappeared into the maw of its shadow. The lights bounced here and there on the uneven dock as the limo crawled along. Its last slow hesitating movements were those of uneasiness, as if it knew at last it was merely a bug that should be terribly reticent to sit next to the monster *Cyclops*. It finally stopped at the bottom of the gangplank.

Here two sailors and Mr. Schonhof had awaited it. The chauffeur was a nimble fellow, and went quickly back to the trunk rather than opening the rear door. The door opened on its own and out stepped an Admiral's aide and then, at last, a portly man in a long knee coat, top hat and gloved hands delicately holding a walking cane. By the way the aide stepped aside, this was clearly the dignitary.

The driver was already removing luggage from the trunk, with the help of the sailors, who at Schonhof's gesticulating orders had quickly obliged.

Or so it seemed from the flying bridge. Worley kept a typical taciturn eye on the event. But he made sure to follow all that went on below. There was no fanfare. Worley ordered no piping, which Mr. Hodge repeated with mildly upraised voice. It was signaled down to the gangplank.

The dignitary waited quietly on the dock, gloved hand reaching up to pat a yawning mouth and smartly trimmed Prussian mustache and goatee. He only acknowledged Schonhof's "good morning Consul General" with a polite nod of his head.

Every bit about the man suggested official aplomb. And yet, well, there was something of "mutton dressed as lamb." There was altogether an air of theatrical mask, something impromptu about the aloof Consul General. He waddled his way up the long gangplank with his retinue of luggage trundling up behind him. His white spats stood out atrociously from his dark attire. Until he reached the golden line of the sunrise near the main deck, his movement along the gang could almost only be traced by the pair of mounting spats.

As soon as he stepped onto the head of the gangplank, his entire right side glowed from the morning sun. He appeared a portly satyr, with his closely cropped goatee giving an angularity his otherwise chubby baby face did not possess. He raised his hat in greeting. His hair was parted in the middle and slicked down. He was a dandy of a devil, with clerkish *pin nez*, the black string dancing about his lapel. As soon as he had stepped upon the deck, Schonhof and the men loaded with luggage appeared behind him. Schonhof now signaled with a demonstrative uplifting of his arm to raise the gangplank.

Captain Worley, who had had more than enough time to reach the gang and await the dignitary, now stepped forward, a very formal air to him. There he greeted the Consul General officially.

Perhaps Consul Gottschalk could not nod more demonstratively because of his tight high collar. Perhaps it was his large paisley cravat and the knot below his Adam's apple. Whatever

A. L. M. GOTTSCHALK,
U. S. consul general at Rio Janeiro

the reason he was as aloof with Worley as Worley was with his men. He was escorted aft to Worley's own cabin. *Cyclops* quietly set sail with one of the leading US diplomats in Brazil, and *nobody* there knew it. An odd event indeed.

As they trundled aft, the ship came alive with men securing for sea. The gangplank was lifting into place by the rail. The tall stacks noticeably belched dark smoke, and the still harbor sea began to churn as the *Cyclops* backed out of her berth. With his anticlimactic arrival, the *Cyclops* had taken leave of Rio. She chugged out of the harbor until she was enveloped in the diamond sparkle of the sunrise.

Alfred Louis Moreau Gottschalk. He was an interesting dandy. Despite his name, he was not from any grand family or background. But he had risen in the ranks of diplomatic service to attain the post of US Consul General of all Brazil. It was his duty to inspect all the US consulates in Brazil and keep them informed, organized and tip top.

Gottschalk remained aloof during the voyage north. A warm evening might see him on the poop deck, far more relaxed without his long coat, one hand in his waistcoat, as he smoked a cigarette. Even in this pose he seemed stiff and aloof. His cravat was no less perfect than before. The long ribbon from his *pin nez* looped down and played on his shoulder, and his spats had so far remained unsoiled. The wind cared to play little in his fastidiously combed and pomaded hair. Parted as it was in the middle, he was paradoxically clerkish, sophisticated— intimidating— and always, as a result, intriguing to the scroungy men working about.

We know nothing of *Cyclops'* northbound cruise. We only know of Gottschalk's personality and his mode of departure. This is enough to tell us that he remained quite aloof. He was, in fact, the type to relish his position rather than conduct the duties of office according to its high requirements. He enjoyed prestige, but did not necessarily have the merits to earn it. He enjoyed the captain's aft cabin, and no doubt ate in the wardroom with the officers, which no doubt required Worley to sit and officiate— a volatile arrangement. But it is unlikely that Gottschalk would have been sympathetic to any complaints, even if he had been in a position to hear them.

Such aloofness, even secrecy, is seen in events that occurred in Bahia. The *Cyclops* came back into the emerald bay on the way north. Fortunately, we have Nervig as a witness again. The *Glacier* had long left Rio de Janeiro and anchored at Bahia. As Officer of the Deck that day he watched the vessel lumber in from the north. He attributed the reverse direction once again to Worley's bad navigation. Since Bahia is north of Rio, the *Cyclops'* gray image should have risen from the dome of the sea to the south. Worley must have simply overshot Bahia again. Was Forbes back in stir? After the *Cyclops* cast a noisy anchor in the jellied reflections of the surrounding jungle, a boat was lowered. But it seems rather definite that Gottschalk himself never left his cabin. He did not even go ashore to visit the local US consulate. A man was to be entrusted with a special sealed letter from him, and this would not be delivered until the *Cyclops* was ready to leave that evening.

This man it seems was young Ensign Page. He came and visited the *Glacier*. Perhaps his visit had to do with Nervig's stay aboard. As Assistant Paymaster he may have had some paperwork that dealt with Nervig's time on the *Cyclops*. Nervig does not tell us. He is, once again, only an observer of things related to him. There is also no mention that Page visited Bahia, however briefly. But the lad appears to have carried a letter with him from the Consul. If he did not go ashore, then he delivered the letter to the captain of the *Glacier*, who will figure prominently in the investigation of the *Cyclops* later, and indeed had figured prominently in Worley's past. In any case, a letter was mailed from Bahia, by whoever's hand had mailed it— either by Page or by an intermediary aboard the *Glacier*. It was most definitely from Gottschalk, and Navy investigators would be surprised by what it had said.

From Nervig we are only given a final impression of what life might have been like aboard the *Cyclops*. After Page was finished, Nervig escorted him back to the gangway. "On leaving he grasped my hand in both of his and said very solemnly, 'Well, goodbye, old man, and God bless you.' I was deeply impressed by the finality, which was truly prophetic in its implication."

Page descended the gangway and waved farewell again. His launched returned to the *Cyclops*. Nervig watched it until it blended with the tip of the long V wake it had cut in the green bay. Up the gangway he went. A man toted the mailbag from the *Glacier* behind him. Nervig had placed numerous letters to his wife therein. The launch was raised, the gangplank, and then the anchor chain clunked up, pulling the soft seabed with it until it locked into place.

At 6 p.m. that very day, *Cyclops* quietly left, her weighty, valuable cargo holding her deep in the water and her single engine groaning along. Next call— Baltimore and home.

However, that was not to be the case. Unexpectedly, on March 3, 1918, at 5:30 p.m., the collier sailed into the British colony of Barbados in the West Indies. It was a great source of surprise to the inhabitants of the many homes terraced up the mountain shoulders when the collier steamed into Carlisle Bay. Out the colonists came, hand to forehead shielding eyes. They watched her slowly wallow in, the little colony quite excited over the unexpected visit of such a big ship. From the flashing of her signal lamp, she was identifying herself to the port authorities. A British gunboat was now circling the vessel and a man was calling out to them to lower their gangplank.

At the same time the port authority was signaling back, Worley ordered his personal launch readied.

From the garden porch of a beautiful colonial home, a balding gentleman in a pale white suit and stiff collar wondered at what all the sight-seeing locals were gazing. The signal codes going back and forth identified the vessel as a US collier, the *Cyclops*, and there were many who could read Morse.

Brockholst Livingston[7] was the US Consul at Barbados. From what he was seeing, he suspected he would be paid a visit soon. He saw a boat lowered from the *Cyclops*, the gangplank lower, and soon trod down three men dressed in their white uniforms. No sooner had they entered the boat when it cut a frothy wake in the deep forest green waters of Carlisle Bay.

Upon landing at the dock, two of the men got out and were greeted by the British harbor officials. The two officers walked with them into the town until it was certain from Livingston's vantage point that they were going to Government House. That made it certain that he would at least hear about this. As the US Consul at Barbados, he would be informed by the British governor.

Indeed, it was less than an hour before Captain Worley stood before Livingston at the "Consulate"— Livingston's quiet colonial home— in his office. Barbados was a small island, and through the French doors behind Livingston's desk Worley

---

[7] Apparently the same as Charles Ludlow Livingston. I do not know if he used "Brock" as a nickname or not. There were a number Brockholsts in the Livingston family, including Henry Brockholst Livingston, a Supreme Court judge. They were all branches of the Livingstons of New York.

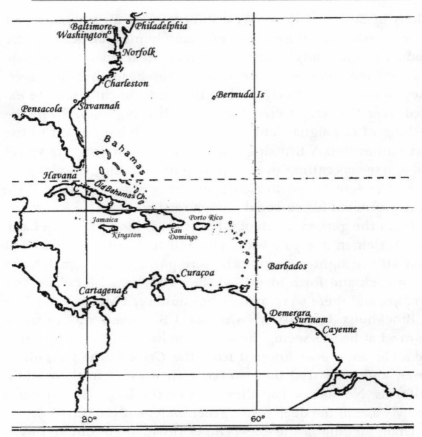

Barbados in relation to the Cyclops' *route home to Baltimore.*

could see almost all of Bridgetown and Carlisle Bay . . . and the mammoth *Cyclops* at anchor.

It was a warm tropic scene Worley could afford to take-in since Livingston was taking an excessively long time to mull over what Worley had just declared. Ensign Page stood at some distance behind his captain, hat in hand, looking very Navy, equally awaiting the Consul's decision. The seadog looked proper enough, but there was altogether an air of expectancy and hurry in him.

Livingston didn't like it. He may not have been the greatest diplomat; the greatest are never on such small islands. But he was a trusted and perceptive man. He was from a diplomatic family. He was one of the Livingstons of New York, and there had been a Livingston in the diplomatic service for 200 years. His ancestor, Robert Livingston, had signed the Declaration of Independence. This also perhaps made him something that the crude but arrogant Worley could not stomach immediately.

Consul Livingston, too, saw no reason to completely hide his annoyance and skepticism. Worley's request was unusual, and it sat ill with the meagerly funded US Consul. Worley requested more money in order to pay for extra foodstuffs and, even more surprising, for more coal in order to make it to his destination. Though appearing offhand, Worley could introduce the young officer as Senator Page's grandson, Chairman of the Senate Naval Committee. This might have made the reluctant Livingston acquiesce. Yet it remained clear that the Consul did not like Worley.

Worley was eager to go and get the loading over with. He had a schedule to keep, and he needed to get to his home port. Livingston shrugged and reluctantly granted his request.

Consul Livingston kept a watch on the *Cyclops* as she purred thin smoke and up-anchored in order to get into her coaling position at the dock. By late afternoon the supplies were being loaded. Truckloads of other supplies were coming and going from the dock.

Night fell on the vessel, and she was well secured with no lights. The low crescent moon's position only made her a distorted figure casting a huge shadow. There was no ship near her size in Carlisle Bay, only the many fishing vessels, yachts, a few inter-island steamers and some British gunboats.

No officer of the *Cyclops* had visited British officers. Worley made no customary calls to various British naval authorities. The *Cyclops* seemed in self-quarantine. Barbadians had a peculiar feeling about the mammoth sitting snuggly in their harbor. But was there anything to the premonition?

10

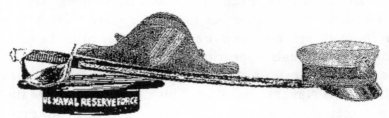

'ALL WELL' TO OBLIVION

"On several occasions I passed some of the Officers on the streets of the town. They did not act as if they wanted to be friendly."
—Lt. Harold Holdsworth, British Naval Exec. Officer, Barbados

THERE SHE WAS THE NEXT morning, still the distant, aloof mammoth like her master. The *Cyclops* was still being fed supplies. Dawn had revealed a few trucks trickling some odds and ends to the vessel, offerings to entreat the massive, primitive brute. Livingston sighed and accepted the unusual event and went back to his work.

By mid-morning he was gardening. The fine view of Carlisle Bay was obscured from sight as he crouched amidst his shrubs and tended his flowers. But in wiping his brow he saw a thin plume of smoke drifting with the wind. Standing up, he noticed that the *Cyclops* was at last belching out smoke from her twin stacks. The gray locomotive of the sea was cleaving the beautiful green bay and heading out. The blemish and her surly master were going. She had spent far less than 24 hours in Carlisle Bay, every waking minute devoted to taking on supplies. Livingston could do little more than shrug, but he was glad the leviathan was gone.

Frankly, the British naval men were just as glad to see *Cyclops* leave. Her seamen and officers hadn't mixed much, and none were too friendly. Moreover, word was trickling back from the loading companies, Gardenier, Austin & Co. and Laurie & Company. Rumors spoke about disturbances, possible mutiny, and that the skipper was regarded by his crew as a "damned Dutchman."

With these rumors already spreading amongst the town, it was an especially curious event to see the *Cyclops* sail out of Carlisle Bay without flying her homeward bound pennant from the bow. Furthermore, as the vessel cleared the harbor, she turned *south*, not north. Yet Worley had made no secret of his sailing to Bermuda, which is far north of Barbados.

Livingston puzzled over this, too, bending back the brim of his straw gardening hat to watch the ship finally disappear around the headland *south*. The dark silhouette faded into the haze of the sea, and at last all that was left was the dark plumes of her smoke tinting the white haze of the tropics as might a very weak solution of ink tint milk.

Shortly after *Cyclops* departed, the Navy picked up another message from her, stating she had left Barbados and was now homeward bound, reaffirming her speed at 10 knots and her ETA on March 13 at Baltimore. At the end the message there was appended the usual official post scriptum: "All Well."

This is the beginning of the mystery of the disappearance of the U.S.S. *Cyclops*. No other message was ever received and no SOS was ever reported. March 13 came and went and yet the vessel never appeared at Baltimore, her actual destination port.

On March 18, the Navy became curious. Operations sent a wireless to her: "Report probable date arrival Baltimore." There was no answer. The Navy now contacted the flagship *Pittsburgh*. Admiral Caperton could offer nothing beyond the message they had sent back on February 22, stating that the vessel had just left Bahia and was due March 7th at Baltimore.[8]

Concern was now raised over the collier's engines, which Worley was on record complaining about. Furthermore, the Navy knew the vessel had put in at Barbados for fuel. Was it possible the great vessel was disabled at sea? But if so, why no wireless message? On March 22, the Navy started sweeping the airwaves with calls to the vessel from San Juan, Charleston, Key West, and Guantanamo. The stations had been alerted direct from Naval Operations. "USS Cyclops sailed from Barbados March fourth. Now about 10 days overdue. Endeavor communicate Cyclops by radio and ascertain location and condition."

On March 24, the 6th Naval District at Charleston, South Carolina, summed it up to Naval Operations: "Have been unable to communicate with USS CYCLOPS by radio from eleven A.M. Saturday to ten A.M. Sunday. Shall I continue attempting to converse?" Operations ordered all stations to continue.

On that very day Operations intensified the search. Orders went out to Squadron One Patrol Force to utilize all available vessels and commence a search for the *Cyclops*. USS *Vixen* was sent to scour the Bahamas around Aves Island. *Petrel* was ordered to San Juan and from there to search straight to Hampton Roads, Virginia. *Albatross* was ordered to proceed immediately "to search the windward side of Bahama Islands from Mariguana Island [Mayaguana] down to the Windwards as far as Barbuda." *Dolphin* was ordered to Guantanamo and to standby.

This search continued well into April. On the 13th, *Dolphin* searched Hogsty Reef, even landing a search party to try and locate an unlikely German submarine base rumored to be there. The next day she searched Caicos Bank and checked with government officials at Cockburn Harbor. Next day Acklin Island, then Samana Cay. Then Long Island and Cat Island on the 16th. Following this, the next day she searched Eleuthera Island and then docked at Nassau where her captain enquired of the Royal Governor for any news. "The Governor of

---

[8] Could be a typo, but according to Nervig the *Cyclops* left at 6 p.m. on the 21st.

the Bahamas states that he would have been informed had any wreckage indicating loss of vessel drifted ashore on any of the Bahama Islands."

With the certainty there was no wreckage in the archipelago, the USS *Eagle* sailed on orders to search Cay Sal Bank.

While this search was ongoing, more radio sweeps were being made. On March 26, the governor of the Virgin Islands was requested to investigate whether there was evidence the *Cyclops* passed there, and two days later, on March 28, the State Department now requested Barbados to sweep the seas within their radio and wireless range. Naval Base Key West kept this up every 2 hours until April 1, finally receiving permission from Operations to stand down.

In all this there was no trace found whatsoever, no clue, and no island base ever reported that it had picked up any SOS, even a fleeting one indicating trouble. The airwaves were so well covered that when an SOS was picked up in late April the Navy frantically tried and locate it. Finally, on May 1, it was discovered to be the *War Queen*, which was suffering trouble and calling for help. No sound from the *Cyclops* made it certain that the great ship had never sent any SOS. *No* US Navy ship had ever been lost since wireless' invention that had not gotten off some message, no matter how brief. It seemed inconceivable the huge *Cyclops* should be the first. But as it stood now in April, this appeared to be the case.

For most of this time not a breath of trouble had been leaked out to the Press. But by April 15, now 1 month after the vessel had been overdue, it was time to make a formal announcement.

The U.S.S Cyclops, Navy Collier of 19,000 tons displacement, loaded with a cargo of manganese and with the personnel on board of 15 officers and 221 men of the crew and 57 passengers, is overdue at an Atlantic port since March 13. She last reported at one of the West Indian Islands on March 4, and since her departure from that port no trace of her nor any information concerning her has been obtained. Radio calls to the Cyclops from all possible points have been made and vessels sent to search for her along her probable route and areas in which she might be met with no success.

No well founded reasons can be given to explain the Cyclops being overdue as no radio communication with or trace of her has been had since leaving the West Indian port. The weather in the area in which the vessel must have passed has not been bad, and could hardly have given the Cyclops trouble.

While a raider or submarine could be responsible for her loss, there have been no reports that would indicate the presence of either in the locality in which the Cyclops was.

It was known that one of the two engines of the Cyclops was injured and that she was proceeding at a reduced speed with one engine compounded. This fact would have no effect on her ability to communicate by radio, for even if her main engines were totally disabled, the ship would still be capable of using her radio plant.

The search for the Cyclops still continues, but the Navy Department feels extremely anxious as to her safety.

The Press, which loves to paint the fangs and wings on anything it sees, published the Navy Department statement amidst long articles discussing several intriguing and potentially lurid possibilities. The *Evening Star* summarized: "No possible theory was rejected by officials in seeking an explanation. Suggestions heard most frequently were that German agents had boarded the ship in port and captured her from her people at sea; that she had broken in two and gone down in a sudden squall; that she had been overtaken by a submarine and sunk without trace, and that an internal explosion had sent her down . . . All of the suggestions had flaws in them, it was said. A theory that she had been captured by a group of German agents aboard appeared to be the only explanation that would account for the silence of her radio equipment . . .The ship had aboard an insufficient quantity of coal for a journey to the nearest German port had she been captured. Some officers think that if the ship was captured her captors may be holding her out of trade routes, waiting for a chance steamer from which to secure fuel . . . It is the absolute silence of the radio that makes the case one of the most mysterious in naval annals. That fact alone inclines officials to the view that the ship might have been captured by persons aboard, for in no other way would it have been possible to silence calls for aid. In case of a storm or an attack by enemy craft, or even if the ship was torpedoed, there would have been time for such calls . . . The possibility was suggested that explosives might have been put aboard, mixed in large quantities with the manganese ore and a time bomb set to explode the mass. In that case, however, the sea would be covered with wreckage."

As sensational or at least novella as some of these sounded, the Navy couldn't discount any of them. Furthermore, they were in for an unexpected and unpleasant surprise. That very day, April 15, Operations sent a secret communiqué to all branch offices of the Office of Naval Intelligence in South America, requesting any information they could provide. Because the vessel stopped off at Barbados, the State Department also sent Livingston a communiqué. The Navy had already ascertained from Admiral Caperton that the *Cyclops'* intentions were to head straight to Baltimore from Bahia. This made the unscheduled stop at Barbados all the more interesting to them. When Livingston received the message, he put his nose to the grindstone to uncover what exactly had transpired for those 18 or so hours the *Cyclops* had remained in port. What he reports constitutes the last solid evidence we have for what conditions were like aboard the ill-fated vessel. It is from this point that a massive Navy investigation began.

11

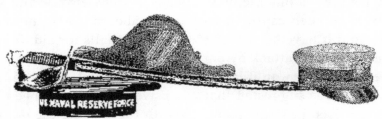

'I FEAR FATE WORSE THAN SINKING'

"That on the last trip the captain had almost starved them to death; that
the boys came pretty near throwing him overboard; that they were not going to stand much more of it."
—James Scroggins paraphrasing his son, seaman Roy Scroggins

ASSEMBLING AND ANALYZING THE FACTS that underpin the disappearance of the U.S.S. *Cyclops* is not an easy task. Originally,
starting with this chapter I had begun what was a laborious
process. This was the strictly coldhearted investigative section
detailing the evidence I was able to uncover in various archives. This was a meticulous (though hopefully interesting)
compilation and synthesis of every report. This included loading and dunnage reports itemizing the manganese down to the
buckets per hold. It also included every little detail of how
George Worley's past was assembled, even from out-of-the-way
comments that led to witnesses, incidentals, in-laws turning on
him, and former Naval officers admitting what it was like to
sail under the old "seadog." Interesting reading though it was,
I became less of an author and more of a compiler. Duty and
history are served much better by getting to the point rather
than just sitting there and repeatedly sharpening it.

But before we delve into the strange case of the *Cyclops* I
should also clarify that much of the information I was able to

dig up was previously secret and confidential. When time came that it should be released, it was unceremoniously dumped in bins at the National Archives; decades, in fact, after the last voyage of the *Cyclops* had faded from popular memory. The contents of those thousands of pages underscore how many different and independent investigative paths merged. Put together they form a vivid and reliable picture of what life was like aboard the *Cyclops*. I should also remind the reader that during its investigation the Navy was completely unaware of Conrad Nervig's experiences aboard. Anybody familiar with Nervig's account is left with quite an impact after going through these musty and neglected documents. They see how many other seamen had independently come forward with equally strange stories of George Worley. The Board of Inquiry had been behind locked doors, as is the custom. The Press knew nothing about it. The contents of those proceedings could not have influenced the recollections of those who related odd encounters with Worley long before the fateful last voyage— and the Navy would uncover many.

There can be no doubt, however, that the very first disturbing information on the disappearance of the *Cyclops* came into the State Department on April 17, only 2 days after the general message to all ONI agents and Consuls to report any discoveries. Such a statement as "I fear fate worse than sinking" could not have had a bigger punch, especially as it was the teasing cliffhanger of Consul Livingston's report. He quickly got to work and fired off to the Secretary of State the findings of his own undercover investigation on Barbados. In it he does not mince words.

Department's 15th. Confidential. Master CYCLOPS stated that required six hundred tons of coal having sufficient on board to reach Bermuda. Engines very poor condition. Not sufficient funds and therefore requested payment by me. Unusually reticent. I have ascertained he took here ton fresh meat, ton flour, thousand pounds vegetables, paying therefore 775 dollars. From different sources gather the following: He had plenty of coal, alleged inferior, took coal to mix, probably he had more than fif-

teen hundred tons. Master alluded to by others as damned
Dutchman, apparently disliked by other officers. Rumored disturbances en route hither, men confined and one <u>executed</u>; also
had some prisoners from the fleet in Brazilian waters, one life
sentence. United States Consul-General Gottshalk passenger, 231
crew exclusive of officers and passengers. Many Germanic names
appear. Number telegraphic or wireless messages addressed to
master or in care of ship were delivered at this port. All telegrams for Barbadoes on file head office St. Thomas. I have to
suggest scrutiny there. While not having definite grounds I fear
fate worse than sinking though possibly based on instinctive dislike felt toward master.

Livingston,
Consul.

The State Department quickly passed this on to Office of
Naval Intelligence. It didn't take much to read between the
lines and find the distressing meaning— mutiny or treason.
Everything about the communiqué gears the reader towards
Livingston's worst fears. Naturally, the Navy didn't care for it.
The US Navy had never had a mutiny before, nor did it ever
suffer anything like betrayal beyond that which was attempted
on the *Rochester.*

The April 15 news release had also tempered any fears,
should they arise, that the vessel could have sailed off to a
German port when it noted that she didn't have enough coal.
That contingent was obviously entirely dashed to pieces now.

Yet while the Navy prepared for the worst, the Office of
Naval Intelligence was remarkably skeptical. Only 3 days later,
on April 20th, a memorandum had been drawn up picking it
apart. "The theory of her being seized by her Master, or by
some German conspirators among the passengers or crew, is
not an impossible one, but seems highly improbable. If she
was so seized, it seems likely that she is being employed as a
raider in the South Atlantic Waters. If she headed for Germany
to take in the cargo of manganese, she must have arrived there
before this." For the idea of an illegal execution at sea the au-

thor of the memo put in parentheses "highly improbable." This, a gut reaction, is the only response. In the Fifth point raised in the memo, it states in parentheses that the Consul considers it "very unusual" that he should be asked to pay funds. The author's clarification is "but it is not regarded as particularly significant, as it might easily happen that a vessel of this kind not carrying a Paymaster would be short of funds." Not only does this overlook the fact that Hugh Morris was the Chief Pay Clerk, it is like all else in the tempering memo the product of gut reactions and not investigation.

For practical purposes, the memo was designed to help give some direction to an investigation and, one can imagine, quell any possible overreaction in upper echelons. But, sadly, it also seems to have come to reflect or, worse, to set the tempo of ONI's approach. Investigation would become a matter of compilation rather than one of analysis leading to an hypothesis and from there to an attempt to solve the mystery.

For instance, instead of conducting an immediate investigation of the situation on Barbados, which in terms of practicality was the obvious starting point, ONI only lingered on their skepticism of Livingston's cable. This was beneficial only to the point of dissecting hints that information could have been conflated and confused before it got to his ears. A clear example can be seen in how "men confined and one <u>executed</u>" is associated with "disturbances en route hither." It seems more probable that Livingston's sources were inspired by the reality of the prisoners being brought north. Coker was to be executed and Devoe had a life sentence on him. Obviously, there were reasons for ONI to ask the question, 'what else may have been distorted in the retelling?' But the answers obviously lay on Barbados. Nevertheless, ONI was lax in conducting its own investigation. Rather than sending operatives to Barbados, or even asking Livingston to recheck his facts, they waited until May 6, 1918, and took advantage of the arrival in New York of the s.s. *Vestris*, a British liner which had stopped at Barbados on the way north.

As soon as *Vestris* started disembarking passengers, ONI

agents were walking aboard the gangway to interview members of her crew. To their initial relief, they discovered that far fewer foodstuffs were taken than Livingston had reported. One of the passengers was "leftenant" Harold Holdsworth. Up until he boarded the *Vestris* for New York, Holdsworth had been the British Naval Executive Officer at Barbados.[9] Although his memory is sketchy on details, he did recall that the officers of the vessel when passing on the streets "did not act as if they wanted to be friendly." Holdsworth also recalled that Worley did not as is customary render an official call to the Naval Office there. Basically, it seems Worley was in a hurry to get his stuff and go. Holdsworth assumed, however, that Worley would have had to go to the governor in order to be allowed to buy coal. Other than this it seems Worley only came to Livingston for the money.

While this is somewhat suspicious behavior, Holdsworth didn't seem to think anything untoward had happened. He states, in almost direct contrast to Livingston:

> Several weeks later when Washington reported the Cyclops as having disappeared, rumors immediately became current amongst the inhabitants in Barbadoes and word came to me that the Cyclops had taken on an excessive amount of coal and provisions, which rumor was circulated to bear out the supposition that the ship had gone to Germany. I immediately made a personal investigation and learned from a representative of the company which supplied the provisions that the ship had only taken on 500 tons of Bunker Coal and 180 pounds of provisions. Neither of these items would I term excessive.

It would not be until June 6 that the Navy would secure its own interview with a member of the Barbados companies in question. Kenneth T. Clark, of the Navy Department's Office of Aid of Information, Third District, New York, made the report. It proved Holdsworth to be . . . *right* . . . partially. "A repre-

---

[9] All throughout his report the operative refers to Holdsworth as "leftenant" following Holdsworth's own English pronunciation for lieutenant.

sentative of this Office interviewed S.C. Foster, general manager for DaCosta & Company, Barbados, W.I., and learned that the *Cyclops* stopped at Barbados where she took on certain provisions and supplies. Two hundred and fifty tons of coal was secured from Gardnier [sic], Austin & Company, and a similar number of tons from Laurie & Company. She bought meats and vegetables from DaCosta & Company, Mr. Foster handling the transactions personally. He states that the order amounted to only about $1000.00 and he considered it a very small order in view of the ship's compliment."

The problem with Holdsworth's and Foster's interpretation of "small" is that neither knew how much supplies the *Cyclops* already had aboard. Holdsworth was certainly wrong about 180 pounds weight. It is impossible that 180 pounds— the weight of 36 five pound chickens or steaks— is going to cost a whopping $1,000.00. Livingston is probably more correct, and the confusion either comes from the British use of pounds for weight and for pounds sterling— money— and from Holdsworth's memory. He also thought that the *Cyclops* was a few days in port.

A ton of meat (400 five pound chickens or steaks) and a thousand pounds of vegetables is still small for a compliment of 309 men. So small it seems to preclude a voyage to Germany. Rather, we might better assume the extra stores were on account of the 57 extra passengers the *Cyclops* was carrying. Also, knowing the Commissary problems the ship had, if more fish or fowl had been rotten it would have been thrown over. Between either possibility we have found more reasonable excuses for Worley needing provisions. One other point may help. Upon leaving Rio, Worley estimated arrival date at Baltimore on March 8th. At Barbados, Worley estimates the 13th of March as the new arrival date. About 400 chickens, a ton of flour and vegetables does seem very minor in light of a few extra unexpected days in transit.

As for the extra coal, however, here rationalizing has to cease. Livingston was right. Worley had more than enough coal. In fact, 2 reliable estimates can be made for how much coal he had. Admiral Caperton told ONI 2,000 tons were taken for her fuel, but he didn't make it clear if this was the amount at Newport News or Rio. In any case, whether estimating 2,000 tons of fuel from Norfolk or Rio the results are disturbing. *Cyclops* burned about 31 ¼ tons of coal a day. Taking the Newport News estimate, she would have burned about 565 tons on the voyage south (18 days in transit at 360 miles per day), and about 500 tons during the 16 days transit to Barbados from Rio de Janeiro on the voyage north (240 miles per day at reduced speed of 10 mph). That leaves her with just under 1,000 tons of coal, more than enough to make Baltimore in 9 days' time (March 4 to March 13).

Is it possible that with Worley's poor navigating the *Cyclops* went far off course and burned up so much of this extra coal? This is, in fact, one of Worley's excuses. An interview with the chief engineer of the *Vestris*, a man Duer by name, revealed he had heard this from none other than the rep. for Laurie & Co, Mr. Lobe. "When his company inquired as to why the need for so much coal, they were informed by the Commanding officer that the vessel had sailed 800 miles off her course, which together with engine trouble, necessitating compounding her engines, had left the vessel with little coal in reserve."

This simply is not the case. What the *Cyclops* had mysteriously lost by Barbados was *time*. No matter how one slices it, 3 days are added to the *Cyclops'* ETA at Barbados, and the Navy investigation didn't try and flesh out the cause. It is necessary to do so now in retrospect to reveal that 3 days were never missing between Bahia and Barbados, and that 800 miles off course could never have.

The entire equation should be easy, but it isn't. ONI compiled the following itinerary.

Left Hampton Roads for Bahia, Brazil January 8th, 1918.
Arrived Bahia, January 22nd.
Left Bahia, for Rio de Janeiro, January 24th, 1918.
Arrived Rio de Janeiro, January 28th, 1918.
Left Rio de Janeiro about February 16th.
Arrived Bahia, February 20th, 1918.

Left Bahia for Baltimore, February 22nd, 1918.
Arrived Barbados, March 3rd, 1918.
Left Barbados, March 4th, 1918.

It works fine until leaving Rio de Janeiro— then it is
"about." Here enters the conundrum of *Cyclops'* departure
from Rio. At first Worley estimated departure the 15th of February. Then he sent a signed message saying he intended to
leave at 9 a.m. on the 16th. But no one is sure if *Cyclops* left
ahead of schedule. Richard Momsen, the Vice Consul, thought
Cyclops left the 15th. Until arriving at Barbados, it's all guessing. According to the Navy itinerary, *Cyclops* arrived Bahia on
the 20th and left there on the 22nd. Nervig was, however, an
eyewitness. *Cyclops* entered from the *north* on the 21st and
left that same evening at 6 p.m. Between Rio and Bahia there is
nothing but mystery and contradiction.

All this disguises the fact that *Cyclops* is about 6 days in
transit between Rio and Bahia. Yet even at the *Cyclops'* reduced speed of 10 knots (about 240 miles per day), she could
easily have made Bahia in about 3 days. (Bahia is only about
750 miles north of Rio.) Three days are indeed missing and at
her speed this amounts to about 800 miles, which is the figure
that the coal company rep on Barbados heard, but this distance
by no means could have been added between Bahia and Barbados. Barbados is about 2,700 miles away from Bahia, and we
know *Cyclops* made it there in under 11 days, indicating she
was maintaining a speed of about 240 miles per day (10 knots
an hour) without any diversion. This underscores for us that
the missing time was between Rio and Bahia. The ship was
merely unaccounted for for 3 days between close ports, and
she entered Bahia from the north.

What was *Cyclops* doing for 3 days between Rio and Bahia?
It is inconceivable that anyone could go that far off course between such close ports. It would mean steaming in circles for a
few days or going a day and a half beyond Bahia before realizing it and turning around.

This was the span of time in which something happened

Broken line indicates what would be the normal course from Rio de Janeiro to Bahia. Solid line represents just one theoretical errant course to explain Cyclops' *3 missing days.*

that must have impressed something very ominous on young Mr. Page. It is at Bahia that he bids such a profound farewell to his buddy Nervig.

Fleshing this out here has not solved it. But it does reveal that whatever happened, ostensibly the catalyst of the "disturbances en route hither," had to be covered up. Coal and Worley's excuse(s) at Barbados make this undeniable. His excuse about going off course may explain the days lost, but that's not how he used it. He uses it to explain why he wants more coal he didn't need. He did not have little reserves left, as

Mr. Lobe recalls Worley claiming. The *Cyclops* had plenty of coal. In fact, the *Cyclops* had so much coal that when those loading the vessel saw how much another improbable excuse is trotted out— it is "inferior."

We don't know how much of it was inferior, if any. Yet with all the coal Worley took from Barbados (500 tons), it doesn't matter if all he already had was "inferior." The 500 tons on its own more than covers a trip to Baltimore. With an estimated 9 days transit to Baltimore, burning 31 ¼ tons per day would only burn up 281 and ¼ tons of this extra coal. He would have over 200 tons of Barbadian coal remaining. This is a bit worrisome, for it is quite an excess.

This fact was immediately put to the Navy investigators when they walked aboard the *Vestris.* "Chief Engineer Duer does not see how a vessel could have gone 800 miles off course between Rio de Janerio [sic] and Barbadoes [sic] and in any event, does not see why such an amount of coal was put aboard, when in his opinion either 300 or at the most 400 tons would have been sufficient to have completed the trip."

It was noted to the Navy by the Barbados company reps. that it wasn't sound economically speaking to even buy coal at Barbados since it was so much more expensive there. There is no question, given the ship's proscribed route, that Worley didn't really need 200 of those extra 500 tons that he bought. . . unless he was headed elsewhere. And *if* all her coal was good, and the "alleged inferior" 1,500 tons (or 1,000) but a lie, then 1,500 or 2,000 total tons would give *Cyclops* at the outside a 64 day steaming radius. She could easily make it to Germany. This is what is truly suspicious.

The varying excuses for wanting coal only indicate Worley was lying. Therefore his coal was probably not inferior. If he intended to return to Baltimore, how would he explain this expensive excess to his superiors? How could any commanding officer do this and expect to survive an investigation upon returning to homeport? Worley would never be able to explain why he took *any* extra coal at all.

In the long run, the Navy investigation at Barbados really

The Rochester, *seen here when still named the* New York. *She is the only ship on which a crewman attempted a plot to prepare a mutiny.*

hadn't dispelled the fears in Livingston's cable. All it had so far done was to tenuously qualify the amounts of foodstuffs taken ($1,000.00 worth as opposed to a couple of tons) and to confirm Worley made various implausible excuses for taking far more coal than he needed. ONI also made no investigation in Rio de Janeiro to try and get any idea of how the coal taken there (or if taken at Newport News, Virginia) could have been inferior. There is certainly no record. Nor did they explain why Worley tried to hide the amount of extra coal he was taking by buying from 2 separate companies. Nor did they try and account for why he was 3 days off schedule. What is now known is that *Cyclops* certainly had enough coal to head to Germany, an itinerary that just did not make sense, and Worley glossed over his needs it with various excuses.

In fact, investigation also showed how Livingston had heard some very accurate information— the 1,500 tons of coal, for example, the amount she would have had upon leaving Barbados. The rest of his information simply could not be acted upon. Without finding the ship or survivors there was no way to determine if there had truly been an illegal execution. However easy and preferable it was to assume this rumor was merely the product of convolution, there is nothing in the fact that

A PASSAGE TO OBLIVION

convicts were being shipped north that could snowball into "disturbances en route hither." Moreover, Livingston does separate between "also had some prisoners from the fleet in Brazilian waters, one life sentence" from the "disturbances en route hither, men confined and one <u>executed</u>" implying he knew the difference. Through various transcriptions, his cablegram also read twice "also conspired some prisoners" rather than "also had." If Livingston's alarming words are not the product of exaggerated confusion about the prisoners aboard, then a real attempt at mutiny must be considered, one that was successfully put down before Barbados.

There is one thing that Livingston's cable gives us that is undeniable but hardly comforting: the men of the *Cyclops* talked to British sailors and dockworkers. From our vantage point today this is perhaps one of the most significant albeit also the most subtle clues in Livingston's cable. There was such little Liberty, if any, in Rio de Janeiro that not even the slightest rumors about conditions aboard reached the Navy's ears from any shore leave scuttlebutt. From what we know of Worley's bigotries, we can surmise that most of those on leave were Auxiliary men who were treated much better by Worley and therefore had fewer complaints. However, the *Cyclops'* crewmen had ample opportunities to interact with other sailors and dockworkers while going about their own work. Yet there is little to be picked up. This indeed makes Barbados stand out even more. The men were truly disgruntled now, more than before, and they were talking to whomever they encountered. Sometime after Nervig and Page shook farewell hands together, between Bahia and Barbados, the tensions aboard had come to a head again.

The question is, what were these "disturbances en route hither" and what caused them? From what we've seen from previous voyages, George Worley was bigoted and disliked, but much of it was actually just petty. However, in later life Conrad Nervig talked at length with venerable Miami journalist Richard Winer. He even sat for film interviews for Winer's upcoming documentary *The Devil's Triangle* (1974). Inspired by

Nervig's recollection, Winer wrote how Worley punished his men by chasing them at gunpoint around the deck. Winer knew nothing of the Board of Inquiry or all the paperwork amassed at the National Archives. Given this, his details seem far more authoritative now in light of the fact that the B of I contained the testimony that Worley chased his men and then the Warrant Officers around the deck. Other contemporary interviews would confirm he chased his men at gunpoint. For enlisted men, it was actually an intentional course of punishment. Winer writes:

> . . . the *Cyclops'* passengers discovered that Commander Worley was not wearing the forty-five automatic because of the contingent of prisoners or incarcerated executive officer. This was punishment day— a day in which those accused of infractions of the ship's (and Worley's) rules were to pay for their misdeeds. As their shipmates watched from an 'at-ease' position, the accused were lined up at attention and Worley read the list of violations. All would be restricted to the ship. But those who had been before the captain previously were ordered to remove their shoes and stockings. Then at pistol point Worley drove the barefoot men around the ship's sun scorched steel decks. After a circuit around the ship, the men would return to their original starting place where the seaman with a fire hose washed down their feet with cool seawater.

Imagine the pain from saltwater in the open wounds.

Contemporarily, in 1918, Yeoman Paul Roberts had already independently confirmed to ONI that such punishments went on, at least by 1915 when he had sailed with Worley. He would state how "disgraceful" it was to see the captain of a ship chase his men at gunpoint. Could the "disturbances en route hither" have been occasioned by such bizarre punishment from which the men finally rebelled or was it from something else and then this bizarre punishment followed, exacerbating the problems aboard?

Yet in either scenario would George Worley have ever committed an illegal execution of a mutineer at sea? It seems hard to imagine. He knew he could never even hope to survive a Court Martial. No captain of a vessel may institute his own proceedings and carry out his own execution order. The only way Worley could have felt safe to execute a man was if he had absolutely no intentions of returning to the United States . . . unless, of course, he did it in a drunken stupor or arrogant rage.

If there is any breath of a chance that this happened, then it is not too far-fetched to suppose that when sober or in possession of himself again that Worley would realize he could not return to the US. What would he have to do then? He would really only have two choices: destroy his own ship and escape, or sail it to Germany and seek asylum. These two choices don't give *him* many options, but a failed mutiny and an illegal execution open the door on many scenarios leading up to the fate that ultimately took the *Cyclops*.

The foremost is that after leaving Barbados the smoldering, angry crew committed a second mutiny that succeeded. The second is that the loyal crew, realizing betrayal by the captain was coming, mutinied to save the ship and bring it to America but something then went wrong.

Although the idea of mutiny seems to be uppermost in Livingston's mind, Worley's behavior at Barbados smacks of intended betrayal. The Consul noted that the men referred to Worley as "Damned Dutchman." The expression back then did not mean a Hollander but a German. Livingston also noted a "number of Germanic names," meaning that Worley could have had enough support to help him in his treason. This was not unreasonable on Livingston's part. He and most any government official knew that the US fleet was chocked full with Germans and pro-Germans, and the incident aboard the *Rochester* was not to be taken lightly.

In order to try and wrestle with the above scenarios, the investigation had to broaden. Of the 2 major theories, mutiny became the easier upon which to follow up. Office of Naval Intelligence contacted all their operatives and all the US Consuls in the entire Caribbean area, asking them to keep an eye out for a large number of white men. In case of treason, the Navy turned to tracing the vessel's possible route to Europe. Kiel, Germany, was becoming a favorite port in the scuttlebutt about the *Cyclops'* ultimate fate. All ships in the Atlantic were signaled and asked to report if they had seen the vessel on a course that would indicate passage to Germany. Neutrals would be approached to see if they had spotted such a vessel in a German port.

With all the rumors and stories now hitting the newspapers in early May, it was a mercy that Livingston's cable remained secret. Enough juicy tidbits were originating from the *Vestris'* crew and passengers to enchant the public. Sabotage rather than mutiny, however, was the main staple of the spreadsheets. But behind-the-scenes the Navy was confronting the worst scenarios of Livingston's cable.

Lt. Commander O.W. Fowler of the Office of Naval Intelligence was in charge of the investigation into the vessel's disappearance and, of course, he had no choice but to follow up on all leads now being sent his way. While Captain Worley's past was becoming more and more colorful, Fowler was the most disturbed when he pulled the Board of Inquiry papers from last August 1917.

Time and time again the witness testimony underscored disquieting facts. Aside from 40 seamen taking the brazen step to petition the Navy against their own captain, the testimony showed that Worley was mean, inconsistent in discipline, and under the influence of alcohol. Not even William Whitted could deny the last fact in his official and confidential report to his superior, Arthur Orenham. Fortunately, this document survives in the National Archives in all the paperwork ONI had retrieved and preserved.

Fowler could see that Whitted hadn't considered much of the testimony. Worley's outright drunkenness should have been sufficient grounds to sack him. After all, he chased Warrant officers around the deck. It was clear that Worley was taking more than "medicinal" amounts of liquor for his beri-beri (Worley's excuse is so cliché it becomes almost comical). If

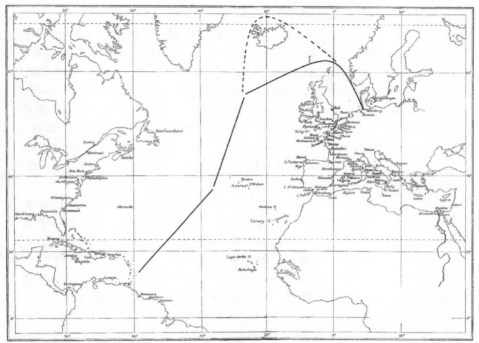

The map represents a possible course to Bremen, Germany. Via the solid line it would take about 29 days; much further if going through the Denmark Straits (broken line). Solid line route would consume about 900 tons of coal. Via the Denmark Straits, about 1,300 tons. The least amount of coal the Cyclops *would need for safety sake would be 1,500 tons.*

Whitted had bothered to read the bottom line of the testimony he would have understood how liquor was the focal point. The bottom line was that Worley was not overseeing the ship properly and was prejudiced in what he did take a hand in.

Revenge for restricted Liberty could hardly inspire all these 40 men to so boldly do what they did. There may have been an ulterior motive in a few men like Asper, but unless something else is going on men just don't join into a private vendetta. Bad food also isn't going to inspire men to blame their captain unless he already had a reputation of ignoring daily operations on board the vessel. Did not Daly boldly testify that there was "no system" of doing anything on board? More than bad food and Liberty issues, the petition was inspired by the fear these issues could not be redressed at all.

Truly unsettling evidence that Worley was passing the blame can be found in his own written defense. He did not bat an eyelash at claiming a plot— several in fact— existed against him. Now, the idea of a plot against a commanding officer is not one that the Navy buys into easily. But a plot is a hazardous tack for any commander to unscrupulously take; and Worley took it easily enough. This should have been regarded as truly bothersome by Whitted and his superior, Captain Orenham.

The petition was just the tip of the iceberg. An explosive atmosphere was brewing in the ship. Problems, deep-seated and unaddressed on far more serious topics than food and Liberty discrimination snuck out at the Board of Inquiry. From the testimony we know that Worley had shown sensitivity to the issue of unauthorized lights on board ship and other evidence of disloyalty and sabotage, although none of these incidents were directly mentioned in the petition. Yet Worley had— and sometimes at the most unusual moments— brought this subject up in cross-examination.

Unauthorized lights did not just imply "lights out" was being violated. A former officer, Ensign Ryder, came forward and amplified the problems in detail in a letter to ONI and in subsequent personal follow-ups. The report by agent C.J. Gass reveals the amount of suspicious activity that crewmen noted on board the *Cyclops* during her last voyage off France, the voyage for which the 40 men finally signed that petition to get an investigation. Ensign Ryder (who was stationed aboard from November 15, 1917, to January 5, 1918) was the Deck Engineer on board the vessel. "That on her voyage from France to the United States he had been told by certain officers of the vessel that the boat falls were found to have been cut and that their patches indicated that this cutting had been performed by someone on board; that while he was in charge of the Deck Engineering Force, Fireman 2nd class Schneidelberg, a German born naturalized American citizen, was under suspicion by officers of the vessel and was transferred from the Fireroom

Force to the Deck Force where he could be under supervision."

Gass goes on to speak about an equally controversial occurrence on board the vessel: "Ensign Ryder also states that he was informed by officers of the vessel that on the same trip from France, a wire was found which was connected with the Deck circuit and which ran up the aft mast and that at its end, near the top of the mast, was found connected a lamp socket holding a white electric lamp. This line and lamp were not authorized to be in this position and it was suspected that it was the work of somebody on board to be used in serving notice to enemy submarines."[10]

Sabotage and acts of betrayal had clearly been committed on board the vessel before her final voyage. An ONI summary report dated February 19, 1918, on Aid for Information letterhead, 5th Naval District, Norfolk, bears out some of the things Ryder would later report. "Learned from Mr. J.S. Glover, in charge optical shop, Building 64, Norfolk Navy Yard that a telescope #2892-Mark 11-Modification 1, had been turned over to him by armed guard office on January 22 for repair; that the cross line lense [sic] and one eye piece doublet were in a reverse position, that he fixed the same and returned telescope to armed guard office next day. Went to the office of the armed guard, where I interviewed Lieut. Meyers, who stated that the telescope in question had been received from the "ARCADIA," and was returned to the ship immediately upon being repaired . . ." Although Lt. Meyers thought it merely the mistake of a mechanic, "Mr. Glover stated that eight telescopes were taken off the Cyclops in practically the same condition as the one taken from the Arcadia. He stated the effect of the reversed lenses was that the gunner was not able to 'get on' [target]. Stated that it took about twenty minutes to change the lenses."

The Navy investigation into this (while the *Cyclops* was en route to Bahia) proved that the gunner's mate of the *Cyclops*

---

[10] It turned out from later questioning that Ryder identified his source as a "Lt. Maquild"— Lt. Maguet, the chief engineering officer under Dowdy. Maguet's name was actually pronounced 'Mcqwait.'

had turned these lenses over to the yard, stating that "his predecessor had recently overhauled these instruments and reported them in good condition." Thus the sabotage had been recent, sometime *after* the embarrassing Board of Inquiry. Or, even more disturbing, that the claim they were in perfect condition was a complete cover by the gunner's predecessor.

In Worley's letter to his commanders dated while off France in 1917, he makes mention of the fact the ship could not keep up with gunnery. Was it the lenses? If so, why were they not checked? And if they were and they had been found put in wrong, why wasn't it reported? Someone aboard was holding out on Worley or the old seadog wasn't supervising well at all.

Hints of Worley' increasing inability to run the ship well and consistently can be found in other places in the same letter. Worley had written this letter to the Commander Destroyer Force and the Commander U.S. Convoy Operations in the Atlantic. It is dated from St. Nazaire, France, on 1 July 1917. In it he stated some of the deficiencies for why his vessel wasn't keeping in line with the fleet maneuvers:

> This vessel up to the present time has fortunately been permitted to retain her trained winchmen and some of the seamen from the Naval Auxiliary 'SERVICE.' All of the enlisted men were assigned to this ship less than a month prior to her departure on this voyage and a large percentage of them joined the ship at New York just prior to sailing. These young men have just recently been enlisted in the Navy for their first time of service and have no knowledge of working a ship or life on board ship. The engine room force have suffered severely from this condition. The compliment in the engine room is deemed quite sufficient provided they were well trained and experienced in the duties they are required to perform. . .The urgent need for trained signalmen has been greatly felt on board this vessel as she has been required to do a great deal of maneuvering with the fleet and it is deemed absolutely necessary that the ship be provided with at least three trained signalmen if her future duties are to be of the character she is now performing.

The *Cyclops* was clearly not toeing the line with the other ships. Worley's answer in July was that the new regular enlisted Navy men were simply untrained, raw recruits. This was the first voyage, in fact, in which Worley had to deal with a large amount of Navy men as opposed to the Auxiliary men he usually had aboard. Amazingly, he blames them. Since Convoy Operations had no previous complaints about him they accepted his answer. The Navy didn't know that Worley disliked regular Navy men and that he was beginning to blame everybody else for problems aboard the ship.

In light of this, one can understand why this was the infamous voyage on which the 40 men had signed a petition requesting a Board of Inquiry. Navy men were being treated badly, likewise the dozens of raw recruits, and Asper, a regular Navy doctor, may have seen his chance to finally get rid of Worley by subtly sponsoring the petition. In poignant contrast to Worley's letter originating from St. Nazaire, Roy Swoveland had testified that Worley was drunk at St. Nazaire.

A captain who claims there is a plot to get rid of him, especially one who has been drinking to excess, should have been a concern to Whitted and Orenham and not the recipient of a whitewash. Rather Orenham wrote that laudatory recommendation to his superiors at Bureau of Navigation, and the result was that Worley remained, and not only remained but perhaps got more and more secure in his eccentric and high-handed way of running the *Cyclops*.

Unbeknownst to Orenham the *Cyclops* had not been keeping up with the Atlantic fleet properly while on maneuvers off France. Equally, he didn't know that Worley had tactlessly blamed it on the crew and on untrained signalmen. Thus Orenham could emit syrupy praise and keep in position a man whose grip on command and reality was weakening.

Fowler was now sifting leads from ONI agents that suggested the Second Mate on the *Abarenda* had had enough information on Worley's complicity in the "beheading affair" to blackmail him. His desire was to be promoted to First Mate. Worley refused, and the Second Mate turned evidence which is what then got Worley tried for negligence. ONI was now trying to find out who the Second Mate had been, and soon they would discover something surprising.

At present before him, Fowler had the disturbing coincidence that after Worley was tried this time, on August 4 and 6, 1917, that he also considered himself the recipient of "shabby treatment." He didn't leave the Navy, but from the testimony of W.J. Jeffers his loyalty might have been faltering. In response to the Navy dragnet, Jeffers, the seaman who had had such an odd encounter with both Worley and Asper on the voyage to and from Halifax, had written in and then subsequently had been interviewed by ONI. In addition to his odd encounter, Jeffers reported that Worley was bringing civilians unnecessarily aboard ship. On one occasion the excuse was given that he was selling his house.[11]

While Worley may have been baiting Jeffers with the blinking light routine that odd night, there is no doubt that the *Cyclops* was a nest of pro-Germans and perhaps even a link in a chain of 5th columnists.

Evidence for just such activity came to ONI soon after the vessel was declared overdue. On April 29 a long letter was received from a former *Cyclops* seaman, Fireman 2nd Class Walter McDaniel. Although his case has already been referred to in general, the details bear some highlighting. McDaniel wasn't a very literary man, true, but he was clear about the strange things that went on and the extent to which anti-Germans were poorly treated. He was transferred to the ship on August 15, 1917, within a couple of weeks of the Board of Inquiry. He had quickly heard about the Inquiry, but without clear details believed it also involved the charges of "pro-Germanism."

---

[11] "He [Worley] was always bringing outside men aboard while we were under way to Halifax, Nova Scotia, Canada. . . .While in Norfolk, Captain Worley had several civilians aboard. The best I could get he was trying to sell his home." ONI's Lionel A. Stahl, who investigated Jeffers, informed his superiors that Jeffers could identify these civilians again, and if it was worth their while he could be sent to "Norfolk for any length of time with the hope that he might run across one of the civilians referred to. . ."

In the long body of his official affidavit he mentions that "The information gained from the engineer's force was that the captain and some other officer and an enlisted man was pro-German . . . While in Norfolk, Virginia, I purchased a 45 caliber pistol. I was asked by some of my shipmates what I was going to do with the pistol, and I told them that if the Cyclops was ever sunk and I was taken prisoner, that it was for the Germans after I was taken on the submarine. The following named persons were mentioned in the general talk about pro-Germanism: Captain Worley, Ensign Shumnugh, Engineer Force, and Wiesenthal, Fireman first-class."

Elaborating, he continues:

On or about October 1, Keller or Kessler Quarter Master First-class came to me and told me that it was the opinion of some of the officers that I had made a complaint about some of them to the Navy Department and wanted to know if I did write to the Navy Department. I told him no, but would if things did not change. About October 18, 1917 I went on the 10 day furlough and after I returned the doctor called me up and told me that he thought me unfit for the service, and asked if I wanted a discharge. I told him no, and the doctor protested and told me that it would be best for me to take a discharge and go home. I told him I would if he thought it best. He said that my health was bad and that would be best for me.

McDaniel was shocked when he got to the hospital (Naval Hospital, Brooklyn) and found that the doctor had put down a general "complaint of insanity against me, and I was confined in the observation ward." After he had been there for 10 days another man, John Emens from the USS *Olympia*, had been admitted with a similar story. "He said the doctor told them to go to the hospital and keep quiet, and he would come out OK. Emens Said That He Was Mixed up in Some Kind of a Spy Deal with the Godfather's and Godmother's Society. I asked him how he first came in connection with the society, and he said that the Chaplain called him up and gave him the name of C. Albert Schaltz, 34 Prospect Pl., Brooklyn, New York, and told him to write and he failed to write, and the chaplain again called him up and told him that he would have to write; and he did so, but thought that C. Albert Schultz was a German spy."

According to McDaniel, Emens finally wrote and in return he received a letter from Schaltz, asking various questions. "What time does your ship leave? I wish you would hurry and get me that pass so I can come into the Navy Yard. You go and see Lieut. Vanmater and he will explain to you how to get the pass for me, as he is a personal friend of mine."

After McDaniel saw the letter, he thought that it "contained information of value to the Government." He and another seaman, Metzler by name, "sent the letter to the Naval Intelligence Department at Washington D.C. or at least we thought we did. Metzler suggested that we send the letter over the doctor's head; and that is the way it went."

In a day or two we were called before the doctor on the subject. Emens told me that a doctor by the name of Volkes had come to him and tried to gain information from him. Dr. Volkes also came to me privately and tried to gain information from me. About November 20, 1917, two men came to the US Naval Hospital to see me. They claimed to be Naval Intelligence men. I told them what I knew of the Scholts [Schaltz] and John Emens case and also suggested to make a statement concerning German propaganda on the Cyclops, but these men refused to hear my statement, telling me they would see me later— they did not see me. After about a month I called at the Naval Intelligence office at the Navy Yard, Brooklyn, and inquired of this case and they told me that the letter received from C. Albert Cholts [sp] was of no importance as John Emens and Metsler had been sent to the "Red House" at Washington D.C., yet I do not see how they could disqualify C. Albert Schaltz's letter.

After the 10 days, McDaniel was declared sane and got transferred to other duties, but for some time he found himself dogged by men who seemed to want to silence him forever. This convinced him that the information he had given at the hospital had been "hampered and was not allowed to go to the head of the Navy intelligence Department at Washington, DC."

On March [November] 27, 1918, he went on Liberty. It was about 7:30 p.m. At the corner of Washington and Sand Streets, Brooklyn, he met two men "dressed in sailors' clothing." One of them said he had a sister living in New York. Since it was Thanksgiving night, they invited McDaniel. At first he said no; but when they urged him, saying there would be girls there and they would have a good time, he relented. They took the subway from the Brooklyn Bridge station and got off at 14th Street. One of them rushed ahead, but when McDaniel tried to follow the other held him back, saying his friend would soon return. When he did, the man with McDaniel asked his friend "Is he there?" to which the other man said "Yes, let's go, everything is alright." McDaniel was now suspicious and lagged behind. When he got at least 10 feet behind "they said 'Let's get the son-of-a-bitch.'"

. . .The largest one of the two approached me and struck at me with all his might but missed me as I was looking for the blow. I had a jackknife in my pocket and quickly to it and got busy— some unknown civilian came up in a rush in all three men attacked me at once. I fought them off with my knife until the three men fled badly cut, at the time this attack was going on I was shouting for help at the top of my voice and a policeman was not more than 20 steps away and he did not come near me until the three men had fled.

On January 11, 1918, I was transferred to the U. S. S. *Lake View* and my ship went to Coney Island for repairs. After we had been there a short while a coxswain came to me and said that he had met two nice young girls in the back of a saloon on North Richmond Terrace. I went with him and the girls lived in Bayonne, New Jersey, and wanted us to come and see them in Bayonne, New Jersey, telling us that we could have a good time. The saloon man found out about our appointment and advised us not to go as we could fall a victim to a trap. I did not want to go and told the coxswain that the saloon man was right. We questioned the girls if they kept any men around the place as the saloon man had said, and they said no. On the date set for our appointment Chief Water Tender Schodbolt and I and the coxswain went to their place in Bayonne, New Jersey and found it just as the saloon man had said and I recognized one of them as one of the men that I had fought on 14th St. New York City, but we got out OK as I was armed and they seemed to know it.

After our ship had been torn up so that we could not sleep or eat on board we had to move ashore. Chief Water Tender Schodbolt and James E. Oiler went to G.H. Mortens restaurant and engaged a room 1914 RI and he told me when he rented the room to me that it was his room but he would move to another. After I had moved all of my clothing to the room and come to go to bed that night I found the Kaiser's picture on the wall in a large frame on the wall. I did not sleep there but left the picture for investigation and reported it to the Captain and he said that he would go over and investigate the next morning. I went over early and found the picture gone.

On or about January 23, 1918, I went to bed at about 10:30 p.m. and at 11:30 p.m., Chief Water Tender Schodbolt and James E. Oiler returned to retire. They found the door locked and had to force the door open and found me in bed unconscious and could not arouse me. An investigation proved that a round hole had been made so that gas could have been inserted. The Postmaster at Richmond wrote to the Captain of the ship (Lake View) and informed him that G.H. Morten was a German.

Elements of McDaniel's story are obviously questionable, but ONI thought enough of it to request he undergo repeated interviews. He was declared reliable. McDaniel's story, though not from a very literary or educated man, true, nevertheless was from an honest man. It opens a can of worms on the subject of pro-German groups in and around the Navy and their attempts to garner information on shipping movements. In McDaniel's case, he instigated what appeared to be the tentacles of one of these spy groups when he was questioned why he brought a .45 caliber on board. As a fireman aboard the *Cyclops* he was in the nest of the ship's biggest area of trouble—the engineer force which would later be dominated by the dreaded Ensigns Stephen Konstovich and Hugo Schonhof (who must be the Ensign Shumnugh mentioned by McDaniel as one of the pro-Germans aboard).

Within the long body of his affidavit McDaniel mentions the *Cyclops'* notorious doctor. Asper deceptively got McDaniel to acquiesce to a "not well" charge but then connivingly declared McDaniel insane to get him off ship. One must accept that it had to be because of McDaniel's obvious anti-Germanness. In his case it resided deeply in a man so unschooled and rough he would most likely have lived up to his promise to use the pistol if it came down to Germans. Members of the Engineer's Force clearly wanted him *off the ship.*

Although I quote from McDaniel's official statement above, in his letter to Fowler (which instigated his cross-questioning), McDaniel stated a few other relevant things worth repeating as regards petty persecutions of anti-Germans. For instance, when he returned from a 10 day furlough (at 10:30 p.m. on October 18, 1917) that on the next morning at 8 o'clock "I was informed that I was on report for having a dirty bag. I was called before the mast and given 6 days restrictions without having a chance to explain that I had been on a 10 day furlough, yet my bag was not dirty." It was three days after this that Asper called McDaniel up and told him he wasn't well.

Pettiness such as this seemed directed solely against the anti-Germans, and there seems to have been a very definite system of reporting them for punishment. Subsequent investigation by the Office of Naval Intelligence proved beyond a doubt that Stephen Konstovich was born in Brod, Austria, but had taken out naturalization papers sometime after 1910 when the Navy had him listed as a coal passer on the U.S.S *Vestal*. At that time he was qualified as an "unnaturalized Austrian." Hugo Schonhof was born in Berlin, Germany, and was discovered to be pro-German, as were a number of the crew: Keller, Wiesenthal, Schmiedeberg.

In a roundabout way, the Navy discovered more alarming information about those on *Cyclops'* final voyage. Inquiries came into the Navy regarding Lt. Albert George Winkle. He was one of the more curious of the passengers. Nervig had actually taken Winkle's position on the *Glacier,* and Winkle had been transferred north on the *Cyclops.* The inquiries came from two women. "Subject is a bigamist," the Navy discovered. Interviews with Lillian Winkle and Beatrice Winkle proved it. Not only this, he left Lillian and their daughter destitute, having disappeared years before while in the merchant service. Lillian Winkle "whose loyalty is beyond question" said that Winkle claimed his actual name was Voight Rex and that he borrowed the name "Winkle" from an Englishman about 1898 and never used his real name again. He was born in Celle, Germany, in 1878, and later came to America.

Amidst the long testimony from both wives, and that which investigators later independently confirmed, it was clear that Winkle was hardly a likeable fellow. He frequently lied about his age and heritage, one way perhaps that a 37 year old man was able to marry a girl in her teens. In the marriage certificate to Beatrice he stated his father was George F. Winkle and his mother Frieda Dewes. Yet even Beatrice declared: "He told me his correct name was Voight Rex, and that he adopted the name Winkle, which was the name of an Englishman." She said Winkle was born in Hanover, Germany. Bureau of Navigation records "show that Albert George Winkle was born in Lorrain, France, February 18, 1883."

The Navy actually secured an interview with Peter Gadeburg, Captain of the *Glacier.* Gadeburg declared that he "never heard Lieutenant Winkle make any disloyal remarks, but that there was something peculiar about subject's character that caused him to distrust him; further, that subject was very evasive when questioned in regard to the place of his birth and his parentage."

This was a big statement to knock out of Gadeburg. ONI investigators had been warned by other Fleet officers that he was so pro-German it would be hard to get information out of him.

Pro-German sympathies, however, were not indicative of friendship within this tight cluster of Navy officers. But they might have inspired more than one man to omit details. Though distrusting him, Gadeburg may have glossed over any other unsavory details about Winkle's past. Gadeburg certainly offered nothing about Worley, and investigators would later learn that Gadeburg and Worley had quite a past behind them.

Civilian neighbors, such as Ida White Van Wagner and Mr. and Mrs. John J. Phelan, however, gave information that indicated Winkle was very pro-German and, in Mrs. Wagner's case,

had boasted of the German U-boat supremacy and Germany's "unconquerable spirit." Supposedly, according to her, as a captain of a merchant ship Winkle had dined German officers who then afterward sailed off and sank a Russian freighter (before America's entry into the war).

"Records of the Standard Oil company, 26 Broadway, New York City, show that subject was born in Pennsylvania, in 1880, and that he was in their employ between February 24, 1915, and July 12, 1915, when he was discharged because of his unreliability and drunkenness," continued the Navy report. "When he applied for his Masters of ocean steamers on January 19, 1915, (passed) he declared he was born in Germany." Finally, the Navy just had to shake its head over Winkle.

The Navy's investigation of Winkle is not listed here for academic reasons. His investigation revealed two connections with the fate of the *Cyclops*, one subjective, one quite real. Subjectively, Winkle's pro-German and unethical background becomes important because of his connections within the Fleet off South America. Most of the sailors shipping home as passengers aboard were from the *Pittsburgh*, the same ship from which the prisoners had been taken to come back to serve their strict sentences. As we know, the men had been tried and found guilty of beating to death an alleged homosexual crew member, and their compatriots might not have deemed their sentences just. Could they have taken advantage of the circumstances aboard the vessel to instigate a jail break of their buddies? Pro-Germans, like Winkle, might have encouraged it as one means to instigate their own contingent mutiny amidst the confusion.

Now, less on the subjective side is the fact that while investigating Winkle the Navy stumbled upon an interesting and unexpected mystery. There was altogether something quite certain in the air of Beatrice Winkle when she declared her husband was still alive. "I do not believe that the 'Cyclops' was lost at sea nor does my father. We both believe that Mr. Winkle is a prisoner of war. I base this belief largely on the fact that Mrs. Hutchison, 1336 W. 30th Street, Los Angeles, whose son was on the 'Cyclops,' claims to have knowledge that her son is still alive, and upon the statement of Mrs. Lillian Bentley, Long Beach, California."[12]

Although the ONI agent believed that the "wish was the father of the thought," Mrs. Bentley was approached, and her statement proved alarming.

My name is Mrs. Lillian Bentley. I live at 321 Ocean Avenue, Long Beach, California. Sometime in April last I received a letter from my brother, Louis E. Samson who is now and was at that time in the U. S. Transport Service, running from the United States to France or England. In that letter he stated that he had been in Paris that he had met there a man Bernard E. deVoe, who told him that his home was in Long Beach, California and that his parents lived there. Bernard E. deVoe was on board the missing Collier "Cyclops" at the time she was supposed to have disappeared. As my brother has never lived in Long Beach and does not know anyone there he could not have invented the story.

Upon receipt of this letter, knowing that the deVoe's were

---

[12] Beatrice lived in Pasadena, California, Winkle's last address.

mourning for their son, I went to their home in Long Beach and turned the letter over to Mr. deVoe's mother. She refused to believe my brother's story but I left his letter with her and I have not seen her since that time.

Of all those aboard the *Cyclops* it is amazing that one of the prisoner's, Barney Devoe, should be reported in Paris.

With the war still ongoing, Fowler was not in a position to confirm or deny the various independent strands of information. However, the information so far didn't allow one to second guess it more than only a couple of ways, neither good. Mutiny was committed aboard, either a shipboard "jail break" assisted by *Pittsburgh* men to get their buddies out, or a general mutiny by the *Cyclops'* own sailors and the prisoners were naturally released afterward. Either the *Cyclops* sailed off to some port unknown afterward or pro-Germans had seized her and, of course, headed for Europe.

"In this connection it may be of interest to ONI to know that there is attached to the staff of my office[13] one Earl B. Meyers, yeomen 2 C, U.S.N.R.F., who last month received a letter from Lieutenant Logan V. Matthews, 139th Squadron, American Air Service, France, in which the following statement appears:

> Cyclops the ship you mention which you believe lost, is
> safe and was a month ago in the North Sea. This
> information from Myron.

The Myron referred to is Lt. Myron C. Close, 1st Lieutenant in the Aviation Section now in France."

This fit with other rumors. Over the entire summer, ONI had been receiving word that crewmen were in POW camps in Germany. One of the most widely publicized cases was in July when much was made in Texas out of reports that Roy Scroggins, one of the firemen aboard the *Cyclops*, was known to be

---

[13] The author of the report is not stated, but since it comes from the "officer-in-charge" of the San Francisco branch of ONI, I deduce it is Lt. Van Antwerp.

alive and well. This information had supposedly come from his friend on the *New Hampshire*, Robert Cooke. Although the Navy investigation was finally able to dispel this (it had merely come from a single line in a letter Cooke had written to Scroggins' family telling them "not to worry about Roy until worrying time came"), the Navy stumbled onto some disquieting information. James Scroggins, Roy's father, told the operative about Roy's last letter home. He had written from Norfolk January 6, 1918, two days before the ship left for Rio de Janeiro. Roy had first written how the ship was loaded and they were prepared to go. The "first part of it indicated that his son was well satisfied, but in the latter part of the letter [he] wrote he was then ashore and could write what he pleased."

> . . .that on the last trip the captain had almost starved them to death; that the boys came pretty near throwing him overboard; that they were not going to stand much more of it; that they were then ready to sail, but the boat was held on account of some sort of Government investigation.

More than this the father couldn't remember. The letter had been sent to Roy's older brother, James Jr., who was also in the Navy and wanted information on his brother.

What is particularly interesting about this is that Roy Scroggins was not on the vessel during the trip off France. He came aboard after the voyage north to Halifax. If James Scroggins Sr. was not confused in his recollections in his son's letter, then the trip to Halifax was just about as bad as the one to France. Otherwise Roy may have been referring to the atmosphere that lingered on the ship after the voyage off France. Both contingencies aren't good. The other interesting point is that crewmen were afraid of being watched while writing or that their letters, half written, might be read by another, perhaps one of the captain's trolls. Roy must have finished his letter ashore and then mailed it.

The rumor that Roy Scroggins was still alive and in a POW camp made such news headlines that even W.W. Swinyer wrote a letter to James Scroggins Sr. (largely to pitch his book) from

California. Other than that, Scroggins received no real official interest until finally an operative from the 8th Naval District Office of Information (R.S. Manley) took down his information.

Irene Porter, too, had heard that sailors were saying their buddies were alive in Germany. Her son Amos had been a passenger aboard from the *Pittsburgh*. She took it beyond the Navy and wrote to the American Embassy in Paris (August 22, 1918), asking them if it was possible that they could find out if the men were alive so that "some communication could be established" back and forth. "This is my youngest child, and naturally I'm very anxious as to his fate."

Irene Porter's impassioned plea would get nationwide publicity and sympathy. In response many families wrote to her. All of them shared her gut instincts. Mrs. Bosher wrote back: "Just as you say I have never thought the boat was lost nor have I ever felt like it was gone. I think after the war is over we will see our dear ones again." Almost the exact same sentiment was expressed by T.V. Lee's mother, "for it seems so impossible for such a large ship with so many souls on board to disappear absolutely without any trace of any kind." Mrs. Ella Tucker, another mother of a man who shipped aboard from the *Pittsburgh*, wrote too, expressing the hope that the vessel was in a German port.

A particularly moving letter was written to her by Mrs. Jennie Hake, whose anguish over her 23 year old son was carried in each word. He is "the idol of our home, a Christian boy and a favorite of all who knew him." Mrs. Hake had gone to Norfolk to find out what happened. There she picked up some of the worst rumor which she then passed on to Mrs. Porter. Not only was Worley married to a 17 year old woman (not true),[14] the Kaiser personally had come aboard his ship while the *Cyclops* was in German waters before the war. Worley, she had heard, had sold his knowledge and betrayed the ship to Germany. "Everybody in Norfolk told me not to worry, nothing but a plot." Mrs. Hake finished: "My boy left crying because I

---

[14] Probably confused with Winkle. His reputation within pro-German circles was ubiquitous.

broke down when I learned he was bound for South America, but knowing that the same God is there just like he is here I look for better days."

It wasn't just hopeful mothers who expressed this faith. F.B. Weltshire, still assigned aboard the *Pittsburgh*, wrote of his friendship with Amos, adding that "My honest opinion is: that the collier is still afloat but in the hands of the Germans, for it has later been revealed that certain persons (both officers and passengers) were strongly pro-German."

Much of Mrs. Porter's views, and even her pleas for information, had been inspired by a correspondence with W.W. Swinyer, who seems from his journey aboard the *Pittsburgh* the year before to have taken quite an interest in the case. By late May, he had already heard of her zeal to find out what happened. He responded to her on June 7:

> I have no recent knowledge of the Collier. Now mark this one fact namely: that those Collier's [sic] all carry fully 20 boats, scores of tables, chairs, etc. and fully 1000 life preservers on the upper deck. Had that ship suddenly gone down then all these articles, all plainly marked with the ship's name, would still be floating and many of them would have been found long since by many of the countless craft that ply those waters. Our Colliers carry supplies all over the world and, especially into the war zone. What would be easier than for raiders to suddenly shoot away the Collier's wireless, then capture the ship and finally sail her under the US flag right through the Allies patrol ship and then on into a German port. Certainly I believe that such a thing happened and that the good fellows on that ship are now prisoners of war. I will issue the 3rd edition of my book August 1st. If you can send me a picture of Mr. Porter, I will try to insert it with the other CYCLOPS men's pictures in that book.

Swinyer was being a bit careless, albeit sincerely careless, in his theorizing. But the facts that he raise rightfully hit home. On his return trip from Rio he had embarked on the collier *Orion*. Thus he had a firsthand experience with the *Cyclops'* sister ship. Altogether it seemed forgivable for those informed and uninformed to believe the vessel had survived.

Activated by family sentiments, ONI learned much more. Irene Porter had inadvertently set their suspicions in motion. The publicity had highlighted all the letters coming into her and she in turn gave them to the Navy to help inspire them to check overseas. So certain had all the correspondents been that their boys were alive that ONI put them on a list and decided to investigate a little closer to home to see how many might have some kind of inside knowledge.

This brought to light young Will Wolf and his telegram home. It was dated from Bahia, sent from the Palace Hotel, January 23, 1918, when the *Cyclops* had made a short visit there on the voyage south. "Will be down here some time for guard duty. Now will be away until next year. We are going across from Brazil." There was nothing, of course, in the *Cyclops'* itinerary that would keep them from Baltimore and the US for a year, nor anything that said they were going across to Europe from Brazil. No matter where that message circulated in ONI that last line <u>We are going across from Brazil</u> was always underlined. None could figure it out. Had Will Wolf and the crew been told a different destination to divert suspicion when the ship left her course and sailed for Europe? If so, betrayal had long been planned.

Thus mutiny and treason remained intertwined in the first months of the investigation— those two fates "worse than sinking." But whether true or not, needless to say, the Navy now knew the *Cyclops* had been at the heart of pro-Germans, either operating under the nose of their drunken captain or assisted by him.

Drunkenness actually never hit the spreadsheets. It was "betrayal" that now ignited them. By early May the fire had kindled. Sunday May 6 newspaper headlines read "CYCLOPS HUN RAIDER NOW." Rumors were hitting every paper. "CYCLOPS SAILOR WROTE HIS CHIEF WAS PRO-GERMAN" read one headline covering the story of Quartermaster James Ryan's letter home before the vessel vanished. "Despite the fact that the government has not heard a word regarding the missing U.S. naval collier 'Cyclops,' which mysteriously disappeared since she left Barbadoes. . .the wife and family of Quartermaster James Ernest Ryan of West Alexandria believe he will come back to them some day. . .It is being recalled now by relatives that Quartermaster Ryan, just before he sailed on the trip from which he has never returned, wrote a letter to his wife at West Alexandria in which he expressed the belief that the commander of the vessel was pro-German in his sentiment, and the feeling exists among relatives that if this were true, it would have been an easy matter to turn the ship and cargo over to a German raider, if one were operating in South American waters. The crew could have been made prisoners and the vessel itself 'sunk without trace,' a favorite naval maneuver of the German sea raiders." The article ends with the notation that the Ryan family had notified their congressman about James Ryan's suspicions of the Captain.

On this same Sunday morning yet another headline "U.S.S. CYCLOPS IS HUN RAIDER NOW" followed with a juicy subtitle: "Latest Developments Make Mystery of Collier's Disappearance Deeper Than Ever— Secretly fitted Up." This short article, like so many that were appearing across the country, introduced two controversial clues in its updates: one, that a funeral mass was announced in a Rio newspaper for Consul Gottschalk's soul *three weeks* before the *Cyclops* was even officially and *publicly* announced as overdue, and, two, that Worley's actual last name was Wichman. "He was a native of Germany."

The Navy was astounded the Press found out. None in ONI themselves had suspected this until April when secret reports started filtering in to agents . . . And yet there had been signs. In Worley's own written defense at the Board of Inquiry in August 1917 neither Whitted nor Orenham, nor anybody else apparently, had noted that Worley consistently spelled names that should begin with the letter C with the letter K. This could mean two things. He didn't even bother with looking at the names of his own officers and (2) it could also indicate a man whose first language was not English but a language, such as German, which has no letter C.[15]

Subsequent Navy investigation proved that George W. Worley was really born Johann Frederick Wichman in Sandstadt, Hanover Province, Germany, in December 1862. At the age of 15 young Fred jumped a German ship at New York and finally made it to San Francisco where older brothers were already living. Agent Robert Burrous of the San Francisco branch of ONI was sent to investigate.

It is indeed time to look into the past of the Navy's crude old seadog, George W. Worley, to see what the Navy found out and didn't want anybody to know.

---

[15] This is particularly evident with J.J. Cain, whose name is spelled variously as Kane and Kain.

George W. Worley

12

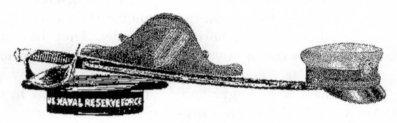

"DAMNED DUTCHMAN"

"Captain Worley was a good sailorman but was practically always under the influence of liquor; his demands upon his crew and officers of his ship were unreasonable and harsh."

—H.R. Treador

"OH, YOU MEAN FRED WICHMAN" was a natural response. Wherever agent Robert Burrous went in San Francisco, Worley's hometown, he repeatedly encountered just such a response from people whenever he asked about George Worley's past.

"Johann Frederick Wichman war in Deutschland geborn" is as explicit as it could be.

Agent Burrous became quite expert at raising a weak smile, acting as if it was a given the Navy had already known that. When it came time to file his report with his ONI liaison, Lt. Van Antwerp, it was another matter. Alarm was irremovably mixed with surprise. There were also rumors of murder and embezzlement, fraud and opium smuggling.

"Pro-Germanism" was so strong in Worley's family that the rumor had been picked up as far away as Washington D.C. Fowler had sent a coded cablegram to San Francisco's Van Antwerp. "Reported that Mrs. A.M. Angerman sister of captain Worley of Cyclops lives in San Francisco. Discretely investigate with view of obtaining any information regarding enemy sentiments or affiliations of family."

Burrous quickly visited the family. Van Antwerp cabled back to Fowler on the 17th of April. "Capt. Wichman of the USS Cyclops, who changed his name to Worley, is the brother of Mrs. Angemann. His brother Herman and his sister-in-law [Minnie Wichman] also live here. As a result of discreet investigation, it has been found that the whole family, including the Cyclops commander, was born in Germany. They have not seen Capt. Worley for eight years but correspond with Worley's wife at Norfolk, Va. They have many relatives in Germany and are pro-German. Mrs. Angemann's son is a lieutenant in the U.S. Army Medical Reserve Corps and is now stationed at St. Joseph's hospital, this city. The family has no social connections and is not very intelligent."

Burrous added that Worley had lived in San Francisco for years under the name of Fred Wichman. "He is said to be able to speak the English language perfectly, and his native language, the German, he knows very well but he has never been known to use it."

Agent Burrous set out to find as many details as possible. From various sources he was able to assemble a sketchy summary for the Navy of Worley's early career at sea. In 1877, at the age of 15 he jumped ship (from being cabin boy) in New York and made it to his brothers already in San Francisco. There he seems to have done odd jobs for them, one of whom co-founded Wichman, Lutgen & Co. Importers and Distillers Agents. Fred Staude, the current president of the company, clarified that the name came from Herman Wichman, who didn't last long in the business, and while Fred worked there the company was always missing items. When he quit, the embezzlement and petty thefts stopped.

From an early age Fred Wichman had developed a fondness for liquor. He went into the saloon business at Clay and Polk Streets, which failed. It was here where Jeremiah Bourk saw Worley manipulate cards, fail, and then take night school navigation. In 1893 or 4 he sold out and went into the grocery business at Broderick and Oak Streets. The whole idea of the sea must have enchanted "Fred." He sold out here too and then went out to the Beach (Barbary Coast) and opened a road-house/saloon. This was called, of all things, "Captain Wich-man's Roadhouse," though it didn't seem he had had more time at sea than a brief stint as a cabin boy and was presently only a night school navigator.

Sea trade rather would be destined to augment Fred Wich-man's income. He didn't excel in business at all, and by 1897 he finally made the firsthand leap back to sea. This began with being the navigating officer on the yacht *Detolna*, a luxury sailing yacht owned by the Austrian Count Rudolf Festetics de Tolna, the son-in-law of the wealthy Haggins family of San Francisco. There had been, however, some problem on the voyage that Burrous couldn't uncover, but whatever happened Worley was ejected from the vessel at Hawaii and didn't com-plete the full cruise.

However, with time the Navy was able to piece together what happened. William Broderson, Vice President of Wich-man, Lutgen & Co., cautiously emerged from the shadows to give his testimony. He made it plain that Worley's background should be thoroughly investigated. "While engaged on the yacht De Tolna he [Worley] told Mr. Broderson that the cargo of the yacht was worth more than the yacht itself, intimating that Count Festetics was engaged in smuggling opium. Mr. Broderson describes the subject as a man with little principle and unworthy of trust."

The incident continued to be pieced together by the most remarkable luck. From New York, J.C. Latham of the Navy Communication Service, sent to ONI this, the gist of which fol-lows: a Mrs. Strobel spent the afternoon with a Mrs. Schoepler in order to meet a Mrs. Peppercorn of Salt Lake City, Utah, vis-iting New York. Well, over tea it comes out that Mrs. Pepper-corn's brother is a Lieutenant Commander in the Navy named Whirley (phonetically), commander of the *Cyclops*. What a co-incidence, for Mrs. Strobel's maiden name was Whirley too! The much more catty conversation of these dames was interrupted now by Mrs. Strobel inquiring of Mrs. Peppercorn if they were somehow related. This prompted Mrs. Peppercorn to explain that Whirley was not her brother's birth name and that he had changed it to Whirley. Mrs. Strobel, the informant, could not remember what the name was, "but knows that it was German as it was remarked upon at the time."

This "by-chance" encounter in New York between a Mrs. Peppercorn and a Mrs. Strobel yielded a valuable lead— Augustus lieb. It was a needle in a haystack encounter, but Mrs. Peppercorn was indeed George Worley's sister. The Navy traced the couple to Salt Lake City and finally spoke to them. It turns out the Peppercorns came from San Francisco, and her husband had a brother still living there on Polk Street named Auguste who had sailed with "Fred" on a yacht years ago.

Auguste Peppercorn was interviewed and in the summary written by agent T.B. Williams it came out that Auguste Peppercorn "served as mate with the subject on the yacht De Tolna." He continues: "Peppercorn states that while he was boatswain on the yacht he believed Count Festetics was engaged in crooked business of which subject had knowledge. Peppercorn accompanied subject back to this city from Honolulu on the ship S.N. Castle, subject telling him on the voyage that the opium carried by De Tolna was abandoned, stating 'that damn fool dumped all of the stuff overboard.' Peppercorn described subject as a very poor navigator when he knew him and he never knew the subject to have taken out more than a Mates' license."

If Count de Tolna was going on a world cruise it would seem unlikely that *he* was smuggling opium . . . but from Worley's condemnation of de Tolna as a "fool" for putting it over the side, perhaps *Worley* was the smuggler. When it was discovered, de Tolna threw it overboard and sacked Worley and told him to take his in-law with him. Worley may only have led Peppercorn to believe that de Tolna was smuggling when in reality it was our rough and ready Barbary Coast roadhouse owner, "Captain Wichman."

Worley was later mate on the schooner *Aloha*, which he was

commissioned to help sail to its owners in the Philippines. This was significant. Burrous' report read: "Worley went to the Philippines on the *Aloha* as Fred Wichman and came back as G. W. Worley." The year was 1898.

Within that factual statement there exists so much. A gap of several months exists here in Worley's life. And this gap interestingly ends when his name is subsequently found on the Navy Auxiliary lists as Ensign George Worley in 1899. At this time he was an officer of the Transport ship *St. Mark* which, though a civilian vessel, had been drafted by the Navy in the Philippines during the Spanish-American War and deployed to service the fleet for the duration.

The significance of this gap, of course, lies in the unaccountability of Wichman/Worley's whereabouts for those several months after he left the *Aloha* and was found sailing the *St. Mark*, and the fact that within that time he saw fit to change his name.

It is actually a fascinating but involved story how ONI and FBI tracked down all their leads, but it is best perhaps to cut from the chase to the results. Two lieutenant commanders in the Navy had served with Worley before, Commanders Burkhart and McKay. Agent H.C. Shull talked with both aboard the *Culgoa*, which Frank Burkhart commanded, while it was berthed in New York. McKay was shipmates with Worley between May 1st 1905 and June 1st 1906 aboard the U.S.S. *Leonidas.* "It was understood aboard ship at the time that subject had shot a man on the yard of a sailing ship and had served time in Australia, that subject ran away from Australia and escaped in a grain ship." McKay continues "that it was an undisputed fact that the subject had changed his name from some German name but that subject had always claimed to be born, not in Germany, but in California . . ."

Worley excelled in brutality toward his crews. Lt. Commander Burkhart elaborated, touching now on that shrouded and bizarre bit in Worley's history— the beheading of his First Mate. His affidavit is dated April 25, 1918. According to Burkhart, Worley "while in command of the S.S. Averenda, [sic] through his influence, secured the services of a man named Witchell, making the statement that he was going to run his ship 'deep water style' and needed a 'bucko' mate." Well, it turned out Witchell was a real bastard of the sea. "This man, Witchell, made a practice of beating the crew on every occasion and finally attempted to beat the carpenter by the name of Dixon, a Scotsman, who killed him with an axe."

Dixon— carpenter— Scotsman— a dead Witchell. End of story . . . or so it seemed. Dixon was tried in Puerto Rico for killing Witchell (actually Witchardt) and was acquitted of the crime as it was regarded as an act a self-defense. According to Burkhart, "George Worley then fled the country and for a time was hiding in Canada, afterwards returning to the United States and being reinstated in the Naval Auxiliary Service."

It's not hard to explain that gap in Worley's career in 1908—Worley was indignant at any oversight— but it is hard to explain why he came back so quickly. It is possible that his paperwork was not in order and he could not get a position in the Merchant Marine. There is no proof he had a Master's license or even of his citizenship. Perhaps he realized he would be less safe in the Merchant Marine, without the authority of the Auxiliary Service behind him.

. . . Then there is the possibility of blackmail. Lieutenant Commander McKay mentioned a number of people who could verify parts of Worley's past. Among them Peter "Gadberg" or "Gladburg" (Gadeburg), captain of the *Glacier*, is raised in an interesting context. He, in fact, was the Second Mate! "In San Juan when Witchard was killed Captain Gladburg was Second officer and he told Captain Worley that he would testify in his behalf if Worley would make him Chief Officer. Upon arriving in Norfolk he was not made Chief Officer so he turned States evidence."

Shull advises Fowler: "Gadberg is a naturalized citizen but born in Germany. It would take, according to Lt. Commander McKay, some very persistent cross-questioning to get Gadberg to divulge any information as Gadberg himself is very pro-German and would not hesitate to protect subject if possible."

The reasons, however, are not friendship. Perhaps not even the fact both were Germans. It is more than likely Worley knew things about Gadberg's past that were equally incriminating. As one would imagine, Gadeburg or "Gladburg" had a very colorful past himself. He "was born in Schleswig-Holstein, and when the U.S.S. *Jason* went across as a Christmas gift ship he was afraid to go ashore in Europe for fear that he would be taken back to Schleswig to serve his time. This man was always anti-American."

The testimony of H.R. Treador of the Weaver Coal Company in New York sheds light on this angle. Treador had served in the Auxiliary and "although never a shipmate of the subject he knew him personally and by reputation." When Treador received orders to ship aboard the *Mars* in 1908 he discovered upon boarding that Worley was the captain. Treador knew Worley too well. "He refused to serve under him because of demands, character and undesirability as a skipper." Furthermore, "he states that subject was a good sailorman but was practically always under the influence of liquor; that his demands upon his crew and officers of his ship were unreasonable and harsh." In regards to the *Abarenda* incident, Treador stated that he was aboard the *Brutus* at that time in San Juan when the incident happened and that he had been a friend of Wichardt's.[16] Treador insisted that Dixon killed Wichardt by mistake. The "man he was really laying for was Worley."[17]

Treador recalled that Worley's birthplace in Germany was the same as Witchardt's. This would seem to add believable authority to McKay's assertion that Witchardt and Worley were brothers-in-law or somehow related. Again, if so, then Worley was brutal and cold enough to sacrifice a relative to save himself. An unusual man was George Worley.

If Fowler's eyes were not spinning yet over the two officers'

[16] Wichardt or Witchardt, not Witchell is the correct name.
[17] McKay says rumors were circulating that Worley was also the "brother-in-law of Witchard, the chief Officer of the Aberanda, who was killed while the vessel was at San Juan."

reports regarding George Worley's past life in the Auxiliary, Burkhart's affidavit would soon set them in motion. Fowler was already sifting through reports of Worley's background with smuggling and embezzlement. Now we hear the "paymaster" story. It turns out that Worley was "very friendly" with a young paymaster in Boston, "going out with him nightly." It wouldn't be long until the paymaster was "short in his funds and put under arrest." No one knows what happened to the money, but it was peculiar that a ship's paymaster would suddenly be short of funds.

George Worley's Chief Officer at the time was a man named Finkey. He had achieved command rank through Worley's recommendations. Yet he was later thrown out of the Service "for using government funds." There's more. Finkey was "arrested shortly after the beginning of the war" [i.e. America's entry in 1917], having boasted of coaling the *Karlshrue*, the famous German surface raider of 1914 that preyed on allied shipping off South America. His arrest took place in New Orleans. He was lost along with Jeremiah Meriethew, formerly of the Naval Auxiliary Service, on board the *C.W. Morse*. "He also claimed to be a lieutenant in the German Navy."

One almost has to stop to either shake their head or giggle at the coterie of roughnecks the Navy had in the Auxiliary. Yet it continues. "On one occasion while in Boston Navy Yard, lieutenant George Worley, while under the influence of liquor, came on board the Naval Auxiliary *Hannibal* and threatened to thrash Captain R. G. Easton, who at the time was not on board. He then used threatening language to James R. Driggs, Chief Officer, threatening to 'clean up' the ship with him. Mr. Driggs resented this insult, whereupon Worley immediately quieted down. In order to get him off the ship," continued Burkhart, "I accompanied him to a theatre and he slept through the whole play. Upon leaving the theatre he met the young Paymaster that afterwards was locked up and also spoke to two cab drivers to whom he was well known, and suggested a trip around town. I returned to the ship and did not accompany him."

Burkhart's statement ends with a loaded single sentence paragraph: "Commander Worley was especially outspoken against any young American who was following the sea." Somehow young Ensign J.J. Cain comes to our mind and Burt Asper who spared him.[18]

Had the agent who took the statement, H.C. Shull, known about the recent shortness of funds aboard the *Cyclops* at Barbados, he perhaps would have recommended reexamining the Board of Inquiry proceedings of last August 1917. Within it there is the testimony of Messman T.A. Lawrence, who stated that there never were enough rations aboard the vessel. An ongoing problem like this indicates that rations or funds were going out the backdoor of Worley's command. Roy Scroggins said as much, too, when he wrote his father and said the captain was basically starving them.

Burkhart's affidavy also underscores Worley's drinking problems and opens the subject of Pro-Germanness. "On the day I joined the ship [Culgoa]," he began, "lieutenant Samuel Dowdy of the Naval auxiliary joined the ship as Engineer Officer, and came to me and made a statement as to the reasons for leaving the Cyclops, showing me a letter stating, as near as I can remember, that he refused to sail on a ship where a commanding officer was continually under the influence of liquor while at sea.

"In the course of our conversation regarding this vessel and commanding officer, who I had formerly known, he made a number of statements as to the wishes of Commander Worley that Germany would win the war, being especially bitter against the English. Commander Worley was to be investigated, which I understand was recently done, after which he was very bitter in regards his so-called ill treatment by the government."

Here we have our only independent glimpse at the fact that Sam Dowdy did write a letter to the Naval Auxiliaries. Though

---

[18] In this affidavit McKay declared the same thing outright, that Worley "never had much use for American boys aboard the ship."

it had not been introduced at the Board of Inquiry, Worley admitted he knew of the letter, for he makes mention of it along with Lt. Hamilton's letter in his defense, declaring these letters began the "Round Robin," though of which plot we're unsure since he also blamed Burt Asper as the center of a plot.

Like many seamen, McKay would testify that Worley "was a good sailorman, but he was always under the influence of liquor." While shipping with him McKay noticed he "imbibed freely a very strong mixture of alcohol and milk which he called 'Deep Sea Punch.'"

McKay then gave the Navy something even more invaluable than a character synopsis— *names*. Amongst these there were two ladies who "ran houses in Norfolk, Va., which were great hangouts for subject when ashore." H.O. Peterson would know a lot, said McKay. He had been Worley's pay clerk on several voyages and was now Chief Pay Clerk on the *Sterling*.

It was not surprising that agent Shull found H.O. Peterson to be praiseworthy of Worley and could think of no charge against him (except he admitted to heavy drinking). By this time, however, Shull knew about what happened to Worley's previous paymaster, and he might have suspected that Peterson could also have been involved in dubious financial dealings with Worley. Shull concludes his report in a cautionary way: "Mr. Peterson was by far the most enthusiastic informant called upon in reference to the subject. He does, however, have the failing of not reporting a great many things and is apt to enlarge upon the evidence at hand."

All Navy men involved expressed the desire that their names should be kept out of the investigation. Not only does this reveal the extent of pro-Germanness in the Navy, the fact such a request could freely be made to ONI revealed what can only be called a mutual understanding of the problem. In a more subtle way, it reveals the extent to which Worley himself was deeply involved in the pro-German element.

Office of Naval Intelligence would learn just how involved. Fred Staude, the current president of Wichman & Lutgen, had been a close friend of Worley's. He gave testimony to ONI on

June 21. He had just rendered valuable service to them in another area, and ONI considered Staude to be very trustworthy. Staude's testimony confirms things of which we are already aware, such as "Fred" disappearing after sailing the *Aloha* and then a year later appearing on the *St. Mark* as George Worley. But what is significant about Staude's relation with him is that after they met again by chance on the *St. Mark* (Staude came aboard at Mare Island, San Francisco Bay, on business) they stayed in touch. To support George Worley's good and loyal character, Staude showed ONI agent S.B. Winram the letters as proof. Staude's motive makes this ironic because there was one letter in Staude's archives of which he had perhaps forgotten the contents. After Winram examined them all, he made mention of this one to HQ: "Wichmann was in Germany in 1913 or 1914, at which time he wrote a very lengthy letter to Mr. Staude describing the details of his trip and, in turn, praising the Germans and Germany."

Since this letter has now been introduced, it is perhaps best to follow it with the affidavit presented to the Navy by Yeoman Roberts. By early May, Paul Roberts had sent a letter to the Chief of U.S. Secret Service. "I believe I am able to furnish information of timely importance on the enclosed case," it read. "At one time I was a member of the ship's company (Cyclops)." The letter originated from Fort Macarthur in Waco, Texas, where Roberts was now a corporal in the Army. The subsequent follow-up investigation was late in starting, but by the end of July agent C.J. Gass personally visited Roberts, who was now a sergeant major at Camp Merritt in New Jersey.

Roberts' affidavit is very significant because it presents a picture of Worley shortly after he returned from his homeland of Germany in 1914, the time just after the letter Worley wrote to Staude. Roberts was aboard in early 1915 and he testified to the extent that pro-Germanness aboard the vessel operated under the aegis of its crass skipper. His affidavit reads in part:

> I used to make up a daily news sheet of wireless reports from the Associated Press, which I daily received from the wireless operator. I

used to render these to the Captain daily in his cabin. At this time the press proclaimed victory after victory for Germany. On every mention which looked bright for the German cause, Captain Worley would become very hilarious and offending. He would oftentimes talk in hopes that the allies would lose.

At this time there were several German liners interned in the Norfolk Navy Yard. Captain Worley made frequent visits to the commanding officers of the ships, and was in daily communication with them. I used to write up all of his private correspondence. Another funny part of it was that he used to have his own Chief Clerk. Despite that fact, he wished that I should write up these letters for him, which were addressed in very endearing terms to the commanding officers of the German naval vessels interned at the Yard. Some of these letters were invitations for parties that were given at the Captain's home in Norfolk. These German officers were entertained many times during this period by him and his wife at their home in Norfolk. His wife lives in an exclusive residential section of Norfolk, the name of which I cannot recall. She often made visits to our ship, and was as decidedly German in her attitude as the captain.

On many occasions during our stays in Norfolk, various German officers, in their full uniform, from interned ships, would come on board and the Captain would accompany them in an inspection of every part of our vessel, from top to bottom.

Many times while in Guantánamo Bay, Cuba, Captain Worley visited the officers of several German liners which were lying at anchor in that harbor. On one occasion about seven civilians from Havana boarded our vessel, in company with the Captain, all of whom talked with decided German accents, were of German appearance, and were undoubtedly Germans of some high position. While at the Newport Navy Yard, he was often in conference with certain German-speaking men in civilian dress who would come on board our vessel, and this greatly aroused my suspicions. The civilians would bring Limburger cheese and beer on board, and they would have a lengthy conference and party in the Captain's cabin.

There was an old ship's carpenter on board of our vessel whose name I cannot recall, and an oiler by the name of Otto Fink,[19] both of whom were often seen in secret conference with the Captain on board the vessel; but when anybody ever approached them their conversation would always cease, and the oiler in the ship's carpenter would leave the Captain. Fink is an admitted former German Army reservist, and the ship's carpenter admitted that he had served his time in the German Navy. This oiler and carpenter also highly rejoiced over German victories. My shipmates and I had to take as much abuse from these two as we did from the Captain, and anything that they said we had to obey immediately or they would report to the Captain and we would be punished.

Captain Worley was an awful crank, and he would frequently drive members of the crew around the ship at the point of a gun.[20] It was a disgraceful sight for a commanding officer to act in this manner. Another peculiarity of the Captain was that when it was his turn to stand watch on the bridge he would take the wheel with an ignorant Greek seaman, and would not allow anybody else on the bridge during his stay on watch. The Chief Officer of the "Cyclops," whose name I cannot recall, was of Russian descent, and was another tool of the Captain's. In my opinion he was a big boob and a dummy.

During April 1915 the Captain discharged the wireless operator of our ship, who was a former United States Navy man and a fine worker, for a trivial argument he had with one of the members of the crew. We were for three or four months with only one wireless operator, and at times we were underway with no one on watch at the wireless.[21]

In my opinion, this vessel was never sunk, but is today lying in some harbor or bay inside the German lines. Captain Worley was noted to be very particular about the workings of his ship, and if anything happened to his engines he would always make for the nearest port and would not proceed until repairs had been made.

---

[19] Probably the loyal paymaster Finkey, but they may be different people. In a May 20, 1918, letter detailing the same general information to ONI, Roberts thought the name was Schmidt.

[20] Another witness to "punishment day."

[21] Illegal after 1912 and the *Titanic*'s sinking.

Roberts' affidavit confirms that two years before the 'Round Robin' would bring the embarrassing Board of Inquiry the same abuses had been of longstanding— that Worley chased men and Warrant officers around the vessel, and it also gives some support for the details of "punishment day" that Richard Winer would later mention after his interviews with Conrad Nervig. We also see Worley's infernal dislike for regular Navy men, which apparently was the deciding factor about why he fired his radioman. By this time ONI had much of this information from other sources. Altogether this bolstered their view that Roberts' testimony was completely independent and reliable. He underwent an intense cross-examination, and ONI accepted his account.

I have not been able to determine if "Worley's wife" referred to by Roberts was Selma Worley or one of the "women who kept a house in Norfolk" that Worley frequently attended. The Worleys did not live in an exclusive area of town, though Colonial Place was a very nice and new community. They lived on Pennsylvania Avenue (the house still exists). According to records it was built in 1918, which must be wrong, but it was obviously very new. It is 2,400 square feet with 9 rooms, including 4 bedrooms and 2 full baths, two floors and an attic. It's a traditional American upper middleclass neighborhood of the time. But for Roberts this might have looked quite exclusive.

Some of the reasons for Worley's many visits to German ships and vice versa can be gleaned from agent W. Bushman. He had been assigned to investigate Worley's doings at Norfolk. On April 22 he had dashed off a letter to Fowler, reading in part: "Further investigation of the above subject is bringing to light undeniable evidence showing that the subject was extremely pro-German, that he acted more or less as a sponsor for the Masters of interned German ships prior to the entrance of the United States in the war." Bushman suggested that Fowler check with the brass in Washington to see if *Cyclops* carried any important papers on board for the Fleet, "as it would seem that this might have considerable bearing on the case."

Even though Bushman's fear that treason had occurred could not be proven during the war, there can really be no question anymore about George Worley's pro-German background. Again, pro-German was common within the US Navy, but Worley was different. He put it into action during the days of neutrality. He was also a rogue skipper who didn't take to discipline . . . and he was capable of murder.

It seems logical to assume he changed his name in consequence of the first of the two deaths associated with his sailing career. Yet not being able to escape his reputation as Fred Wichman he often employed various excuses for why he changed it to Worley. He told Fred Staude somewhat confidentially on the *St. Mark* that Worley was "the name of his real father, his mother having remarried." He told others that it was the name of a seaman who had befriended him in his youth. All well and good, but none of them true. He hadn't been befriended in his youth. He had been a cabin boy for one trip over to New York where he jumped ship. He hadn't gone back to sea until manipulating cards at his saloon didn't get him anywhere. Then he studied navigation, and that's about it. One doesn't just pull a name like 'George Worley' out of a hat. Treador was of the opinion (whether from Witchardt or not it is not clarified) that Worley stole his naturalization papers from a "drunken or dead sailor" and "by means of these papers was able to obtain his license; in truth he had never been a naturalized citizen of the United States."

As it stands, this is probably the case. Only two things subtly repeat in *all* witnesses' recollections, both pro and con Worley— the voyage of the *Detolna* and whether they knew the name *Aloha* or not the voyage of some yacht to the Philippines. That's it. This is not a very stellar career at sea. With those credentials and experience it seems well nigh impossible Worley could have suddenly become First Mate on the *St. Mark*, his next ship and the first where he is now suddenly George Worley.

To back up his statements, Treador gave names that could verify what went on in Worley's past . . . but we need not delve more into it. Both murders are shadowed in rumor and hearsay, mixed with confused and circumstantial evidence. But the timing of Worley's name change and the *Aloha* murder is too coincidental, and there can be no doubt about Witchardt's death by an axe, and that the Scotsman, Dixon, literally cut off his head. Suffice it to say that "damned" went very well hand-in-hand with "Dutchman" when it came to George Worley's character.

Was Worley capable of turning traitor? Was he that brutal? Was he that proud that the indignity of a Board of Inquiry would cause him to become proactive during the war in his Pro-German views?

The history of George Worley was a convoluted mystery at this point. Some of the witnesses, if not most, were very good. Though details and recollection of names sometimes varied, and some scenarios came from different perspectives and angles, a few things were undeniable. These were: Worley was German, pro-German, coarse, brutal, and most definitely given to drunkenness. A few things were not certain but likely. It was not certain whether he was actually even a U.S. citizen. At least one death was verified in his career, that of Witchardt. But the one for which he must have changed his name is still obscure. "He shot a man on the yard on a sailing yacht." This must have been the *Aloha* . . . and in attempting to defend him his friends would unwittingly give us more clues into the past of the murderous old seadog.

13

ALL HELL
AND
LIMBURGER TOO!

"It is a wicked old world nevertheless and only in trouble are friends actually tested."

—Selma W. Worley

BY JUNE 1918 THERE WAS no newspaper wherein it was not stated that the Captain of the *Cyclops* had been pro-German and was born in Germany. All said and done "Fred Worley" was now number 1 traitor in the nation. In the outcry of accusations the defense of the old seadog proved but a burp in a whirlwind. But a defense there was; and it would be wrong and an injustice to inquiry if some of that defense is not presented here. And yet it too would be an oversight not to mention a great irony, that is, that as well-intentioned as it was meant to be, what some family members and friends said actually and unwittingly reveal even more disturbing facts about our seadog's character.

The public defense began when a piece came out in the *Literary Digest* containing the scathing rebuttal of Selma Worley against Captain Worley's detractors. "Do you think my husband would prove a traitor to America, to his wife and little daughter? My husband was an American through and through. He hated Germany. He came here seeking freedom and he would fight and die to maintain that freedom. He is just as good an American as any man born in America, and a whole lot better than many of those who question his patriotism now. I hope he lives to settle with his traducers."

It was an emotional and passionate defense, but it was not a persuasive one since the *Digest* also brought up some of George Worley's last actions before his final voyage, all of which appeared suspicious and were indeed offered as suspicious by the paper. "Before Captain Worley sailed on his last voyage on the Cyclops he disposed of some property he owned in Norfolk, Va., including the home his wife and child live in. He told friends that when he returned from the voyage he intended to get an extended leave of absence and go back to California and rest. He said he had to have an operation performed and it would take about six months for him to recover his strength."

Frankly, such a medical claim is suspicious, for it does not require one sell their home on such short notice yet go on a long voyage. Not only did Selma not touch on surgery in any of her defense, she committed the blooper of declaring how her husband refused to call a doctor for their sick daughter, Ginny, even when fearing it might be scarlet fever. She offered it in the vein of deep patriotism to America, but it struck others as a callous and suspicious act on her husband's part.

Robert Burrous' words seem to ring true that the entire Wichman/Worley family was not very intelligent. From our vantage point today, Selma's excuse just confirms that Worley did everything he could to make this voyage to Rio.

Worley's nephew Lt. Dr. Ewald Angermann would enter the scene next. His claims unintentionally provoked a closer examination by the Navy. Newspaper articles carried quotes in which Angermann presented himself as the one family member who would know all about his uncle's affairs. Such a claim naturally induced the Navy to actively pursue interviewing him in private.

A few days after these news articles hit, ONI's Robert Burrous was there to take down Angermann's evidence officially. Agent Reed declared Angermann to be "the closest in touch with the affairs of George Worley due to the fact that Angermann was in charge of Worley's legal documents since the Spanish-American War when Worley was away." Despite this phenomenal claim, Angermann's statements are either concocted by himself to save his family's reputation, protect his own position in the Army or, quite possibly, reflect only what his uncle told him.

The *Digest* mentioned that Worley was to undergo an operation. This operation is completely unknown by Angermann. Rather, it seems to be as cleverly woven an excuse as Worley's excuse to explain that gap in his life when he changed his name, which we now hear from Angermann. "According to Dr. Angermann it was when subject was an officer on the U.S.S. Transport St. Mark, during the Spanish-American War, when he was taken to the Second Base hospital, P.I., suffering from beri-beri,[22] that he (Dr. Angermann) received a letter in which subject told of changing his name from John Frederick Wichmann to George Wichmann Worley, explaining that he was sick of being called 'Dutchman' and that he took the name of George Worley because it was that of an old sea captain who had befriended him in early days. According to Dr. Angermann, subject referred to the German colony in San Francisco, Calif. as 'tight nosed Dutchmen' and resented any remark made to him about being a 'Dutchman'— declaring that he was an American citizen and sorry that he was born in Germany. In one letter to Dr. Angermann, subject made the statement that he had plenty of guns aboard the Cyclops and 'if we sight a U-boat, we will make all Hell smell like Limburger.' In other letters, after the United States entered the war, subject expressed the hope that all his nephews would join the American forces to beat the Kaiser."

This is, of course, offered here in defense of the old seadog. But there are several reasons why we should be wary of An-

---

[22] Worley mentioned beri-beri in his Board of Inquiry defense (See Chapter 3)

germann's family defense. For one, Angermann claims "that the letters from which the above quotations were taken were destroyed by him when he was leaving Queen's Hospital, Honolulu, about 7 months ago, to come to San Francisco." Thus not only is there an absence of substantiation, there are facts which contradict Angermann's claims . . . and the Navy was well aware of them.

First and foremost is the fact that the Navy never knew that "Uncle Fred" had changed his name, something they most definitely would have known had he already been a drafted officer on a U.S. Auxiliary Service transport ship when he changed it. Worley's Auxiliary career officially began on May 20, 1900, on the USS *Nero*. When the civilian *St. Mark* was "drafted" in 1898 Worley was only temporarily a US Navy Auxiliary Officer. But they still would have looked at his ship's papers and his i.d. Therefore he had changed his name sometime before he became Mate on the *St. Mark*.

The real time period has already been established by several witnesses. Worley's change of name occurred in that blank period in his life between sailing the *Aloha* in 1898 and his subsequent appearance in the Auxiliary as George Worley.

There was no onus in being German in 1898. From Staude's later letters and the testimony of several seamen we also know Worley never hid a German background.

Ironically, it is this last point (and not Angermann's misguided claims) that can be used as a better defense of the old seadog, at least as a better defense against treason. No contemporary in the Navy or amongst his friends was ignorant of George Worley's German background. Down to a man all knew his original name had been German and it started with a W. H.O. Petersen, though very praiseworthy of Worley, had frankly declared he knew Worley was born in Germany "and that his name was originally 'Wieschman;' that subject had always signed his name as 'George W. Worley' and made no pretense of the fact that the initial 'W' stood for 'Wieschman,' his original name." I have indeed confirmed this in Worley's own records at the Military Personnel Archive in St. Louis— George

Wichman Worley.

It is wiser to assume that in changing his name the old sea-dog was hiding misdeeds in his past and not hiding a German background. His bragging of being German even became pronounced after his visit to Germany in 1913-14 when he developed an admiration for his homeland. The correspondence with Dr. Angermann is probably purely fictitious or the vehicle Worley used to explain his actions to his family in 1899.

The above is not a digression from the purpose of this chapter which is, of course, to present a consistent defense for Captain Worley. Defense is against the accusation, however. The public accusation against Worley was treason, and the probability of that is what is being examined here. Past murders and the brutality with which he commanded his ship were not something found in the newspapers, and cannot and should no longer be doubted. The problem is that family and friends put up such a lousy defense it is hard to defend the seadog consistently. And it seems this was because Worley's excuses had varied from person to person in order to cover past misdeeds.

Moreover, none of those who defended Worley had any clue as to how much ONI and FBI crept about asking questions. Thus they were little aware of how informed the agents interrogating them really were. This is especially true in Norfolk. What agents received in reply here tells us much. It is from Norfolk alone where the stories of George Worley being sick or needing surgery began. Nowhere else. This is not surprising. This was a Navy town. Here and nowhere else acceptable excuses had to be given for selling the house and quitting the Navy. Agent C. Avery: "Immediately before leaving on his last trip, Worley was complaining to Mr. Rotholz of being in ill health, and expressed a desire to retire from active service 'when I get back from this trip.' Mr. Rotholz expressed the utmost confidence in Worley's loyalty to the United States." Another Norfolk man, Mr. J.H. Scrivener, of Bramble & Scrivener, Ship's Chandler's, "was questioned along very much the same line as Mr. Rotholz had been, with practically the same results." Mr. Scrivener, too, "was apparently rather intimate with

Worley's family . . ."

Avery was understandably a bit suspicious by April 22 (when he was compiling the summary of interviews). Neither of the informants had any details, which is not surprising. The *Cyclops* had berthed back at Norfolk at Christmastime 1917 and then left January 8, 1918. This gave Worley only 2 weeks to get his house up for sale and make excuses. It also wasn't difficult to notice the above two men were of German heritage.

Avery set out to find out just why there was such a rush to sell the house, but Selma wouldn't talk to him or any investigator. It had taken only a couple of days for Selma to become gun shy at publicity. She had foolishly invited the negative publicity herself. When the *Cyclops* had just been reported overdue Selma had strobed with many excuses that gave her nationwide headlines, each excuse shoving her foot deeper in her throat and retreating her further into her own private closet. She had visited a number of families in Norfolk and had told the parents or spouses that the mystery would soon be cleared up. Then on the night of April 17, she came to the local newspaper and told them "the mystery of the *Cyclops* would be cleared up in the next twenty four hours.")

Encountering a closed door with Selma Worley, Avery therefore carefully asked Scrivener why Selma had displayed such confidence. It was his opinion "she had no reason whatever for saying that her husband was safe, this being inspired only by the hope that he was safe. She had now given up all hope of her husband's safe return and was thought to be breaking down under the strain."

Selma, in fact, had reasons. Norfolk was, once again, a premier Navy town and George had been very openly pro-German. It hadn't been optimism that had given her the positive appearance. Rather she had been unnerved by the suspicion with which some she had visited greeted her. She was now reacting to the local belief that her husband had betrayed the ship. She then put up a good front in Norfolk, playing roulette with theories that the *Cyclops* was drifting at sea with a disabled wireless or that they were safe in a "South American port, and an official announcement regarding the vessel would be made shortly."

When she had come into the newspaper office, the crucial step to inadvertently launching her stupidity nationwide, she actually had a specific motive. "Mrs. Worley visited the office also to request the suppression of an interview she had given about her husband's change of name and his birth in Germany." There probably was no "also." She came to stop it and the reporter probably got her so worked-up she declared a solution within 24 hours.

There can be no doubt this was all clumsily done by Selma to stave off the fears of treason. Personally, she believed George was dead. As soon as word came out officially on April 15, 1918, she had quickly telegrammed one of George's old friends in San Francisco, J.A. Goodwin: "Think Cyclops lost, my heart is broken."

Of all people to give up immediately, it is amazing that it was George Worley's own wife. On the surface this helps his defense better than her ungainly proffering. This doesn't suggest a woman who is aware her husband was going to commit or was even capable of committing treason.

However, it would have been better if Goodwin had not entered the picture. He immediately organized his own defense of George Worley. One of the curious things about it is how he felt the need to quickly defend his old friend in a long letter to the Navy only 4 days after he got Selma's telegram. This letter took some time to organize and write, so it seems he got right to it after receiving it. As a part of his defense, Goodwin presented his encouraging replies to Selma, telling her perhaps the ship was drifting without wireless and that she was not to give up. "Fred too resourceful."

Goodwin gave her some of her early theorizing (she had repeated the drifting without wireless theory publicly), but he had only helped her put his foot in her mouth. Goodwin, too, wasn't the sharpest tool in the shed. As with the others, with Goodwin we find that those coming forward to defend "Fred Worley" actually let some very damning information about him slip through. What makes Goodwin's long letter to the Navy very interesting is that it was penned before any kind of public outcry, but some of Goodwin's defensive comments show he is anticipating accusations against his old friend.

Goodwin goes over Worley's career at sea. But again, like Angermann, one is not sure whether it is just poor memory on Goodwin's part or just relying on what Worley had once told him. Goodwin's recollections don't even recall the voyage of the *Aloha*, other than we must deduce that this is the schooner he refers to when he said Worley took it "to its owners." For the voyage of the *Detolna* he merely says the Count was starting on a world trip and Worley sailed with him "but for some reason or other Wichmann left him at Honolulu."[23]

Vague rumors of a murder of a man "on the yard" and opium smuggling are not things, of course, that Goodwin would mention, even if he knew such rumors to reflect genuine facts. His recollections are general, to be sure, and possibly quite sincere. Imprecision, however, as innocent as it may be, gains some of the guilt of evasion when one is hesitant or lacks the forethought to offer any reason for important actions, such as why Worley had changed his name. Goodwin does not even stop to think it important. What Goodwin also understood of the Wichmann family is hard to make out. He states "Fred" had *two* brothers named Herman and one other brother named John (that would make 2 Johns and 2 Hermans in the same group of siblings). One of the Hermans was in the saloon business as well, at Commercial Street.

Goodwin does admit to Worley's heritage: "I am sure that Worley was either German or Prussian born; I was with him almost all of the time he was in San Francisco and I know him about as well as anybody in the world, and I consider him one of the best friends I ever had. He was always against the nobility and many times remarked to me how much he hated the German government. Notwithstanding these facts, about eight months ago, I went to a government official in the post office

---

[23] Again, with Goodwin we see that Worley only had 2 voyages prior to the *St. Mark*; and the *Detolna* was not a complete voyage.

in San Jose (his name I do not now recall) and told him that Worley was a German by birth and master of our largest collier. He laughingly told me 'never to fear that the government had combed him with a fine tooth comb.'"

It must have been hard for O.W. Fowler to repress a self-conscious look while reading this letter.

Goodwin concluded:

> He was madly in love with his wife, and devoted to his daughter Virginia. At the time he left on the present voyage of the Cyclops I received a letter from Mrs. Worley – in January I think it was – in which she said she never seen him break down before, but that as his daughter was sick and they were afraid she had scarlet fever, he feared to leave. They would not call the doctor for fear that Worley might be quarantined and be unable to make the trip. Worley always spoke of the United States government as having the finest navy in the world.

Before Selma had even used that remarkable example of his loyalty in the public forum, Goodwin here had presented it to the Navy. The Navy therefore followed up these astounding claims by sending agent B.F. Cranfill to personally interview Goodwin. Although Cranfill thought him to be a "loyal and conscientious informant" because his wife was very active in Red Cross, Goodwin was clearly not the smartest man. While Goodwin may not have known Worley was not a devoted husband, enjoying a couple of "dubious houses" on the sly, it is still hard to see the devoted father image that Goodwin and, indeed, Selma had been promoting. Both admitted— Selma in newspapers and Goodwin in private— that Worley's greatest fear was not being able to make this voyage to Rio. A devoted father would call a doctor immediately if he thought his daughter had *scarlet fever*! So what if he is quarantined? Worley is, in fact, portrayed as openly worried about not making the trip to Rio. Yet poor Selma and poor Goodwin couldn't scrape up enough IQ between them to see why the Navy was now doubly worried. Goodwin and Selma went so far to build up a patriotic image to defend the accusations of treason that they let a terrible cat out of the bag. Why was it so necessary for Worley to make this trip?

A better defense comes from Worley' German friends in Norfolk. They were so certain of his loyalty that they easily confessed to how open George Worley had been about his sentiments. Jacob Rotholz had more to tell ONI. "Worley had not concealed the fact that prior to the time when this country entered the war his sympathies were pro-German. While the two German raiders were interned at the local Navy Yard, he had become rather intimate with some of the officers and frequently visited those ships. Mr. Rotholz recalled that sometime during the interval between the severance of diplomatic relations and the declaration of war, he asked Worley what had become of Captain -----, one of the German officers and the latter replied that he 'did not bother with those people anymore.'"

George Worley was so crudely pro-German in Norfolk that he becomes an unlikely candidate for the fulcrum of a plot. Even to the Germans interned in port, Worley must have seemed a drunken oaf. An incident is related by Charles Aydelotte. He was another shopkeeper, one obviously of French heritage. He had known Worley 20 years and frequently saw him while he was in port. Aydelotte naturally upheld the Allies side in the struggle. Prior to the outbreak of the war this led to lively discussions with Worley, who "invariably expressed a belief and hope that Germany would win." While the two German raiders were interned in the port, Worley came into his store with one of the captains, Mund by name. "Worley, who had been drinking, began a discussion of the war with Mr. Aydelotte. Worley became very much aroused and was severe in his denunciation of the British and French, referring to Mr. Aydelotte in the jocular way as a 'damned Frenchman'. At which point Capt. Mund requested Worley to refrain from further discussion of the topic, saying that Mr. Aydelotte had as much right to his opinion as either he or Worley had to theirs." After war was declared, however, Mr. Aydelotte too "had not heard Worley give vent to pro-German sentiments . . ." Nevertheless, he "was unwilling to express unqualified confidence in his loyalty to the United States."

Regardless, was such a crass boozer as this really a good matrix for any treasonous plot? It would appear not.

But then there was that one undeniably strange act on Worley's part— the sudden selling of his house and possessions. There was no question that it was as suspicious as it looked. Ensign Ryder, who had provided ONI with much information about suspected sabotage aboard the vessel, had come across a Mrs. Vernon Cannon on a ferry ride. *Cyclops* was the center of talk then, and he had mentioned he had been stationed aboard. This led to an interesting conversation with Mrs. Cannon about her encounter with a man in Norfolk while she was visiting her mother. This man had told them of Worley suddenly selling his property. His name was Russell something. Based on this alone, ONI actually tracked him down and he proved to be Ned Russell, Worley's own nephew. He confirmed that the sale and the disposal of many possessions was rather hastily done.

Excuses on Selma's part should have been frank in order to assuage suspicion. But, sadly, they weren't. Already by April 20th, only 5 days after the official announcement of the vessel's loss, ONI was being coaxed into believing Selma Worley was solely responsible for the sale and not her husband. Therefore it could not indicate any premeditation on his part to sever his life in America and betray his ship to Germany. Mr. Scrivener had quickly offered agent Avery that "Mrs. Worley was a native of the West and had long desired to return and be among her own people"— yet another excuse.

When through intermediaries the question was broached, Selma Worley only confirmed what ONI had already been told. As General M. Churchill, Director of Military Intelligence, summed it up for A. Bruce Bielaski, Chief of the FBI: "She stated that Captain Worley did not dispose of his property prior to making the last voyage, and that the property in Norfolk is hers, and that she has disposed of it since Captain Worley left port, and that he did not know of it."

A weak, understanding smile or a roll of the eyes may be all with which the investigators had responded. Avery, Bushman, their boss Fowler, all knew better. They already knew that Jeffers had remembered Worley had civilians on the ship when trying to sell his house in late December/early January. They had also dug into real estate records, and Selma should have suspected that they would. Yes, indeed, the property was hers, but George had transferred it to her for $10.00 and "other valuable considerations by deed dated April 7, 1917, and recorded April 12, 1917."

This was a nice thing for him to do. War had just been declared and he was making it easy for Selma to inherit by giving it to her first just in case he was lost . . . or even better disappeared. She should have stuck to her story that they were going to move to San Francisco. But she didn't. It was ignorant of her to think she could have fooled ONI by making it sound as if selling the house was her idea.

The records show the deal was completed just as the *Cyclops* left Rio for home. "Mrs. Selma Worley, wife of the Commander of the *Cyclops*, by deed dated February 15, 1918, recorded February 26, 1918, in consideration of $2,500.00 cash and the assumption of a debt of $4000.00 made a transfer of the same property to L.F. Hobbs [or Holbs]." Quite a chunk back in those days. Worley seemed to do better than most captains.

Selma didn't stay in Norfolk long after the *Cyclops* was officially posted overdue. By May 7 she was already back in her native Washington State, listing her address in Port Orchard, just across the inlet from Bremerton from where she had come.

While on the subject of those in Norfolk, it might be prudent to bring up Worley's extracurricular affairs, to put it politely. ONI didn't leave it at rumor, of course. They tracked the prostitutes down. There were 2 women, both in Norfolk.

In some ways this fact may explain the sudden selling of the house. Did Selma get wind of these "romances"? If she and George suddenly separated, the selling of the house and the leaving of Norfolk seem a little more expected and far less than an indication of treason. She didn't return to San Francisco to await her husband's possible return. She went home to

Washington. Naturally she would never wish a smudge on her name. Nor would she wish her daughter to know this. She would never want to admit what George had been up to.

On a more solid note of defense, the Navy finally tracked down Lt. Myron C. Close. It was now already around Christmastime 1918, and he was at Tours, France. He was asked about the cablegram that he supposedly sent about the *Cyclops* being seen in the North Sea. Somehow a rumor was started and one of the men, Carroll Myers (same as Earl B. Meyers), found out "the *Cyclops* was safe and passed this information on to Lieut. Close, who, in turn, informed the others." Close said that he personally did not know if the *Cyclops* had been seen in the North Sea, but "he suspects that this statement was added to the information by Carroll Myers, who always was apt to exaggerate."

On April 22, 1918, Walter McDaniel had willfully submitted to a psychiatric examination. Although he wasn't insane, "he is a rather peculiar, egotistical and boastful type of individual who might be classified as a psychopath. . ." but it wasn't bad enough to diagnose him as Constitutional Psychopathic State, whatever that was. The upshot is that "persons of this type are prone to suspicions and exaggerations. . ." What it came down to was that McDaniel might have had some persecution because of his anti-German attitudes or the men just might have been unnerved by his behavior and got him off the ship.

It would be nice to accept that Goodwin's slant on the seadog as the actual fact of the man's character. Such lurid stories that surround Fred Wichman could ironically be the result of the seadog's propensity to spin tales. He was incredibly wry and subtle in his humor, and given to telling tall, humorous stories, from the stories about de Tolna to those of the tame lion aboard ship. Some of the second- and third-hand information now circulating about Worley could indeed have been started by his own storytelling. He might indeed have told people that he shot a man while skippering the *Aloha* to make a good, fearful story of himself. His beri-beri episode might not have been to cover up prison in Australia but his drunkenness, which does seem to be well testified to.

Nevertheless, we have the undisputed fact of Witchardt's head rolling about the *Abarenda* without its usually accompanying body, Gadeburg seeing enough in the situation to blackmail "Fred," and Worley being tried at Norfolk. We also have the many different stories of why Worley changed his name and why he came up with "George W. Worley" in the first place. So many of the stories in Worley's past, in fact, seem to be covering facts and not the product of haphazardly dreaming them up.

The Navy was so confused by this time whether Worley was a real US citizen or not they finally went and talked to Herman Wichman, one of the Hermans anyway. This Herman was still in the booze business at 239 Lexington Street, San Francisco, and was glad to tell them what he knew. Yes, indeed, John Fred Wichman was George Worley's real name. He supposedly changed his name legally in some city in Kitsap County, Washington State, about 1898 (where Selma came from). He was securing his naturalization papers ("it is thought") in San Francisco at the same time.[24]

The records, however, were not available and the Navy knew it had reached a stone wall: the earthquake and fire in 1906. Therefore it could not be determined if Worley was really a naturalized US citizen.

Herman also offered his opinion that the *Cyclops* was lost in a gale and lamented that he "would never see his brother again." This was the new and big defense the family was using. It is based on a report that a gale had hit off the Carolinas on March 10. Without any other explanations handy, those trying to downplay treason latched onto this vague storm.

Other points in Herman's testimony helped some. . .or did they? Edwin L. Reed in his long summary to his superiors in

---

[24] Herman may have gotten this from Selma. She had said that George changed his name as a young man in Port Orchard. This is obviously not the case. But he may have married Selma in Washington when he was still named Wichman, as that remained her middle name too. Lt. Burkhart saw the marriage certificate aboard ship and remembered it showed George married her in Pensacola in 1906. He may have married her again that year under the Worley name.

Washington noted that the Wichman name in the company of Wichmann & Lutgen comes from Frederick Wichman, an elder "brother now deceased." That would make 2 Johns, 2 Freds, and 2 Hermans all in the same family, a number of the doubles conveniently now deceased.[25]

ONI was so damned confused more back-working had to be done. It seems so many reasons were needed to cover up past business that "death" was the common excuse amongst the Wichman family. Herman kicked off a couple of times. So did a "Frederick." Now in 1918 it wasn't even certain that Fred AKA George Worley was dead!

Only Selma Worley was certain. In May she wrote a long letter to her sister-in-law, Mrs. Angermann, and nephew Dr. Ewald.

May 27, 1918
My dear Sister & Nephew

Just now received your letter and am truly pleased at what you say in regard to my taking a position for I felt that way too but it seems everybody worried me so about it and at last I said, well if I got better I might try. To tell the truth I'm not what I should be even mentally or physically. This terrible anxious time has left me a nervous wreck. If I could have one bit of hope but no I cannot think it possible for them to be safe they must have had to put into some port for coal, supplies etc. and in so doing so someone surely would have seen them and reported. No Ewald they were sunk in that storm. There may be reasons for the attitude which the Navy Department seems to hold for instance they knew the size of the "Cyclops" holds and the weight of the ore and how it would shift also that her one engine was not in good condition also may be Fred even said it would not be safe to take the ore without dividing her holds etc.. Of course this I do not know to be a fact but I knew other times they have loaded him so as to be really "top-heavy" and he reported that he did not consider it safe and still they have sent him so maybe he did the same now, who

---

[25] "Rufnamen" can be confusing in German, but this seems beyond even that practice.

knows. All I know is that whatever has happened Fred did his best and the best anyone could do. Why no one knows how he tried to always please the Department and to be on time at all times. Really it is terrible for the papers to be allowed to print such articles as I am sending you (Clipping Attached) I would like so much to have a visit with you both and will try and come in a few weeks. Yes I've heard frequently from the Goodwins and always letters full of hope. Do you know this fall when the second Liberty loan came out we didn't have much cash on hand and I suggested that Fred take out only one one-hundred dollar bond but he even then said "No, I must do five times as much as the others who were born here" so took out five hundred dollars and since then I have taken two thousand so we have twenty-five hundred in liberty bonds. Virginia, give up her pet Polly to the Red Cross and they realized about forty dollars. From this house they got over seventy-five in the last drive. Have a letter from a clerk[26] which had been with Fred the time he took the "Cyclops" until October of this year and in it he says "I could and would willingly stake my life on Capt's. loyalty." All who knew him felt that way at heart. It is a wicked old world nevertheless and only in trouble are friends actually tested. A man who Fred has befriended and helped in every way yes, and for years too has proved himself to be wanting. You heard Fred speak of Captain Shunliffe[,][27] well he and his wife both. She went even so far as to express herself in a large gathering of people that Captain Worley was a pro-German and that she didn't expect anything better at him. Old Shunliffe has supported another lady for the last five years up in Philadelphia and Fred knew it all the time and to shield her denied not only his knowledge of it but said he knew it was not so. That's only one of the things and then for him to say one word. Oh, where is there any justice! Will this terrible wrong done him ever be righted? And I that would do anything, yes, and everything am absolutely helpless. If people only knew him as I did! Why if he could come back [and] heard all the contemptible things said of him and that even his folks said years ago turned against him why he would die of that alone. Yes, I'll come down some before I must talk to you

---

[26] H.O. Peterson.
[27] Shunnliff or Shutliff, captain of the *Nero* when Worley was its First Mate.

both and I'm glad you feel so about my working for I didn't believe Fred would [not] have approved but since everyone thought it best I begin to think maybe I'd better. With a little economy Virginia and I will be able to live on our income and so it shall not worry us. With love to you both, I am always yours,

Selma W. Worley

Some caution should be entertained for Selma's letter. Ewald Angermann presented it quickly to ONI in San Francisco as part of the family's defense of "Fred." Solid evidence for the patriotic claims, obviously, is lacking. All it implies is that Worley's background in Germany was well known and he tried to outdo all those born here to prove his loyalty. This seems incongruous with facts. Officially (that is before the disappearance), as far as the Navy knew San Francisco was his hometown and birthplace. He was already an officer in the Naval Reserve with a very English surname like Worley. What was there to prove about his loyalty that required outdoing "others who were born here"? Most of those officers and men who had known he had changed his name from something German still thought he had been born in San Francisco.

Just like Herman Wichman, Selma took comfort in that gale that had been reported off the Carolinas on March 10 that year. The Navy seemed to be banking on it as well, according to her letter. For Selma this too seemed the better death. Any death in the line of duty was better than the charges of treason. The letter was a round-about way of giving her final words to a Navy she would no longer address. Of all the crew's wives and mothers, it is odd that the captain's wife alone believed, even insisted, her husband was dead and held out no hope. Could it be her sure belief her husband could not have betrayed America? All other families held out hope for their loved ones' lives *because* of their belief Worley betrayed the ship and took the men to a German POW camp.

There is no denying that Worley's last actions are suspicious and that circumstances can favor the idea that he could have turned traitor after the indignity of the Board of Inquiry. But it is inference and acrimony that surround Worley.

In any event, the Navy seemed rightly prejudiced against Worley by this time. He was crude, rough, brutal at times, mixed up with two deaths that could not be clearly explained in retrospect, given to drinking (which even friends could not deny), pro-German, and the last voyage of the *Cyclops* had an unexplained, unscheduled stop at Barbados where he took on more supplies and fuel. He was a strict disciplinarian, good sailorman, but poor navigator. He was like Nervig observed—some old bucko sea captain. When it comes down to it, he was an old seadog, not a fine seadog but a seadog nonetheless.

14

REQUIEM FOR A TRAITOR?

"I am ready to take my oath in court that, in my opinion, the same A.L. Gottschalk is (or was, if now dead) a man of no integrity of character, a man given to misrepresentation and lying according as it suited his purpose."
—J.E Conner, US Consular Service

IN THE SUMMER OF 1918 there was one thing and one thing only that vied with the theory that the *Cyclops* was betrayed to the Germans by "Fred Worley." This was the idea that German spies or saboteurs had planted a time-bomb aboard the vessel and succeeded in destroying her at sea. Had it not been for this, the public verdict would have long been in and firmly fixed on the seadog.

On May 6 the news had hit. The *New York Sun* broke the story with the arrival of the *Vestris* into New York harbor. The article stated in part: "Passengers from Rio called attention to a story that stirred Americans and anti-Germans in the city two weeks after the Cyclops had been reported missing. An advertisement appeared in one of the Rio dailies printed in Portuguese, saying that at a certain date a Mass would be said at a leading Catholic church for Alfred L. M. Gottschalk, American Consul-General at Rio, who was a passenger on the Cyclops and who was referred to as a 'distinguished north American

Consul.' The advertisement bore the names, as signatures, of one of the principle members of the American consulate at Rio and other friends of Mr. Gottschalk. Investigation the next day revealed that none of the men whose names were affixed to the advertisement knew anything about it, and the pastor of the church declared that no one had arranged for a Mass for Mr. Gottschalk."

Aside from this mystery, there is a major problem and the Press and the Navy picked up on it right away— the notice was declared to have appeared in the Rio newspaper about 3 weeks *before* the *Cyclops* was even posted overdue on April 15. At this time nobody but the upper echelons in the Navy knew the vessel was late.

The *New York Times* elaborated the next day: "Mysterious Advertisement In A South American Newspaper Hints Cyclops Was Sunk." The article called attention to a parallel, reminding readers that the German ambassador in New York placed advertisements in newspapers warning American passengers not to embark on the *Lusitania* before she left on her final voyage from New York and was torpedoed off Ireland. "While the advertisement at Rio was not in the nature of a warning it may have been another recourse by German agents to the advertising columns to transmit a report of their operations. It was the first time that an intimation had been given that the Cyclops had been sunk."

Passengers from the *Vestris* suggested that it was placed in the papers as a way of alerting the large German colony in Brazil that "the German government was still active and to spread and keep alive the German propaganda in Brazil, whose participation in the war so far has been passive." In doing so, the hopes would be that the government would rethink the price of loyalty to the Allies. Preserving their pre-knowledge of the *Cyclops'* sinking with a fake ad for a requiem mass "for the repose of the soul of Consul Gottschalk who was lost at sea when the Cyclops was sunk" was really the only way the saboteurs could have surreptitiously signaled their success to the greater German community.

The *Times* article itself ended on the note of the mysterious. "There have been many strange features concerning the disappearance of the Cyclops. She disappeared in a well traveled sea lane, but no other vessels saw her, nor did any of them pick up a wireless message. Had a bomb exploded on board, marine men say that she certainly would have had time to send a wireless appeal for aid.[28] If she had gone down, naval men said that her lifeboats and deckworks would have floated and would have been picked up by other vessels. Nothing was heard or seen . . . therefore the story has persisted that there was a mutiny on board and the Cyclops either was converted into a raider . . . or that she started for a German port . . ."

And, of course, the value of her cargo and its desperate need in Germany for armament production is next brought up, then Worley's heritage. Strangely, all assignations were directed back to Captain Worley again, though betrayal would seem a contradiction with the requiem notice implying spies destroyed the vessel.

For all the significance of the Rio newspaper requiem ad, Alfred Louis Moreau Gottschalk is quickly glossed over; so is the potential mystery inhering in the fact *his* name was used in the ad. Oh, yes, indeed, the article hinted at it; that his name might have been used because of some "animus" against him, but it quickly added what it did not know: "but there is no known basis for it, and he was a highly respected and well liked man in an important government position."

ONI wanted to find out. It was a natural course of events that the Navy had already started an investigation of Alfred L.M. Gottschalk's past. In a coded message sent to Rio on April 16, 1918, the investigation had been ordered with a brief: "Cable your confidential opinion as to the loyalty of Consul Gottschalk."[29]

It was an unpleasant surprise for the Navy to receive in reply on April 18 from their agent Hil in Rio de Janeiro the fol-

---

[28] Recall Paul Roberts' statement that Worley sometimes had no operator on duty, at least in 1915.

[29] It was sent by Navy Intelligence (Lt. Commander Fowler).

lowing: "Before entry into war, he was very pro-German. He endeavored to transmit German Red Cross Funds, of which he was the custodian, to Germany, through the National City Bank of New York. I cannot give any instance of his lack of loyalty to the United States. His chief fault lay in his being a newspaper man and secondarily Consul General. This, together with a disagreeable personality, caused Americans and other foreigners to dislike him intensely."[30]

Not the most reassuring response to get.

Another ONI operative (not mentioned by name in the report), based in New York, made a supplemental report on May 13 after the above newspaper articles had been published. In it he reported the results of his interview with another passenger of the s.s. *Vestris*, Mr. W. Van Dyke, who was a representative of the General Electric Company. Van Dyke doesn't make mention of the ad, but he did contribute to the theory of betrayal. He stated that he had been en route to Buenos Aires when the *Cyclops* was at Rio. When he returned the *Cyclops* had already headed north. "Sometime thereafter reports were current in Rio de Janeiro that the Cyclops had disappeared." Among the many rumors it was said that the ship had sailed to Germany. Van Dyke's account stands independent of the requiem ad, and as such it confirms that rumors of the *Cyclops* disappearing were in circulation in South America before she was being publicly reported overdue.

Van Dyke also states something quite intriguing, and his source was qualified to know. "He further mentioned that officially Consul General Gottschaulk [sp] was supposed to have boarded the Cyclops at Bahia, yet he had been informed by a United States Naval attaché, C. Jungling stationed in Rio de Janerio [sic], that Gottschaulk [sp] had actually boarded the vessel in Rio de Janerio [sic]."

The operative, unnamed on the report surviving in the National Archives, now speaks of personal knowledge. "Mr. Gottschaulk [sic] whom the Operative knows personally was

---

[30] This reference to a newspaper man implies a man who catered to publicity but in substance did not do his job. Gottschalk had been a reporter some 20 years before.

not very popular with the members of the American Colony in Rio de Janerio [sic]. No one knew of his departure until a letter was received from him by members of the American Colony in Rio de Janerio having been mailed in Bahia."[31]

"American Colony" is a rather broad term, and it is safe to assume it included the consulate staff, for if he had told any of them certainly the rest of the "Colony" would have been aware when they inquired of his whereabouts. Being late arriving at Bahia means this was 3 extra days in which nobody in Rio knew what had happened to Gottschalk. One can well imagine why the staff was upset about being informed only by letter after days of wondering where their boss was.

It is hard enough to try and explain how Worley could have gotten lost between Rio and Bahia for 3 days without now trying to figure in all the coincidences that arise with Alfred Gottschalk's secretive departure from Rio. Foremost, why is this the only port from which the *Cyclops* left secretly? Vice Consul Richard Momsen admitted Gottschalk left from Rio, but only incidentally, in his letter of April 27, 1918, to his superiors. But he also stated the *Cyclops* left on February 15. In another letter he said February 16. There is no departure notice. There is only Worley's signature on a cable saying he *intended* to leave the 16th.

In addition to the mode of Gottschalk's departure, there is another mystery. There are clues that he did not intend to return. After Momsen sent his formal letter of April 27 on the state of affairs, he sent a telegram to the Department of State asking to be kept informed about the investigation "as I have personally assumed the up-keep of Consul General's house which I cannot continue indefinitely on present salary, but at same time wish to protect his personal interests." The telegram was sent May 1. Since Momsen didn't know Gottschalk had been declared missing until April 15, he could only have as-

---

[31] Van Dyke seems wrong about an "official" departure, since according to this none knew ahead of schedule that he was leaving. He also knew that Gottschalk was "an admirer of German methods," but didn't give credence to the rumor he was pro-German.

sumed the upkeep after that time. And since it seems very unlikely that Gottschalk could have returned to Rio by this time,
it is evident he had retained no one to take care of his property
and personal business.[32]

Newspapers reported that Gottschalk had said he was returning in order to enter the US Army to do his part in the
war. The US ambassador from Argentina, William Robertson,
had done that. He was given great fanfare when he returned,
but he had resigned first. The papers even noted he had given
up a $12,000 dollar a year job to do so. But Gottschalk hadn't
resigned. He had merely left without telling anybody.

What was the motive for Gottschalk's stealth? There was no
need for such a clandestine and deceptive departure as he took.
This was completely at odds with his penchant for publicity.

Prior to entering the Diplomatic Corp., Gottschalk had been
a war correspondent for the *New York Herald*. During the
Spanish-American War he was attached to General Brook's di-
vision conducting the Puerto Rican campaign. The *Herald* had
a flattering spread on him in their April 15 edition, stating that
in 1899 he left the paper. "Seeing the opportunities in Latin
American commerce," he became a sugar planter in Haiti "but
was discouraged by successive revolutions." That's a nice diplomatic way of saying "going belly-up." He then became the
Collector of Customs at Monte Cristo, Santo Domingo. Then in
1902 at the age of 29 he entered the consular service.

For all Gottschalk's brief stint as a reporter, the moniker of
"newspaper man" still clung to him. Though he hadn't worked
on a paper for almost 20 years, he had apparently kept the attitude of a publicist; the implication of his detractors was that
this was more often for himself than for his country's service.
Taking into account Hil's secret report stating how disliked
Gottschalk really was, the *Herald's* view of Gottschalk appears
all the more like a tailored publicity release, reflecting an image Gottschalk alone preferred to paint of himself. "Since go-

---

[32] Transit would have been about a month to and from the United States.
Since he was due to arrive mid-March he would have had to board a ship by
the end of March in order to get back by mid-April.

ing to Brazil Mr. Gottschalk had been credited with having had much to do with swaying the feeling of the people against Germany. He was a popular speaker there and possessed great influence."

If Gottschalk is to be regarded as a clever spinmeister and a camp follower of cheap newspaper spotlight, a military enlistment might be a logical step on his part. Politically it would put him in a better light, certainly in his hometown of New York where he was well known. He might indeed have been feathering his nest for a political platform in post war elections. Would this not seem smart? However cunningly he may have been able to manipulate the press and public opinion, the military establishment had seemed wary of him. He had tried to get enlisted before at the outbreak of the war, but apparently nobody in the military had helped him.

Based on a solitary but significant letter this fact was discovered. A Colonel Brainard came forward and showed the Navy a letter sent to him. It is dated February 6, 1918, nine/ten days before Gottschalk boarded the *Cyclops*.

Dear Colonel Brainard:

I am expecting shortly to be in Washington on a short leave of absence.

There are a great many interesting things happening the world over, concerning which it is difficult to write and one of the pleasures which I have in anticipation on my arrival, is being able to meet you again and having some conversation with you. It is my hope to leave here so as to arrive in Washington in early March. During my absence the office will remain in charge of the Senior Vice Consul, Mr. Richard O. [sic] Momsen, who will act in my place in case you should wish anything here in Rio de Janeiro.

With kind regards,
Yours faithfully,
A.L.M. Gottschalk
CONSUL-GENERAL

On the surface not much of an illuminating letter. In fact, it is so pointless it is hard to see Gottschalk's purpose other than confirming he is coming north and wants Brainard to set aside some time in early March. All it underscored for the Navy (and indeed for us here) was Gottschalk's unprofessionalism inasmuch as it proves he had intended to travel north and yet had not bothered to inform his own associates except by letter after he left. He also needlessly provided Brainard with a Vice Consul's name, a man he'd really not need to contact anyway, no matter what happened.

But Gottschalk was quite out-of-touch. Brainard was now a Brigadier General and stationed abroad in Lisbon.[33] In his cover letter to the Secretary of State, in which he turned this letter over "as a matter of interest," he told him of the previous letter of some 10 months before. Shortly after the outbreak of the war (April 1917), Gottschalk had written to Brainard at the War Department. "In this letter, Mr. Gottschalk asked whether it would be possible for me to assist him in obtaining a commission in the National army, as he wished to do his part in the war." There is no clarification given by Brainard as to why Gottschalk did not obtain his commission in the army when he first requested assistance.[34] But Brainard (or anybody else) obviously did not help him with his commission or Gottschalk didn't follow through.

There is thus little evidence that Gottschalk was returning to the United States to enter the army as the rumors said. He had already tried 10 months before when war was declared and apparently received no response or help. It is even less likely now while only returning to Washington on a short leave of absence.

The newspaper reports of him joining the army, however, came from other sources, for the letter to Brainard was long in forwarding since he had been transferred to Lisbon. It appears

---

[33] Brainard forwarded the letter on November 25, 1918. He was now military Attaché in Lisbon, Portugal, the reason why he was tardy in transmitting it.

[34] We declared war on April 2, 1917, almost 10 months prior to Gottschalk's letter to Brainard.

only tardily in the investigation. Therefore Gottschalk had set rumor in other places, couched in far more definite terms, about entering the army than he did to the colonel, a relative stranger, to whom he sent the oddly ambiguous letter.

Perhaps his reasons were in his letter to the Consulate that he had mailed from Bahia. It is unlikely it contained much. It had already been thrown out when news came that the *Cyclops* was overdue on April 15, for the letter does not survive and there is also no communiqué between agents (many handwritten memos survive) mentioning the contents of this letter. It is certainly not preserved in the archives.

The fact is that Gottschalk— the *Consul General*— silently left Rio, a premeditated decision by at least 10 days, and left no other excuse than traveling north. More significantly than this, since the embassy had not arranged it, nor apparently had Admiral Caperton, Gottschalk must have had mutual contacts with Worley in order to board the *Cyclops*.

By February 6, when Gottschalk had written his letter to Brainard, only one person knew the *Cyclops* would be shipping north relatively soon because he knew he was going to be coming back on her— the pro-German Albert Winkle. Also, in Caperton's messages to the *Cyclops* the Naval attaché (possibly C. Jungling) and the USS *Glacier* were copied.

However, Jeremiah Bourk, whose first contact with Worley went back "close to 29 years" when he first saw him manipulating cards at his saloon, was very dissatisfied with the Navy investigation, especially agent Edwin L. Reed's approach to it. Bourk now lived in Chicago, and Reed was the local agent there, Chicago being the head of the 9th, 10th, and 11th Naval Districts. When he turned in information, it was Reed who had to take it all down. When visiting Washington DC Bourk made a stink about it being "superficial" and as a result Captain R.S. Day was sent to interview him in detail. Bourk, too, understandably has some trouble with memory, but he recalled that Worley had done a lot of "plying between Atlantic ports and South American shipping points." He "was in my opinion undoubtedly in close contact with the leading political and business Germans of the Southern continent."

As the investigation proceeded, ONI would learn just how much Gottschalk too was in contact with German businesses. On April 27, Thomas C. Latham of the Naval Communication Service sent a dispatch to the Director of Naval Intelligence in which he notes: "This office is in receipt of a communication from the Censorship Intelligence Officer, referring to an intercepted letter from Marden, Orth & Hastings Corporation, 61 Broadway, New York City, to a Mr. Victor Schochet, Caixa Postal 359, Rio de Janeiro, Brazil." The letter read:

> As you have certainly read in the local newspapers of Rio, the collier Cyclops, which had on board Mr. A.L. Moreau Gottschalk, is missing since March 4th. That explains why we did not receive any answer to the three letters of ours directed to him at Washington. If any mishap has happened to him, or we hear any news of his whereabouts, we will not fail to communicate with him.

Obviously, Marden, Orth & Hastings knew Gottschalk was coming back to America and would be in Washington. Strange they should know this when Gottschalk was so stealthy about leaving Brazil on the *Cyclops* he didn't even tell his own associates except by letter from Bahia.

Naturally, the Navy wanted to know what all this meant. Investigators visited the firm and started asking a surprised group of men just what their connection was with Gottschalk. Everybody there answered the same: that Schochet was their rep. in Brazil. "They claim their interest in Gottschalk was due to the fact that he was considered to be in a position to assist them in extending their business connections."

Further investigation showed that the personnel of Marden, Orth & Hastings were "largely German." ONI ran to ground the former rep. of the company in Brazil and discovered that "one Weicker," head of the export department, Von Hess, head of the dyestuff department, Mr. Orth himself, president, and Mr. Trepp of the Brazilian department were all "sympathetic to the German cause." Nonetheless, the agents concluded there seemed to be little connection to anything serious.

Had this branch of ONI known that Gottschalk had been telling other businessmen in New York a different story as to why he was coming home they might have probed deeper. Guy Wellman was another of Gottschalk's New York contacts. "He [Gottschalk] made a statement to him that he was contemplating a trip down the coast in connection with some intelligence work for the Navy. Wellman, however, was informed by other people that Gottschalk was in reality going to New York and that his real movements were being carefully concealed." More mystery, it seems, and some of it Gottschalk's own doing. Why?

There was no question Moreau Gottschalk was very pro-German and *very* disliked. General sentiments from staff in Rio de Janeiro were one thing, but a startling letter was received at the Secretary of State (May 13, 1918) from a member of the US Diplomatic Corp., making specific allegations against Gottschalk and the newspapers' claims he was enlisting in the Army.

The letter was from Mr. J.E. Conner. It contains a scathing opinion of Gottschalk based on his behavior at other consular posts. The letter went silently through channels. The Secret Service (Captain Burke) delivered it in person to the ONI New York office. From there it was forwarded to Washington. Leland Harrison soon forwarded to Captain McCauley, in charge of ONI, Fowler's boss.

> If it is desired to solve the mystery of the Collier "Cyclops," I would suggest that you begin upon the theory of the complicity of the Consul General at Rio de Janeiro, A.L. Gottschalk.
>
> If there was any foul play anywhere in the shipping of the seamen it must have been from the last port of call, Rio de Janeiro, and with the cognizance of the Consular Officer there. Reports to that effect have appeared in the New York papers namely that there was foul play, hence mutiny and the loss of the vessel, though I have as yet seen no intimation as to the complicity of the aforementioned Gottschalk. Quite to the contrary, indeed, was an announcement of the loss of the vessel, to

the effect that the said Gottschalk was returning to offer his services in the war. In other words his press agent was on the job. My theory as to the loss of the Cyclops is that through the connivance of the same Gottschalk, the vessel was handed over to the Germans, who either destroyed her after making themselves secure, or possibly interned her in some out of the way port of the world, and that in any case the same Gottschalk will later turn up as the central figure in a romance of his own construction, claiming to have been under duress all the time.

These things I know about the self same Gottschalk: that he was too much of a coward to fight on any account. Second, that before the war he was an ardent pro-German and I have no doubt that he continued to be so while in Brazil. I have myself heard him speak most disparagingly of our country while praising Germany inordinately, and that too as an official at the time of the U.S.A. The former Consul General at Vienna (Mr. Denby) might have something interesting to contribute as to his conduct in that city, where he spent something like three months, doing nothing apparently, while he was supposed to be around inspecting consulates.

I am ready to take my oath in court that, in my opinion, the same A.L. Gottschalk is (or was, if now dead) a man of no integrity of character, a man given to misrepresentation and lying according as it suited his purpose. I had abundant proofs of his lying in my possession at one time, and with the assistance of the Department of State can prove the case; I am ready to go further into this if you send a representative to see me.

J.E. Conner

The Navy didn't waste time following up on this. In the subsequent interview at ONI's New York office, Conner explained that he had served 7 years in the Diplomatic service. "He was in St. Petersburg when Gottschalk was in Vienna and later St. Petersburg." Conner's attitude hadn't changed from his instigating letter. "He further stated that he believed Gottschalk to be unscrupulous and a man who used every effort to further his own interest, rather than those of the government he represented." Conner also noted that Gottschalk spent all his vacations in Berlin and preferred to associate with Germans. There were also other statements that Gottschalk made that led him to believe he was completely pro-German. "Mr. Conner gave the impression of being absolutely honest and the information as given was not due to any personal spite, although he fervently stated that he thoroughly disliked the man." Conner also gave the name of "Mr. Harris," the former Consul General at Stockholm who could speak of Gottschalk along the same lines.

At this point the Navy investigation was still suffering from the compile and file attitude. Investigation was weak, just as Bourk had complained. There is no record whatsoever in all the papers amassed at the National Archives documenting an attempt to contact Denby or Harris, though it may have been done much more unofficially. On the contrary, the above report, dated May 31, 1918, was only 14 days before the Navy would officially do something remarkable. They would declare all aboard the *Cyclops* to be dead, "lost at sea."

There is nothing to indicate what made the Navy take this action. They may have preferred the gale off the Carolinas for public consumption (even Selma Worley mentioned it in that vein), but it was probably safe to say that part of the reason was for insurance, both for the families and the Navy. The cargo was valued and insured for $500,000 dollars.

Despite the bureaucratic maneuver, official interest was by no means dead. "Loss" had certain legalistic meanings, and attorneys even wrote to the Navy to inquire just what the definition was since they needed it for their cases. On June 15, the Secretary of the Navy himself responded to one bereaving mother, Mrs. J.R. Wilkinson: "While we must face the fact that the return of the ship is very doubtful, it has not been entirely given up as sunk."[35]

---

[35] Investigation continued throughout the summer. On August 26, ONI drew up a long list of "persons with whom Lieutenant Commander Worley would probably try to communicate." On September 12, 1918, Captain Lowry had stated that he had "seen a cablegram which stated that Consul General Gottschalk was in Germany."

Publicly, theories were not intertwining Gottschalk with betrayal. The requiem mass announcement was merely being viewed as a tip-off by German agents. With what ONI had now learned, however, a different view had to be taken. Could Gottschalk have been an active key or dupe to carrying out the diabolical plan of mercilessly destroying the ship and its precious cargo? No time bomb could be rigged in Rio to go off weeks later. It would require someone aboard to set the mechanism at the right and crucial time. It is hard to imagine that Gottschalk would set sail on a ship he knew was destined for destruction, so if he had any part he was a dupe or a small cog in the greater wheel that intended and could insure its members would survive the sinking.

The date of the requiem announcement was placed at about March 17. This is around the time the rumors began that the *Cyclops* was missing, both only days after the ship was due at Baltimore. This was an unsettling coincidence, for it indicated a close watch was kept by spies on shipping arrivals and departures. If so, this then raises a disturbing question. How did spies find out her destination in order to be watching for her arrival or non-arrival?

An interesting connective strand between Gottschalk and this question might be drawn from an offhand statement. In his long letter to the Secretary of State (April 27, 1918), Richard Momsen notes that his office contained the "Invoice No. 112, certified February 7 at the Consulate General, that the U.S.S. Cyclops carried 10,000 metric tons of manganese ore consigned by the Companhia Morro da Mina, to order, destined for Baltimore, Maryland." This reveals the fact that even embassy people knew the ship's destination. Aside from the consular service only Worley, the Navy, and the United States & Brazil Steamship Company would have known.

"Complicity" was an incisive word for Conner to use, but how much was necessary? We cannot imagine that the "American Colony" was not a leaky sieve. It did not require Gottschalk, but thanks to his letter from Bahia (which later vanished) the information probably got about. That's all that would be necessary. Or is it?

No one could have known about Barbados. That was purely a surprise stop. But it was *only at Barbados* where the ETA at Baltimore was updated. When the *Cyclops* left Rio, her ETA at Baltimore was the 8th of March. In order to communicate the new ETA to an accomplice in Rio or Bahia or America, there would have to be a culprit aboard the *Cyclops* who would of necessity have to cable it there. If one of the many cables coming from the *Cyclops* at Barbados contained the revised ETA of the 13th even in a harmless form "I am arriving the 13th," the accomplice, already knowing the destination, would now know the new ETA.

Consul Livingston mentioned that many cables directed to or coming from the ship were held at St. Thomas. Thomas P. Bryan of the Office of Chief Cable Censor sent a memo to ONI on June 18, 1918. The Cable Censor at San Juan had examined them and declared that he was "unable to find in them anything that would give any information as to the probable fate of the U.S.S. Cyclops." From our perspective today, the substance of Bryan's investigation all depends on what he was looking for. Within them there may have been an innocent "Expect me the 13th." I have found the cover letter in the Archives when the cables were sent to ONI, but as yet the actual cables remain elusive.

Their existence is actually quite intriguing. No family member ever came forward and said their loved one had telegrammed them from Barbados. The Navy didn't even know the ship had put in there until Worley had left at 11:45 a.m. March 4.[36] Just who could have been sending cables over what? It is interesting to note that only Gottschalk would probably have been told the updated ETA before they left.

But this would still be independent to any spy network that could put information in action. Who could possibly be so in tune to the sailing, departure, cargo and arrival of a particular

---

[36] The exact message: "Arrived Barbados, West Indies, 1730 [5.30 P.M.] for bunker coal. Arrive Baltimore, Md, 12013 [March 13,]. Notify Office Director Naval Auxiliaries, Comdr. Train (Atl), 07004. CYCLOPS."

ship as to organize and be a focal point of communication between agents in Brazil and in America?

Office of Naval Intelligence discovered Franz Hophenblatt. He "is the New York agent for the South American Shipping Company." The South American Shipping Company was owned by none other than E.G. Fontes of the Morro de Mina which supplied the manganese ore. "It is alleged that he [Hophenblatt] handled the whole transaction."[37]

The problem with getting a statement out of Hophenblatt was that he now took it on the lam. He was a foreign alien from Germany and he had only taken out his first naturalization papers. Now the Navy and the FBI were after him on the recommendation that he be interned. One witness, Harry Lambert, came forward and confessed that Hophenblatt had told him that he had no intentions of taking out his final papers. He was completely pro-German and had no interest in becoming an American anymore.

Another informant, Benjamin B. Murray, also told the FBI that "Hophenblatt is not only giving aid and comfort to the enemy, but is also supplying them with information as he has access to the cables and understands more than anyone else in this country the need of manganese ore and the shipping of same." Murray also claims "that on or about May 1st, Hophenblatt came into his office and upon seeing a service flag said, 'What the Hell is that for?' Murray explained that it was a service flag for the company's employees who were in the service, and Hophenblatt said, 'Damn every one of them, they should be shot. They are fools for fighting for this country.' When Murray said that he was willing to fight for this country, Hophenblatt replied, 'Damn you, if you do I will shoot you first.' And then Hophenblatt continued to express his regrets that he could not return to Germany to fight. Murray states

---

[37] To keep everything clear, United States & Brazil Steamship Company chartered the *Cyclops* to haul the manganese to the US. The Brazilian Coaling Company loaded it (Cory Brothers), E.G. Fontes' Morro de Minho had consigned it. It was sold to United States Steel Products Company, of which United States & Brazil Steamship Company was a subsidiary.

that these statements were heard by" . . . and then names followed.

A number of informants didn't even know they were lending information, for ONI agents were surreptitiously snooping around the New York businesses of German aliens. A.C. Gross of Bullock and Gross is one example of German aliens still doing business in New York. Gross was even overheard to say that "his friend" (Hophenblatt) had handled the *Cyclops* transaction, and it is from this tidbit that ONI was able to identify Hophenblatt's participation in the whole shipping of the manganese. However, information leaked both ways. It is no doubt through some of the German aliens that Hophenblatt learned there was an investigation and he was being sought for internment. As soon as he found out, an ONI aid in New York heard he had "destroyed 700 letters (from Germany) stating 'They won't get anything on me.'"

And apparently the Navy didn't. Hophenblatt disappeared in Mexico, Scott free. With him he took his secrets.

The requiem mass and its timing anchor the whole idea of premeditation and collusion in the loss of the vessel and therefore anchor this with an act of sabotage. If anything has been regurgitated in the legend of the *Cyclops*, it is the existence of this ad. I have introduced it seriously. But to be fair we must come down to brass tacks. For all of its rather obvious importance, it could never be traced, that is, there is no solid evidence the ad *ever appeared*. Had the Navy ever found solid evidence for it, they never would have pursued so many different angles and theories. Hil at Rio never mentions it (there is no record anyway). There are numerous clippings from Rio newspapers in the State Department papers dated April 15 or later. All cover Gottschalk's life, his South American career, and praise him warmly. He definitely was popular with journalists. But in none of them, though my Portuguese hangs on my rusty Latin, can I find a mention of the mysterious requiem mass.

This rumor appears to stem solely from passengers aboard the *Vestris*, and from there it cannot be traced except as Brazilian scuttlebutt. What paper? No name is ever given. Those aboard the liner had merely heard of such an advertisement. It would seem that such a thing would and could be quickly backtracked; just have the embassy send a clipping . . . but there is no official word from Momsen either.

Even more peculiar is Momsen's own letter to the State Department giving details of how the *Cyclops* was loaded. This letter, dated April 27, makes no mention of the advertisement. If he had not yet known about it surely Washington would have informed him in early May when on the 6th the *Vestris* arrived New York and the newspapers carried the story. But there is no subsequent dispatch from him detailing an investigation to discover the truth of it. The papers also said that the chief diplomat at the embassy had signed the advertisement for the requiem mass. That would be the ambassador or perhaps even Momsen himself. Surely had he heard of such a claim he would have sent a dispatch refuting it or confirming it. Yet there are none. Until April 15, the embassy staff apparently didn't even know the *Cyclops* was overdue.[38]

ONI should have proven or disproven this ad explicitly, but they didn't. They kept it on their long list of clues until the very end, but they never confirmed it, which does rather reflect a superficial investigative approach, at least superficial analysis. But the fact that Momsen never heard about the loss until the official announcement more or less tells us the ad never happened.

The requiem mass ad was probably journalistic sensationalism; their yellow form of incarnating those rumors in Brazil that the *Cyclops* had vanished . . . but rumors there truly were.

There are many things about Gottschalk's participation in the last voyage that leave open the mystery of some kind of premeditation in the fate of the *Cyclops*. Why so much lying? Why the deception? Why the stealthy departure? Why 3 miss-

---

[38] "On April 15, 1918," wrote Momsen, "I was very much surprised and grieved to see the telegraphed reports in the newspapers of this city that the U.S.S Cyclops, which had left this port on February 15th carrying as a passenger Consul-General Gottschalk, had not been heard from for many weeks."

ing days along the coast to Bahia?

Lies are in Worley's excuses for selling all his property, including his car, before his final voyage; he gave varying excuses for needing supplies at Barbados. Lies are in Gottschalk's excuses for simply returning to America for a short leave of absence. Germans and Pro-Germans abound at every point in the voyage, even in the shipping of the manganese. Hophenblatt absconded. What really happened?

By Fall 1918 the question had not been answered. So much of the "investigation" had been "compile and file." Now there seemed little reason to finding an answer. A world event happened that closed the book on the case of the *Cyclops*: the war, The Great War, had ended.

15

ONLY GOD AND THE SEA

"Will the sea give up the mystery of the lost boat and its 300 men?
Most of us will hope so. Mysteries of any sort fascinate the human
mind, sea mysteries most of all."
— *Philadelphia Record,* July 4, 1930

NOTHING BANISHED THE MOST CONTROVERSIAL and sensational
theories about the *Cyclops'* disappearances like the end of
World War I. Pro-Germanness and treason were irrelevant now,
a closed book slammed shut by the process of elimination. The
lack of finding the *Cyclops* in a German port was proof of that.
Admiral Robison of the Navy delegation of the Armistice
Commission was also put in charge of finding any evidence in
German records. Admiral Goette of the German High Command complied with Robison's requests and searched the files.
Perhaps it was not a diligent search, but it was certain that he
could find no records indicating that subs, raiders and mines
were operating in the area the *Cyclops* had been sailing. The
German government also didn't seem to know anything about
a plot to sabotage the vessel. Altogether this meant the Germans actually had nothing to do with the *Cyclops* mystery at
all.

Mutiny was the only other "exciting" theory; and now with

the end of the war it too seemed of little merit. None of the 309 men were ever found; none came home, however secretly, and were recognized by neighbors who then quietly reported them. Ultimately all this translated down to one thing: the *Cyclops* must have merely foundered in a gale or storm, that blow that swept the Carolinas on the 10th of March. It was a filler in the papers, and not all of them at that. By spring 1919 the story with all the newspaper litter skipping down the street was swept from the public mind.

Behind the scenes, however, the Navy didn't buy it. With a refreshing deferral to the facts, it declared the *Cyclops* was a true mystery, the "greatest in its annals." The Navy had known the gale could have nothing to do with it. Given the known speed of the *Cyclops* (less than 250 miles per day), she could only have been around the Tropic of Cancer on the 9th of March and off Florida on the 10th, far south of the storm off the Carolinas.

Notwithstanding this the Navy had investigated the publicized rumor that the small freighter s.s. *Amalco* had sighted the vessel battling heavy seas off the Carolinas. This all stemmed from a shadowy informant in Boston, a Mr. Freeman, who wrote them and declared: "log of ss AMALCO shows that on night of March ninth USS CYCLOPS was about five miles distant. March tenth heavy gale damaged the AMALCO."

The Navy immediately tracked down her captain, Charles Hillyer. An agent of ONI interviewed him and confirmed that while 80 miles south of Nantucket Light Ship on the 9th or 10th of March Hillyer encountered what he called the worst gale ever. "The heavy seas which washed over the ship strained the hull and machinery badly, stove in the lifeboats, wrecked the bridge, carried away the topmost light, and all but sent the *Amalco* to the bottom." Unfortunately, Hillyer also immediately denied that the *Cyclops* "was seen by himself or by the men aboard the *Amalco*. He assured me that no such entry had been made in the log. He stated that each night he read over the day's log, and if correct he signed it. If it contained a mistake he had it corrected before signing."

Thus ended the only alleged clue to link the *Cyclops* with a storm. Selma's last hold-out to link her husband with an honorable albeit prosaic death in the line of duty was gone.

The theory that the *Cyclops'* heavy cargo of manganese somehow shifted and sent the vessel to the briny had little practical merit as well. Richard Momsen's letter explaining how the *Cyclops* was loaded set in place many specifics, from the number of buckets of manganese loaded in each hold to the number of stevedores working on loading the ship; and even more important to the discussion at hand Momsen set down a description of what the *Cyclops'* holds actually looked like and how she was loaded.

Momsen's information was based on his personal interviews with E. G. Fontes, "who handles most of the manganese ore" for Morro de Minha Manganese Company, the contractors for the ore. Fontes reminded Momsen that The Brazilian Coaling Company (Cory Brothers) were in charge of loading the vessel and that they have been loading manganese since 1901, "practically from the beginning of the export business in Brazil." Momsen clarified for his superiors that it appears the "only ship loaded by them that was lost was the 'Cambire' [Ed. *Gambier*], a British sailing vessel which was sunk— some years ago— immediately outside of the harbor of Rio . . ." and which, Momsen clarified quickly, was "without any crew having been lost in the disaster."

Gambier was a far cry from the huge *Cyclops*, and not just in hull design and size. Mr. Fontes praised the great vessel as a "self trimmer," meaning a ship equipped with "special dunnage" (stowing, insulating or other material to adjust and trim her holds and secure cargo). This special dunnage consisted of a section of horizontal wooden platform "to prevent the ore from coming into contact with the ship's plates." On the port and starboard sides of the holds "there were two diagonal, sloping board platforms to prevent a like pressure on the ship's plates." Momsen added: "This is considered to be ample dunnage." The diagonal wood platforms would also prevent a dangerous shift of cargo if the *Cyclops* should roll at sea, and this

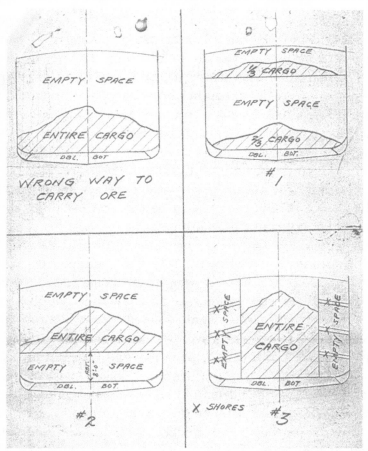

The one wrong way and 3 better ways to load manganese. Cyclops *was loaded in a combination of No. 2 and No. 3.*

would aid in preventing the ship from capsizing. Also, it would tend to separate the manganese from any coal dust remaining at the bottom of the hold, as that would have settled on the plates underneath the wood dunnage (which was 8 feet over the bottom of the hold).

The only problem Fontes could see was that there were no between-deck holds, so that the "ore was necessarily all laden in the bottom of the hold." Since the weight was on the bottom of the vessel, could it have broken in twain? This, too, is a popular theory, but it is effectually nullified by Momsen's report.

When the *Cyclops* sailed, she "drew 33 feet of water aft and

29 feet at her bow." Fontes was certain that the *Cyclops* could easily have "drawn 35 feet of water without being overloaded." Worley personally supervised the loading. The night before sailing, noticing she was heavy in the stern, he ordered more cargo in the bow to "equalize her buoyancy." Fontes stated that the ship carried 10,800 tons of manganese and could have carried at least 2,000 more. This would seem to be correct, as he recalled Worley saying the *Cyclops* could handle 12,000 tons. However, Worley did not want to sign for more than 10,000 tons (no doubt due to its weight and contract specifications). The difference of 800 tons would be determined upon arrival in the United States in the usual manner.

Both the supervisor of loading vessels, Manual Pereira, and Captain William Lowry, verified Fontes' statements. Worley was well aware of the heavier weight of his cargo and, though the Cory Brothers were in charge, he knew the *Cyclops* and he made sure the cargo was evenly loaded. We can almost hear the voices of all those who gave evidence against Worley's personality: that he was a drunk, poor navigator, brutal and strict . . . but that he was "a good sailorman." The seadog truly knew ships and cargo. . .and especially he knew the *Cyclops*.

There was also little chance the wood dunnage was crushed. When the loading began the buckets (which contained 900 kilos each of manganese) were lowered all the way to the dunnage and then dumped. When the hold began to fill, the buckets were dumped 25 feet over the rising manganese pile.

From the records, the *Cyclops* was loaded as follows.

Hold

1 forward	1,624 buckets
2	1,995 buckets
3	2,250
4	1,875
5 aft	2,870
	10,604 by tally
	10,835 by draft

Thus Momsen ends his 7 page report with a certain amount of frustration, stating he has not been able to find any evidence that this vessel was improperly loaded. His subsequent conversations with "shipping men, naval men, and other competent persons" provided no clue what could explain the mystery of the *Cyclops*' disappearance. He must only consider that perhaps some defect in the *Cyclops* allowed her to break in two, as happens "to steamers on the Great Lakes." This he attributed to the heavier nature of her cargo. Momsen's referral to this is rather weak, given the *Cyclops* was shy 2000 tons of cargo by contract.

Improper loading is but one theory that remains with us to this day. The post popular theory along these lines is that coal dust from *Cyclops*' previous cargo of coal mixed with the manganese. A mixture of coal dust and manganese dioxide could actually provide a very volatile and combustible atmosphere in the ship's holds, one that could without warning suddenly blow the vessel to bits. It is ironic that this theory has been perpetually recited in any regurgitation of the *Cyclops* saga for the last 95 years as the logical and "scientific" solution, for it was dropped by the Navy, to their credit, after only a few days of research in 1918.

On May 7, 1918, Richmond B. Levering of the Department of Justice, sent a letter to Captain Edward McCauley, head of ONI's investigation. This letter puts it all in context, and it is best to quote it *in toto*.

Dear Captain McCauley

In going about the investigation of the loss of the Cyclops upon the theory which is chemically sound, suggested by Lt. Commander Wilkinson's office, that the cargo of manganese dioxide would be highly incendiary when mixed with some of the material which we are working with, hexamethy-lene tetramine, I secured samples of the actual ore, as it is being shipped from Rio on these ships.

The laboratory reports to me today that it is exceedingly unlikely that sufficiently ideal conditions could have been created to cause any great incendiary effect with hexamethylene tetramine, and they advised me that they consider this particular theory of her destruction as almost untenable.

However, in working with the material, similar to the Cyclops' cargo, they have come upon what appears to be a very much more practical suggestion. This ore is an extremely oxidizing agent, and that a mixture of this material with coal dust forms a highly inflammable compound. Inasmuch as this ship was a collier, it is possible that no great care was taken in cleaning her out before taking on the cargo of manganese dioxide, and there might have been sufficient coal dust accumulated in her storage spaces to have made the combustible combination.

They report to me that a mixture of coal dust and manganese dioxide can be set on fire very easily.

I have arranged for a very thorough investigation of the conditions attending the loading of this ore at Rio, as the underwriters of vessels here inform me that the manganese cargoes have proved very troublesome from many aspects to all of the ships which were in this trade, and that there is good ground for watching the situation.

I have arranged for the cooperation of Mr. H. E. Inman, who is Lloyd's executive officer at Rio de Janeiro, who will give us the benefit of the service of several of his inspectors who may be relied upon. We have an additional arrangement with the representative of the oil company at Rio.

I am sending a copy of this report to Mr. Bielaski, and would appreciate very much if you would give me any information you have bearing on the question of how thoroughly the coal compartments of the Cyclops were cleaned out before loading the manganese ore.

Yours very truly,
Richmond Levering

McCauley, however, already had Momsen's letter. He wrote back on May 10, two days after receiving Levering's letter, and it is reproduced here.

<u>Personal & Confidential</u>

My dear Mr. Levering,

I am in receipt of your letter dated May 7, 1918, in regard to the results of your investigations into the loss of the Cyclops.

The Navy Department has accurate figures showing the amount of coal on hand at the time of loading manganese and the amount taken on board subsequently. And for that there is a suspicion in your mind that coal may have been left in the bunkers and covered with manganese, the result being a combustible combination. This theory, however, is untenable, due to the fact that the cargo was not stored in the bunkers but in the regular cargo space.

I shall be pleased to receive any information obtained by you in the course of your investigations, especially any details which may lead to a plausible conclusion regarding the loss of the Cyclops.

Levering wrote back on May 14, 1918, stating in part:

We will drop this theory from the investigation as suggested by you. I merely emphasized this once more as our laboratory feels that in the future any ship which has carried coal should be carefully cleaned before loading manganese dioxide in the same space.

It was cut and dried.

Amongst the many theories trying to explain the *Cyclops'* disappearance there are two theories of particular importance. Both come from Naval officers who served aboard the vessel at one point. The first was from Lieutenant Commander Mahlon

S. Tisdale in an article published by no less than the *Naval Institute Proceedings* for January 1920, in which he made what appeared to be an ironclad case for the *Cyclops* capsizing.

This article *Did the Cyclops Turn Turtle?* has proven to be an influential source for a number of reasons. One, it influenced Josephus Daniels, the then-Secretary of the Navy, to support this notion; two, when the Bermuda Triangle enigma gained such popularity in the 1970s Triangle fever inspired an entire genre of books and documentaries which resurrected the old article and used it as one of the logical theories to account for the ship's disappearance (other than that of the Bermuda Triangle enigma, of course). The entire article was even reprinted in the 1977 paperback *Riddle of the Bermuda Triangle*, edited by Martin Ebon, a compendium of theories, articles and interviews on the Bermuda Triangle phenomenon. Ebon accentuated the article's authority by noting it appeared first in 1920 "and therefore has an immediacy and closeness to the subject that cannot be equaled by narratives written at a later date." Therefore Tisdale's article is much still with us, strengthened by the fact that it appeared in the prestigious journal of the US Navy.

Regrettably, what anthologists into the Bermuda Triangle didn't know was that in the April 1920 issue of the same *Naval Institute Proceedings* Tisdale's theory was laid to rest, in such a way, one must add, that it reflected badly on Tisdale. Commander I.I. Yates was the author. He took exception to something that Tisdale recalled Worley saying. It was actually the cornerstone upon which Tisdale's arguments were built.

Tisdale had recalled that while on his 10 day stay on the vessel he noted the topside tank hatches had been left unsecured. When groping forward during heavy weather he was shocked to find that each one could potentially fill with water as the great vessel shipped seas over her deck. He secured each one as best he could and then reported on the bridge. The sea-dog wasn't concerned at all. "He laughed at my earnestness and said that they were *always left off* in accordance with instructions from the navy yard (I won't mention the yard, as I never saw the circular during my time in the colliers), as the air was 'better for the bitumastic.'[39] The skipper was worrying not at all about the tanks. We were cavorting around the old ocean like a frisky colt, but, true enough, were taking no green seas over the main deck. As I have said, we were light and high out of the water. The Captain wasn't worrying about his cargo."

Tisdale's theory for her final voyage depended on the top-side tanks also being unsecured. He speculated that if the *Cy-clops* rolled to one side, sending her heavy cargo shifting, the topside tanks, with their hatches unsecured, would have filled with water and increased her roll until she quickly capsized. This would have plunged the vessel keel over, capsizing her before any could get out.

It seemed plausible until Yates' article refuted it a few months later. Every Navy man knew that the *Cyclops* was berthed at Norfolk. Feeling compelled to defend the Norfolk Navy Yard, Yates wrote his article. No such instruction had ever been issued, he declared, and after exonerating the Yard he included interviews with the captains of the *Neptune* and *Jupiter*, sister colliers to the *Cyclops.* Both officers made it plain that in a light condition, as the *Cyclops* was when Tisdale was aboard for a short stay, the topside tanks were probably filled with water anyway in order to maintain ballast. So it was immaterial whether the hatch covers were secured. Also, it seemed certain that Tisdale didn't understand Worley's notorious sense of humor. "Captain Worley was always making jokes," W.J. Kelton, Captain of the *Neptune*, recalled, "and was author of the celebrated 'Tame Lion' story of 1910-11 which was given such publicity that the Department wrote him to put ashore any lion he had on board. It is probable that Captain Worley answered Lieutenant Commander Tisdale in jest on being taken to task for leaving his covers off."

Tisdale looked bad, hasty and ill-informed. The idea about the *Cyclops* "turning turtle" was essentially laid to rest.[40]

---

[39] Meaning it was better to let the asphalt coating of the tanks breathe.
[40] Amazingly, Yates also proposed the *Cyclops* capsized, but his theorizing didn't even have clues let alone evidence.

The next Naval officer to offer his own theory is none other than Conrad A. Nervig, and the conduit for his claims is also the *Naval Institute Proceedings*. For that reason alone his theory that the *Cyclops* suddenly split in twain has never been challenged as a solid, reliable theory. It is the last theory offered from a firsthand eyewitness, but its survival and prestige is probably more due to the fact that no other firsthand witness was around anymore to challenge a theory that was in essence more unfounded than Tisdale's. As already noted, Nervig's influential article was published in 1969.

Memory lapse after *51 years* is quite understandable. But there are some things that Nervig simply had never known, especially about what went on in Rio de Janeiro after he was transferred. His theory hinged on improper loading. In his article, he declared that only Forbes knew how to load manganese. Since Nervig assumed he was still under arrest, he asserted that Worley had carelessly assigned some junior officer to load the vessel. Not only is this contrary to Worley's character, it is obvious from the facts that Nervig had no idea about how the ship was actually loaded and he didn't have a genuine working knowledge of how expert his bucko sea captain really was. Moreover, the ultimate authority was by contract the United States & Brazil Steamship Company, and Admiral Caperton had relayed written orders to Worley on how the ship was to be loaded. In essence, Worley basically wasn't in charge. The Cory Brothers took over and controlled loading. Worley only stopped the loading at the contract limit and ordered more loaded forward.

Nervig's memory problems are also cause for caution in other areas. By the time this article came out, he must have been 82 or 83 years old. His honesty should not be questioned, but there is much in his memory that should be.

Examples of Nervig's poor memory include his complete avoidance of Worley's alcoholic problems, although having been close to him on watch he could hardly have avoided the smell of liquor others frequently mentioned. Coming away from reading Nervig's article, *The Cyclops Mystery*, one is struck more with the idea that Worley could have been pro-gressing toward insanity. But considering that drunkenness is the most incontrovertible aspect of Worley's career at sea we would be better to suspect drinking or the DTs as the cause of some of his unusual episodes rather than lunacy. Worley was, to Nervig, merely a ruthless, "bucko" sea captain from days long gone. As true as this character synopsis is, alcohol un-questionably played a role in some of the captain's unusual behavior and outbursts.

Nervig's theory of the vessel breaking in two was also based on his remembrance that he saw the deck undulating, that is, conforming to the swells and the synchronicity of the waves. These were signs of "bad contractions," meaning the ship's back could break at any time. Although he brought it to Wor-ley's attention, he recalled only his superior dismissal: "Son, she'll last as long as we do."

This is not a small point at all. The Navy investigated every lead, including Albert Winkle for bigamy, but in all the pa-perwork amassed there is no statement where another seaman ever reported this "undulating" problem developing, and there were many who wrote in.

The whole notion that the *Cyclops* had a "weak back" stems from a series of articles in July 1930 that looked back on the mystery. The source was an unnamed former officer who was transferred off just before the vessel left Newport News, which makes it sound like Ensign Ryder. He was now living in Maine. There simply is nothing to Ensign Ryder's (presumably) claims 12 years later.

Likewise there are reasons to be wary of Nervig's memory. In later life his memory may have been contaminated by other experiences in his career at sea (or even the 1930 series), and he applied these to his last voyage on the *Cyclops.* It is possible therefore that what he recollects of "bad contractions" 51 years after-the-fact applies to other, older ships on which he served.

Speaking about the *Cyclops'* launching in 1910, Captain Kelton of the *Neptune*, who was one of her first officers under Worley, was quoted in Yates' 1920 article as follows: "The Cyclops had just been delivered from Cramps and was unusually well built, in fact Cramps lost money in building her, and no caulking of seams or butts was found necessary after her first cruise to Europe to coal the squadron at Kiel. The Cyclops was the most seaworthy of her sister ships, but she rolled to wide angles."

One significant gaff in Nervig's memory underscores the caution that must be taken in accepting some of his details. His presence is most significant in the documentation by his absence, and this extends to a gem of a find— the officers' list for the voyage *south*. Bureau of Navigation pulled the jackets and there was a communiqué listing all aboard. Nowhere was Nervig listed. He was not an officer on board the ship!

It took some time to get all the officer records from the Military Personnel Archives in St. Louis. In the meantime I toyed with the idea that Nervig was actually Albert Winkle and that he had survived the sinking of the *Cyclops* and was, in his own way, giving us her final moments couched in theoretical terms. I thought this, perhaps an unforgivably romantic idea, because there is much in Nervig's recollection which proves he was acquainted with Worley and the conditions aboard. Yet the records show he was not aboard. When I finally got them, having inserted Nervig's name in my request, I discovered through his record of movements that he had actually been "a passenger only" on the *Cyclops* on the voyage south. He had no assigned duties whatsoever. This fact Nervig never mentioned in later life. His memory of the voyage was that he was an officer on board with assigned duties. It may be that when Cain was committed by Asper that Nervig was asked to take over his duties. This is natural to expect and easy to accept. But nevertheless that is not Nervig's memory. He even claimed that because Worley had liked him so much he had tried to prevent his transfer at Rio, when all the time Nervig was already assigned to the *Glacier* and was in transit to take up the duties of none other than Winkle.

The attempt by Worley to prevent Nervig's transfer is a confusing point as well, if it really did occur the way Nervig remembered. One would think if the Navy found out that Worley went to Admiral Caperton and tried to prevent a transfer they would have tracked down the officer— Nervig— and questioned him. But there is no evidence they did. However, blame for this may be attributed to ONI's attitude of compile and file at the time, for it seems Nervig did try to communicate. Momsen sent a cable to the Secretary of State on April 30: "Information here indicates that Assistant Paymaster Carroll G. Page was aboard the CYCLOPS, when ship departed for United States. Commander in Chief [Caperton] suggests Navy Department consult United States ship GLACIER for possible further information." Sadly, there is no evidence they did talk to Nervig. His interview could have clarified so much when his memory was still fresh.

Nervig also claims that a man was drown by being knocked over at Rio. This may be the case, but there is no record of this. Worley's own signature can be found on the request for a Board of Inquiry over the engine cylinder, but there is no B of I over the death of a crewman and no mention made in the Press of such a death.

Out of all the letters Navy men sent into ONI, there are also no stories of Worley walking around at night in longjohns and wearing a derby hat. Worley was well-known to carry a walking cane while on land, but did he walk around the *Cyclops* at night dressed in such a manner? It is very possible, and this in itself would argue that his problems, either mental or with alcohol, were getting worse on this final voyage.

Yeoman Roberts declared that Worley would shoo everybody off the bridge, take an ignorant Greek and pilot the ship himself. Walking around in longjohns, topped with a derby hat, and poking a walking cane, seems far more innocuous to the ship's safety than this, but it is just as odd.

Nervig is clearly confused at some points. Moreover, in those 51 years since his strange voyage with the mad seadog he had become one of Hollywood's top editors, editing such films as *A Tale of Two Cities, Northwest Passage, King Solomon's Mines* and *The Bad and the Beautiful*. He is the first recipient of an Oscar for editing (in 1934) and shared an Oscar for editing *King Solomon's Mines*. A bit of that dramatic world could have influenced his story of the *Cyclops'* last voyage. I have incorporated some of his observations in the reconstruction of the voyage, but it is only fair that we hold some in reservation. With time he may have confused the details of sailing on another ship and another voyage. He died in 1980 at the age of 91 after a long and accomplished life.

On the other hand, we may wonder if we would not have more disturbing details from Nervig had the Navy acted upon Caperton's suggestion. Whatever Nervig told his superiors, Caperton thought it worthy to have Momsen alert ONI.

Jeremiah Bourk's criticism of superficiality seems to ring true in many avenues of the investigation. On one occasion Bourk was particularly irked by Edwin L. Reed. He was a main conduit in Chicago, where Bourk lived, for information passing between San Francisco's ONI and Washington. He virtually retyped every report and sent it along. However, the only pavement pounding he had to do was to visit Bourk. He was so fatigued, he asked to take off his jacket and recline on Bourk's sofa. Bourk kept a narrow and disapproving eye on him as he gave his long story. Another time he borrowed 25 cents off him. All he ever took was notes. This superficiality that irked Bourk was not just in Chicago. He was able to see more documents in Washington DC and still thought the investigation was superficial. In many respects this seems to be true. There is no evidence that ONI talked to Denby or Harris regarding Gottschalk. They didn't make an effort with Nervig.

Even a year later, officers didn't know what had finally been accepted and resolved in the case. As late as March 14, 1919, long after the war was over, a tip came into the Navy's Third District (New York) Communication Service. A Mr. Slechta of Gano, Moore & Company had received a letter from a friend overseas. "Suppose you knew Gottschalk has been summering in Kiel." It seems absurd. But the district superintendent, J.C. Whitly, in a personal note asked his subordinate Ensign Lee to "kindly keep this pretty close until we unearth something more. Want to have bulletin give first info regarding the missing Cyclops." Nothing came of it. Compile and file.

Two years after the war, in 1920, things had changed greatly. The Auxiliary was basically gone. Versailles had changed the post war world. The boys "over there" had long come home and marched under Washington's triumphal arch in New York. The Spanish Flu epidemic had taken its toll. Prohibition and modernism had come, paradoxically at the same time. The post war boom was upon us. People wanted to forget "The Great War" and all its ugly reminders of what the future held. If people wanted to remember the *Cyclops*, it was only because she was now a great unsolved mystery of the deep. Various epilogues had been given the last voyage by crank writers in the usual outlet for crank writers: notes in a bottle. So many off base stories had circulated and gained notoriety that the *Cyclops* had become fodder for the tabloids. Finally, newspapers resurrected that old storm off the Carolinas and acted as if it was just discovered. "Fate of *Cyclops* solved at last."

Behind the scenes, however, a far more intriguing clue had truly surfaced, and this led to a secret epilogue. Not secret because of any conspiracy. The events remained secret because the *Cyclops* wasn't news anymore.

A graying gentleman moored his boat at Kansas City, Missouri, on his way home to Chicago. The deep green of the Mississippi, the variegated colors of its banks in early spring, and the smell of the musty old docks were quite a contrast to where he had been sailing in the bright tropical waters of the Bahamas. Suntanned and whiskered, he was now eyeing the local citizens in hopes of gaining the address of the local Navy outpost. At last he was given the address of the recruiting station. He held mesmerized Lt. Commander John K. Richards. On March 18, 1920, he wrote to the Chief of Operations.

Subject: Possible explanation of loss of U.S.S. CYCLOPS.

1.   This a.m. Mr. Donald J. Fraser of 110 N. Menard Ave., Chicago, Illinois came into the Navy recruiting station at Kansas City, Missouri and imparted to me the following information, which is for-

warded to the Chief of Naval Operations for whatever it is worth.

2.   Mr. Fraser, while cruising off the banks of the Bahamas in February, 1920, was caught in a small hurricane and forced to take shelter behind the nearest land. This land happened to be Gun Key. While exploring the Key and vicinity he went to what is known as the first Riding Rock, a small Key of about 15 acres situated about 8 or 9 miles southwest of Gun Key in the following approximate position: Latitude, 25° 34' 30" N., 79° 15' W. While exploring the beach of this first Riding Rock he came across a quarter of a clinker type boat whose dimensions were approximately those of a Naval lifeboat. Printed on the bow of this piece of wreckage where the letters U S, then a blank, then CYCLO. Mr. Fraser also stated that there was signs of other letters or letter following the O. The above leads me to believe that the final translation could have readily been USS CYCLOPS.

3.   Further, while exploring in this vicinity he found a section of a notebook of the size that is normally used by Naval Navigators in keeping their rough notes. There was considerable writing in this notebook but the action of the sea had made all of it illegible. Mr. Fraser did not bring this notebook with him but carefully buried it under a rock about 25 yards up the beach. Further, he states that there was on the beach a large copper circle which had been smashed until it was absolutely flat, but was of about the size of the normal Naval Franklin Life Buoy.

4.   In addition to this wreckage which he described, he stated that there was a great amount of wooden wreckage that might readily resemble a coaling boat, which he could not definitely identify because of his lack of knowledge of Naval equipments. In exploring waters of the immediate vicinity Mr. Fraser stated that about 2000 yards from the Key first described there was in the water a long dark object which might have been a reef, but which he did not think was one. He stated that if he were to guess as to the identity of the dark object he would say that it was the hull of some vessel.

5.   The Recruiting Officer believes that Mr. Fraser would be on-

ly too pleased to definitely mark a navigational chart of this area in order that the exact situation of the Cyclops described above could be located if the Naval Operations would send to the address given in the first paragraph a chart of this area. Mr. Fraser further states that he would be only too glad to furnish any information that he may have which might enable the Bureau to better corroborate and verify statements given above.

6. From my conversation with Mr. Fraser this morning his attitude and his familiarity with nautical terms, phraseology and other things pertaining to the sea would indicate that the statements given above were based on facts and not conjectures.

John K. Richards.

There seemed no reason for the Navy not to take this seriously. And indeed they did. Admiral R.E. Coontz himself, Chief of Naval Operations, sent a letter to Fraser in Chicago. On April 1 Admiral Coontz received a letter from him.

In reference to your letter dated March 23, concerning Op-16 B, FFR-AM:

Just received your letter this morning. Have been out of town or would have attended to it sooner. Will mark chart to the best of my ability, but will not be able to mark on chart where I placed the navigator's book. To the best of my knowledge I placed the book about 100 yards due west on the beach (North Cat Cay), placing a piece of coral rock weighing about 100 weight. The remains of the whale or row boat lay nearly in a direct line southeast from Gun Cay lighthouse to the nearest point of North Cat Cay, visible at low tide. This is a matter which is rather hard to explain on paper. I intend to get in touch with the Admiral commanding Great Lakes Naval Training Station tomorrow, and perhaps between the two of us we will be able to figure it out. About 500 yards east,[41] by straight-line, from the point North Cat

---

[41] This letter is quoted from the many that the Navy typed out and copied. It contains a significant mistake.

Cay, it looks to me as if there might be the remains of the vessel which lays in about 40 fathoms of water, though it may be a reef, as I did not pay much attention to it at the time.

If there is nothing more to explain at present, I will close for this time. Will do all in my power to help you in this matter.

I remain
Respectfully yours,
D. J. Fraser.

Without waiting for Fraser's details, on April 17, 1920, Coontz decided to act. "You are hereby directed to dispatch some suitable and available vessel of those under your command to Gun Key, Great Bahama Bank," read the order to the Commandant of the 7th Naval District. "There is a strong possibility that the U.S.S. Cyclops would have passed within a short distance of Gun Key in the course of her voyage," continued the order. "The information is of such a definite nature that it seems most important that efforts be made to determine whether or not there is sufficient wreckage there to determine what vessel was wrecked if not the U.S.S. Cyclops."

Admiral Benton C. Decker, the Commandant, decided to go and investigate for himself. His cruiser cast anchor and away he went with a retinue of junior officers and men, some armed with shovels, to land on the desert island.

While he was combing Gun Key, a letter came in from U.S. Naval Training Station, Great Lakes, Illinois, to Naval Operation in Washington. Coontz read:

Mr. D.J. Fraser, 110 Menard St., Chicago, Illinois called at the station recently in compliance with suggestion made to him by the Department that he come here with certain charts. The object of his visit was to secure assistance in indicating on these charts the location of a spot in which Mr. Fraser claims to have found certain material which he believes might have belonged to the late USS Cyclops.

Mr. Fraser was interviewed by Lt. Commander E. J. Foy, who recommended to him that he return one of the charts to the Chief of Naval Operations, showing the point in question. Mr. Fraser while apparently a man of considerable intelligence seemed rather hazy when questioned about the articles which he claims to have discovered; consisting of what he thought might have been the log of the Cyclops and possibly the bow of one of her boats. The impression left here was that there was little probability that Mr. Fraser had discovered anything of value. Still in view of the importance of the subject, it is believed that even a remote possibility might with advantage be investigated.

As this matter has been the subject of correspondence between Mr. Fraser and the Chief of Naval Operations, it is reported now simply to inform the Department of the impressions left here by Mr. Fraser.

What happened to make Fraser so hazy and bestow such a reaction on officers? True, there was significant inconsistency already between Richards' letter and Fraser's own later letter to Coontz. (Richards' letter did not say that Fraser found anything on North or South Cat Cay; he said it was at the First Riding Rock about 9 miles to the southwest. In Fraser's own letter to Coontz he said it was on the Cat Cays, which are a part of the Biminis.) But his recollection of the "articles" he found was still "so definite," as Coontz had put it, that this discrepancy should only have inspired broadening the search.

Admiral Decker also noticed. While walking up and down the Cat Cay beaches he was carefully comparing copies of both Richards' and Fraser's letters. So far they had found nothing. Now bored and tired, lips chapped by the Bahamas salty trade winds, his men were leaning on their shovels awaiting his verdict. Inasmuch as he had so far found nothing on the cay, they would return to Key West. On April 30, he wrote a long letter to Fraser.

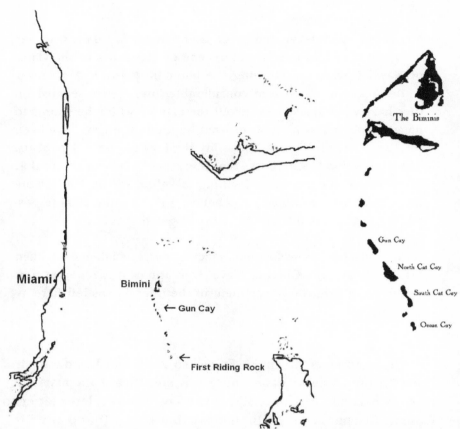

Fraser confused the Navy. According to his account as written down by John Richards he found the debris at the First Riding Rock, the southernmost islet south of the Bimini Islands. The inset shows where Gun Cay is situated in the Bimini chain.

Dear Sir:

There was referred to me a copy of a letter from you to the Chief of Naval Operations dated April 1, 1920, and the letter from Lieut. Comdr. John K. Richards to the same officer, all referring to your experiences in discovering evidences of the wreckage of the U.S.S Cyclops.

I visited Gun Key harbor and walked over the Northern and Southern end of North Cat Key and South Cat Key, for the purpose of discovering the evidence you speak about. I was unable to find any remains of a row boat, tho passing these points about low water. At the Northern end of North Cat Key, I found two or three large stones, possibly two feet in diameter, that showed signs of having been moved, but did not discover any book under them, nor did I see any signs of wreckage of the boat, nor were there any evidences of any wreckage such as you've made in the statement to Lieut. Comdr. Richards. This leads me to make further inquiries from you, with the purpose of securing further information on so important a subject.

(1) During the hurricane, did you anchor in Gun Key harbor?

(2) How did you recognize the harbor?

(3) How did you determine the latitude and longitude given by you in your statement?

(4) How far from your anchorage did you proceed before you sighted this boat, your statement to Lieut. Comdr. Richards, stated that you went to what is known as first Riding Rock, a small Key of about 15 acres, eight or nine miles southwest of Gun Key.

(5) How did you measure the distance; did you proceed in your boat outside or inside; was there any surf?

(6) How did you land and what was the appearance of the small Key from a distance?

(7) What was the characteristics of the beach where you landed: sandy or rocky; smooth or jagged?

It appears that the description given Lieut. Comdr. Richards, and the one contained in your letter, cannot be reconciled; however, if you can, it would be a great favor if you would explain to me the difference.

The last part of your statement of April 1, you speak of a reef or the possible remains of a vessel about 500 yards east from the point North Cat Key. This, of course, is impossible considering the shallow water to the eastward.

I trust you will find it convenient to answer these questions, because it is of great importance that I should clear up this matter, as your statements about the letters on the bow of the whaleboat indicate almost to a certainty that this boat did belong to the Cyclops.

Hoping you will be able to answer my questions, in order that I may continue the investigation, I remain

Very sincerely,

Benton C. Decker
Rear Admiral, U.S.N.
Comdt. 7th Naval District.

It is not surprising that Decker received no reply. Fraser had been cooling for some time. By the time he had hauled himself into the Great Lakes base (a remarkable 20 days after he had promised Coontz), something had already happened to cool his zeal to help the Navy. There, as we know, he gave them a "hazy" recollection. Fraser had succeeded in making the Great Lakes' officers skeptical. But Decker had those astonishing letters in hand. Decker, too, was certain there was something to what Fraser had discovered. Fraser must have received his letter. He must have known the Navy wasn't giving up. But it is clear he never responded.

On paper Fraser was and had been too "definite" despite the slight inconsistencies. Decker was right. The letters on the whaleboat, spelled out by Fraser, definitely meant this wreckage came from the *Cyclops*. Fraser's response was perhaps to simply not respond and leave the Navy with confusion.

Why?

I suspect Fraser's haze and then silence was his defensive reaction to the unexpected interest the Navy showed in his innocent but dutiful report of wreckage. To cut to the chase, should we frankly ask a single pointed question? Namely, was our dear Captain Fraser a rumrunner? In 1919, Prohibition was passed and clandestine rum running into the United States from the Bahamas became a big and profitable business for old mariners. Some even came out of retirement to run the "devil's brew" into the US from the Bahamas. A central staging and storage area was none other than Gun Cay in the Bahamas. A major destination was Chicago. Seeing it as his duty to report the famous ship's wreckage, did he then get nervous in Chicago that a Navy investigation might spoil the hideout and trade of a growing (and in Chicago, violent) business upon which he depended?

Well, one can second-guess it forever. However, either way one slices it the type of wreckage should have compelled Decker to a thorough search of the surrounding islands. If Fraser was confused, Decker was clearly lax. He should have checked out First Riding Rock where, in Richards' summary, Fraser found the bulk of the items.

According to Richards' summary, it was 2000 yards from "Gun Key" where Fraser saw the "reef" that could possibly have been a sunken ship. In Fraser's own letter to the Navy, he got specific and said it was 500 yards *west* from North Cat Cay. Why did Decker make the mistake about "east"? The reason is uncovered in the many triplicates the Navy had of Fraser's letter. "East" exists in all the copies of the letter, but the original is still in the same archive drawer with them, with Fraser's own signature. On this original it clearly reads "west." There had been a typo when a Navy clerk copied the letter for distribution. Therefore Decker had looked in the wrong direction and saw only the very shallow water of the Great Bahama Bank.

What then did Fraser make out of Admiral Decker's letter to him? He must now have been more confused by the Navy's mix up. By May 24, he hadn't yet responded to Decker . . . nor would he ever. Nothing is recorded afterward in the Navy's records, but we may safely surmise the Navy gave up the investigation. The upshot was that Decker scoured the wrong islands, and had a copy of Fraser's letter with a significant, indeed, critical typo.

As it stands today, we know the hulk of the *Cyclops* does not rest 2,000 feet off any of the Bimini cays. It would easily have been found by now. But for a short period wreckage

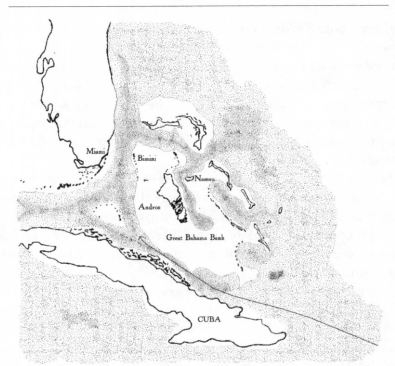

The Cyclops' *course through the Old Bahama Channel, the likely place where she was lost.*

appeared. For a brief window the sea gave us a clue, a clue as to where the *Cyclops* met her fate. It is somewhere in the deep channel off Andros Island, south of the Riding Rocks or possibly further south in the Old Bahama Channel.

Does this location offer any other clues? One thing is incontrovertible. The *Cyclops* was not headed to Germany. She was also far south of any storm. With this understood, we have to accept the *Cyclops* was lost in perfect weather very close to the Bahama islands, Cuba and southern Florida.

This coincidence raises the disturbing questions of Livingston's worst fears— mutiny and treason. Where would be the best place to scuttle a ship and still escape? Somewhere right along here would actually be the perfect location. Could mutineers have waited to blow the ship up here? A small group could get back into the United States relatively easily in the Captain's launch, since it had a motor. Passage to the US wouldn't take long. It would require crossing the Florida Straits to the Keys or sailing the Old Bahama Channel to Cuba and from there to any port of call. Mutineers might head home through Florida; traitors might ship from Havana for faraway places and eventually to Germany or back to plush Brazil.

It is hard to believe that mutineers could do this. Passage requires money. Total destruction of the ship requires skill. To willfully kill hundreds of one's comrades takes something most people do not have. It would also take opportunity most, if not all, of the passengers and select members of the 'Round Robin' did not possess. It takes someone who hates and who has nothing to lose. It would take someone who knew how to blow the ship to bits. And it would have to be a very small group. They weren't trying to create a mystery. They would care less about debris. It might even be in their favor. But they could not afford survivors. There could be no witnesses. How do a few passengers, convicts and crew plan something like that?

Frankly, it seems impossible. Even if the manganese and coal could have been rigged to be a massive bomb, it would still take more than spleen and skill; it would need some command protection. This means treason and not mutiny.

Mutiny also does not explain the actions of Captain Worley at Barbados. No matter what excuse given, he did not need that extra 500 tons of coal, and this coal was not something he would be able to explain away if he intended to return to Baltimore. But all the evidence says that it was not used to take *Cyclops* to Germany. She remained on course. Could it have been used to fuel the bomb?

Perhaps.

But something a little more logistic comes to mind. We have no proof Worley was truly short of funds. Livingston believed 2 and a half *tons* of foodstuffs was taken. Holdsworth's investigation tells us there was much less. Dacosta & Company said it was $1,000.00 worth. Livingston didn't get his figure direct from the source. He had to investigate. What had Worley told him? If the discrepancy is as large as it could be, and Worley certainly had had good relations with 3 paymasters, two of whom went up on embezzlement charges, then Worley could have had lots of extra cash now thanks to his bookkeeping at Barbados. This now gives him and a small group enough passage money out of Cuba.

The tattered whaleboat suggests massive destruction. It seems to be the captain's own launch. As noted, this would have been easiest to launch. A rather poetic sense of justice makes me like to think that if treason occurred the traitors fled the ship in the captain's boat but were captured in the explosion and the boat destroyed, their lives forfeit by the unseen hand of fate, thus wiping out any survivors to ever tell the tale.

Barney Devoe in Paris. This I cannot explain unless it was merely a confused identification. In the early deciphering and transcriptions of Livingston's cablegram, twice the deciphering of the statement after "disturbances en route hither, men confined and one <u>executed</u>" is followed by "also conspired prisoners from the fleet in Brazilian waters" before it was changed to "also had prisoners from the fleet in Brazilian waters." Could disgruntled elements aboard have assisted *Pittsburgh* men in a jail break to free their buddies? Maybe to jump ship, yes, but to completely destroy the vessel this is nigh impossible to believe.

Maybe both happened. That is hard to swallow, but the clues say both. There was some form of disturbance aboard the ship before Barbados. There are lots of clues because of Barbados hard to explain except as premeditated betrayal.

These fit in too neatly with the idea that George Worley had nothing to come back to in America. The excuses about selling everything can more logically be explained by Selma having found out about the two prostitutes in Norfolk that Worley frequently visited on the sly. Separation is suggested by her actions thereafter. She moved to Port Orchard and there remained. She put up as good a face as possible to assuage any belief her daughter's father was a traitor. Maybe she had hoped to get back together. Maybe she didn't want divorce. But from George Worley's point of view he probably had nothing to come back to. He needed no surgery. But he needed to make this voyage.

It might be better and more honorable to close by deferring to a more prosaic end of the vessel. The amount of lumber indicates that what Fraser saw was the dunnage, the trimming the *Cyclops* carried to insulate the manganese in her holds. Had the vessel capsized, it would seem certain the manganese would burst open the hatches and rain down to the bottom. Most any capsizing ship experiences a 360 roll underwater in which it comes back right side up and settles on its keel or side on the bottom of the briny. The wood dunnage would then float up and drift with the prevailing current. Given the Old Bahama Channel's current, this would be northward to the Riding Rocks. Considering that Fraser saw the wreckage almost 2 years after the disappearance of the vessel the wreckage could have drifted for some time or, very possibly, remained on the beach for quite some time.

There are problems with both scenarios, but it is fruitless to debate it. We can only be sure that the wreckage wasn't floating around when the Navy scoured the islands in March and April 1918.

There I have to leave it, for it is not a story that can be told any longer. The *Cyclops'* fate is an empty sea preceded by dark clues, circumstantial evidence, and followed by rumor. Germans and pro-Germans may surround every facet of the final voyage, but this nation is built upon millions, if not over 100,000 million Germans. They've proved fiercely loyal. In neutrality it was their privilege to pick sides, and there were many Americans who preferred the Kaiser to the King. Worley was indeed one of them. But he seemed too much of a dolt to be valuable in a plot; too drunk for a spy cell to depend on . . . but, alas, drunk enough to be a dupe.

George Wichman Worley really belongs to us and not to Germany anyway. He jumps from the pages of Jack London's San Francisco rather than Faust. He was an essentially American character, perhaps the last true seadog of which America can boast. He was clearly a complex personality. He could command admiration for his sailorly skills, earn respect from those he could use, while at the same time be completely inadequate as a navigator, hopelessly under the influence of liquor, brutal as a skipper and, in his last voyages, inconsistent and without purpose in his discipline. The latter might be explained by the fact he had so many regular Navy men on board. He couldn't stand them and he clearly discriminated between his own Auxiliary men and the Regulars. He didn't take to having authority over him, and the encroachment of the regular Navy implied that oversight was not far behind. And there is no doubt that he began to shift blame onto his men, even to the point of claiming a plot existed against him. The first time the Navy tried him (for Witchardt's beheading) he left. The last time, just before this major cruise, he complained bitterly and said he would leave.

Yet there is no denying that throughout his life George Worley had likeable qualities, though toward the end they became but a pocket in a very dislikable jacket. In later life he seldom reached into this pocket to retrieve anything of his sarcastic humor. When he did, he could entertain most anybody with his "fund of tales." There was truth to them and there was exaggeration. All had entertainment value. It was probably as important to Worley that he was entertaining himself as that he was entertaining the hearer. Humor had a purpose. It allowed him to mock decorum and establishment.

It is easy to succumb to Livingston's gut instinct to dislike Worley and imagine a "fate worse than sinking" based on this. But even with what we have discovered we must concede that as dislikable as Worley might have been, logical explanations can be given for stopping at Barbados and for all he did when leaving it. It is true that Worley turned south at Barbados and did not fly the homeward bound pennant. In light of Fraser's tip, which indicates the vessel was on course when she sank, Worley's actions upon leaving Barbados could even be construed as clever. The old seadog knew how infiltrated the coasts were with spies. He could merely have been leading them off his actual trail before heading northward. The same can be said for implying Bermuda was on his course. To his credit (and defense), it can be easily imagined the old seadog was throwing red herrings about to protect his course. He might have left Rio quietly for the same reason. He might have asked Gottschalk to refrain from admitting he was leaving until after they were underway, in this way protecting his time of exit from local spies. One might even view his overshooting of Bahia on the trip south to have this purpose behind it. With very little leapwork in imagination this could also explain why the *Cyclops* came in from the north at Bahia when Nervig saw the vessel lumber in on her return trip. The seadog was not one to justify himself to his crew and officers. He may have intentionally not told Forbes what he was up to in order to bait his executive. It may have provided Worley with some entertainment to chew a man out and send him to the brig.

But without a doubt 500 tons of extra coal and some extra foodstuffs raises suspicious brows. Livingston says it was a ton of meat and vegetables. Harold Holdsworth says in was only 180 pounds. It is hard to imagine only 180 pounds of foodstuffs, the weight of an average man, costing near 1,000 dollars. Truth lies somewhere in between both figures . . . unless Worley padded the amount to embezzle some of it.

The old seadog *was* a bastard to his men. Even his officers hated him. The fact Dixon got off at trial at Norfolk condemns Witchardt as the beast other Navy men said he was. It also condemns his master who so wanted a bucko mate to keep his seamen in line.

To say Worley was the American Captain Bligh, however, does Worley and Bligh a great injustice. Worley was a crude Barbary Coast tavern keeper who hated authority whereas Bligh was an overbearing martinet maintained in power by an establishment. Our seadog is a rogue. But he was possibly less of a Captain Bligh because of the era in which he lived more than because of any temperamental differences. It is very possible that had Worley lived 100 years earlier, as Nervig fancied his character should have, that he could have been the victim of any number of mutinies. The existence of wireless in Worley's days severely curtailed the incentive for crews to mutiny. It would be too easy for an officer to call for help. Too easy for other ships to set course and come alongside the mutinied vessel. Too easy for a mutineer to swing on the yardarm back at Norfolk.

But had there been no wireless in 1918, I think it certain the *Cyclops* would have succumbed to one. The world of the sea was in the throes of changing. It was at the threshold of a new era governed by new communications. Marconi vanquished the old world of the silent, mysterious abyss. Yet into this new era the remnants of that old era of Captain Ahabs and Blighs were still treading. In that silent era such stern characters were the force that bent an iron crew to their will and kept the vessel on course and to its purpose far from a friendly port.

This was the world of young Fred Wichman. At age 15 in 1877 he had already seen the seas as a cabin boy. All the elements of two different eras came briefly together at the time to allow many Fred Wichmans to get into the new Auxiliary Navy in 1899.

Who can tell what such an atmosphere was capable of instilling in the crew between decks? It is the lack of finding a mutineer that dissuades us, albeit hesitantly, to believe there could have been mutiny or treason. Yet the location of the debris makes for an odd and unsettling coincidence. For if it did happen, it could only have been pulled off where Captain Fraser spotted the debris. Only from this area, remote but accessible to southern Florida, could an escaping crew get back into the United States, Cuba or the Bahamas, and then disappear.

Maybe it happened. Maybe a small group did get away. One would have to try and investigate each crewman's family to find if there is any hint that one of their boys came back for any period of time under a new identity. That is beyond my desire. I leave that to some other in the future.

At this late stage in the mystery of the *Cyclops*, let us rather give George Worley all the benefits of the doubt. But innocence is a big word. It is not probity. It carries with it no intention of perseverance. Nothing in the state of being innocent implies anything proactive. In the end, even Worley's defense must concede he was very dislikable. The seadog could have been a very loyal American, but it didn't change what he was. He was a brutal, mean, drinking bucko captain. And for every cause there is an effect. The fate of the *Cyclops*, whatever it was, cannot stand independent of the character of her taciturn master.

What to make of it? In the long run, what to finally say? Who knows? But something happened aboard the *Cyclops* that was neither prosaic nor expected. The US Navy boasts today it has never had a mutiny. They may still officially do so. But when considering the strange last voyage of the U.S.S. *Cyclops*, who can be sure? To this day, the only true statement remains that of then-President Woodrow Wilson: "Only God and the sea know where the great ship has gone."

Epilogue

The Navy Department drafted various versions of its official opinion to be given out to all who continue to enquire. After going through a few versions, its opinion was finally settled. The following is still handed out today to any curious person asking about the loss of what is now called "The Greatest Mystery in the Annals of the Navy."

Since her departure [Barbadoes] there has been no trace of the vessel. The disappearance of this ship has been one of the most baffling mysteries in the annals of the Navy, all attempts to locate her having been proved unsuccessful. Many theories have been advanced, but none that satisfactorily accounts for her disappearance. There were no enemy submarines in the western Atlantic at that time, and in December 1918 every effort was made to obtain information from German sources regarding the disappearance of the vessel. Information was requested from all attachés in Europe with the result that it is definite that neither German U-boats nor German mines came into the question.

Length: 520 feet. Beam: 65 feet. Depth of hold: 36.9 feet. 12, 900 gross tons.

Naval officers of the vessel	15
Naval enlisted men of the crew	221
Naval officers carried as passengers	6
Naval enlisted men carried as passengers	64
U .S. Marines carried as passengers	2
U.S. Consul at Rio carried as passenger	1
Total	309

Bibliography

Due to space it is impossible to list every document, including each telegram, from which some information was gleaned. However, those listed below are the most important and form the focal point of the investigation. The reader can consult the Record Group 59 for State Department papers, and Boxes 1068-1070 at the National Archives for the Navy investigation paperwork.

2nd Endorsement, No. IO-F4-2 Bureau of Construction and Repair, *Cyclops* – Stability (Standard Oil Co's let. To Sec. Navy, April 17, 1918).

#2061 United States Pacific Fleet, USS Flagship *Pittsburgh*, 4 February 1918, to Commanding Officer *Cyclops*, instructions on how to load manganese while in Rio de Janeiro.

Account of interview with Thomas John Davies, Chief Officer of the British s.s. *Vestris*

American Embassy, S Rue De Chaillot, Paris XVIE), relaying the letter from Mrs. Porter to Berne's US Military Attaché, Berne, Switzerland, August 31, 1918, C.L. Chandler.

Assistant Supervisor Naval Auxiliaries, transfer of officers' records, January 23, 1919.

Avery, C.S., (Operative), collection of reports, Office Aid for Information, Fifth Naval District, Norfolk, of local people regarding George W. Worley.

Bassett, F.R., US Naval Training Station Great Lakes, Illinois, Report on visit by D. J. Fraser, 20th April 1920.

Burrous, Robert,   RE: G.W. Worley, missing commander of the collier 'Cyclops,'   April 26, 1918.

Bose, W., Bureau of Construction and Repairs, letter to Commander I.I. Yates, February 2, 1920, in regards request for *Cyclops* loading information and Tisdale article.

Brainard, D.L., US Military Attaché, Legation of the US, Lisbon, Portugal, letter to Secretary of State November 25, 1918.

Bushman, W., report to Director of Naval Intelligence Re: Captain George Worley.

Cable from F.W. Taylor, captain of s.s. *Lydie*, concerning conversation with Captain Lowry of the Brazilian Steamship Company, September 18, 1918.

Caperton, W.B., Admiral, January 29, 1918, to Captain John E. Pond, commanding officer *Pittsburgh*, ordering Board of Inquiry aboard *Cyclops*.

    "   "   Report of Board of Investigation on Damage to Main engines of *Cyclops*, Feb. 4, 1918.

Cipher telegram, Department of State, March 27, 1918, to American Consul Barbados: "Telegram present whereabouts of U.S.S. CYCLOPS or explain delayed arrival Baltimore. Lansing."

Cipher telegram, Department of State to American Consul, Barbados, April 15, 1918: "CYCLOPS believed to be lost. Consider very carefully all circumstances surrounding her and crew and passengers while in Barbados and telegraph full report with opinion or relation to disappearance of vessel. Were any suspicious or significant remarks or actions of master or crew noted? What messages did master receive and how much coal and supplies taken aboard? Answer urgent. Lansing."

Clark, Kenneth, report on interview with Barbados rep S.C. Foster, general manager of DaCosta & Company, June 6, 1918.

Clephane, Louis, report on interview with Charles Hillyer, captain of the s.s. *Amalco*, June 7, 1918, Fifth Naval District, Norfolk.

Commandant, B.F. Hutchison, Acting, to 7th District, April 20, 1920, ordering search of areas specified by Donald Fraser.

Confidential dispatch, Livingston, Consul, April 17, 1918, to Secretary of State. Time 2 p.m., Rec'd 9:25 p.m., Washington DC.

Conner, J.E., letter to Captain Burk, US Secret Service, 30 May 1918.

Coontz, Admiral R.E., Chief of Naval Operations, to Commandant 7 District, Subject U.S.S Cyclops; possible wreckage from.

"   "   letter to D. Fraser, Op. 16-B FFR:AM, 23rd March 1918.

Churchill, M, Director of Military Intelligence, to A Bruce Bielaski, Chief, Bureau of Investigation, investigation of G.W. Worley and *Cyclops*, September 13, 1918.

Decker, Admiral Benton C., 7th Naval District, letter to Donald J. Fraser, Chicago, Illinois, 30 April 1920.

Decker, Denton C. , From Director ONI to Officer-in-Charge, Mail Censorship Office, "Persons with whom Lt. Commander Worley would communicate if possible," August 27, 1918.

First Naval District, Aid For Information, Subject: Information concerning U.S.S. Collier *Cyclops*, 9-7-1918.

Fowler, O.W., to Intelligence Officer USS *Cyclops* informing him of tampered lenses and requesting a report be made.

Fraser, Donald J. letter to Admiral R.E. Coontz, April 1, 1920, in reference to letter of March 23rd concerning OPP16-B FFR AM.

Gass, C.J. Report of Ensign Ryder while aboard *Cyclops*, Custom House, New York, April 21, 1918.

"   "   Report on Paul Roberts., August 10, 1918.

Glover, J.S., Machinist, Optical Shop Norfolk, Navy Yard, letter to Bureau of Naval Intelligence, Washington DC, February 11, 1918.

"   "   RE: ASAT *Amphion* gun lenses and possible correction of problems, if not sabotage, 3-11-1918.

Gottschalk, A.L.M., Consul General, letter to Brig. General David L. Brainard, February 6, 1918.

Haley, Henry S., letter to War Department RE: Cyclops and G.W. Worley, June 15, 1918.

Hengstler, Herbert C., Acting Director of Consular Service, letter to Miss Clara Aimee Gottschalk, regarding brother A.L.M. Gottschalk's effects, September 3, 1918.

"   "   letter to Richard P. Momsen, Rio de Janeiro, September 10, 1918, regarding disposition of A.L.M. Gottschalk's unfinished business.

Hil, (ONI operative), Rio de Janeiro, response to Navintel cable April 18, 1918.

"   "   Rio, May 13, 1918, report of interview with W. Van Dyke.

Lansing's cipher telegram to Livingston, Barbados, March 20, 1918: "Has U.S.S Cyclops sailed, if so when? Answer immediately." Livingston's response March 21, 10 a.m: "CYCLOPS sailed fourth for the United States."

wireless, Tho. C. report of interview with Lt. Commander Burkhart and later Ensign Ryder, regarding George Worley and the *Cyclops*, April 25, 1918.

" " report on Gottschalk and Marden, Orth & Hastings, Navy Yard, New York, April 27, 1918.

Levering, Richmond, Department of Justice, Bureau of Investigation, letter to Captain Edward McCauley, Office of Naval Intelligence, Washington DC., May 7, 1918.

" " May 14th, 1918, letter to Edward McCauley of ONI.

Livingston, Barbados, telegram March 28, "Nothing is known here whereabouts CYCLOPS since departure fourth March. Cannot account for non arrival at destination. Have asked the Colonial Governor institute wireless search West Indies waters."

" " Telegram to Secretary of State, Received 9:25 p.m. Washington DC., regarding investigation.

Lt. Scott, Operations, to Barbados, March 27, 1918: "USS CYCLOPS sailed from Barbados March 4th due to arrive Baltimore March 13th period CYCLOPS now fourteen days overdue period Can you advise Navy Department of present position of CYCLOPS or give any information which might explain delay in arrival?"

Lucas, DeWitt B., Graphologist, report on handwriting of Stephen Konstovich, June 14, 1918.

Maguet, Glenn, Report of accident to starboard H.P. Engine. January 28, 1918.

Marvin, W., United States Department of Agriculture, Weather Bureau.

McCauley, Edward, letter of May 10, 1918 in response to Richmond Levering of May 7th.

"   "   RE: Tampered Lenses, Arcadia, Cyclops, 3-20-1918

Memorandum for Lt. Johnstone RE Walter McDaniel Psychiatric Examination, September 19, 1918.

Memorandum for Captain McCauley, "Six Theories suggested to account for the disappearance of the *Cyclops*," June 29, 1918.

Momsen, Richard P.,   Concerning the U.S.S. *Cyclops* on which Consul-General Gottschalk was a Passenger, April 27, 1918.

"   "   May 1, 1918, RE investigation and stating he has taken to up-keeping Gottschalk's affairs.

"   "   letter to Secretary of State regarding disposition of A.L.M. Gottschalk's personal effects, July 25, 1918.

"   "   Transmittal of newspaper clippings covering the Cyclops story and A.L.M. Gottschalk in Rio, including well wishes and condolences, August 8, 1918.

Muster Roll, August 1, 1917, U.S.S. Cyclops, Auxiliary Service list.

Navy Department, Third Naval District, District Communication Service, Memorandum for Ensign Lee, March 14, 1919, RE: "Gottschalk Summering in Kiel."

Naval Institute Proceedings, April 1920, "Discussion." Vol. 46, No. 206.
Navintel, April 16, 1918, coded message to Hil, Rio de Janeiro: "Cable your confidential opinion as to loyalty of Consul Gottschalk."

Newspapers, U.S.

Brooklyn Eagle, 9-3-30, "How were 293 Lives Lost?"
New York Herald, April 15, 1918, "The Cyclops Loss Likely to Rank Among Unsolved Mysteries of the Sea."
New York Sun, May 6, 1918, "Mysterious Advertisement in South American Newspaper Hints The Cyclops Was Sunk."
Official Bulletin, Washington, Monday, April 15, 1918., "Navy Collier Cyclops Overdue . . ."
Philadelphia Record, July 4, 1930 "Voice from a Lost Ship."
Press Herald, Portland, ME 7-9-30, No Mystery About the Cyclops.
San Antonio Express, July 11, 1919, "Fate of Cyclops May Be Cleared By Bottle."
The Evening Star, April 15, 1918, "Collier Cyclops Probably Lost."
The Union, Manchester, N.H, 7-4-30, "Another Cyclops Mystery Clue."
Washington Herald February 4, 1919, "Cyclops Went Down in Says Navy."
Washington Herald, 4-8-1920, "Nature's Dr. Jekyl and Mr. Hyde."
Washington Post, Feb 3, 1929, "Naval Record Offers Solution for Disappearance of Cyclops."
Washington Post, 7-13-1930, "A Wartime Mystery of the Sea."
Washington Star, July 30, 1921, Cyclops Victim of U-Boat, Says German Officer."
Waterbury Republican, Conn. 7-4-30, "The Cyclops Mystery."

Niblack, A.P. , Memorandum for Chief of Naval Operations recommending 7th District undertake search of areas indicated by Donald Fraser, April 17, 1920.

Office of Aide for Information, Fifth Naval District, Norfolk, Va., Case No 400/76 Subject: Tampered Telescopes, Report of March 20, 1918, and request for investigation, February 19, 1918, by O.W. Fowler, Office of Naval Intelligence.

Office of Naval Records and Library, Historical Section, Navy Department, "Loss of the U.S.S. Cyclops" (undated).

Orenham, A,   Bureau of Navigation, August 10, 1917, Subject: Report of Investigation on Lieut. Comdr. George W. Worley, Commanding U.S.S. *Cyclops.*

Operative #1,   Case# 8D-22, May 11, 1918.

"   "   Supplement to Case #8D-22, May 14, 1918.

Porter, Mrs. A.M., letters to:

Mrs. W.T. Bosher, Richmond, VA., July 27, 1918.
Ella Granberry Tucker (undated)
Mrs. Jennie Hake, Richmond, VA., July 30, 1918.
Mrs. John F. Lee, Baltimore, MD., September 3, 1918.
M.F. Rawle, Paris, Sept. 11, 1918.
H.C. Tucker, American Bible School, Rio de Janeiro, July 2, 1918.
W.W. Swinyer, Oakland, Ca., June 7, 1918
F.B. Weltshire, USS Pittsburgh, Oct. 16, 1918.

Proceedings of a Board of Inquiry, Hampton Roads, Virginia, August 4 & 6, 1918. Bureau of Navigation.

Reed, Edwin L.   Subject: John Frederick Wichmann alias Lieutenant Commander G.W. Worley USN (RF), Commander of the U.S.S. Cyclops." 6-15-1918

"   "   U.S.S. Cyclops and Lt. Commander G.W. Worley, U.S.N.R.F, Commander of, May 17, 1918.

"   "   Information gleaned from J.F. Burke (sp) RE: G.W. Worley, Hyde Park, Chicago, 6-13-1918.

Report from CinC Pacific to Secretary Navy RE H.P. engine aboard

Cyclops, February 1, 1918.

Report of Board of Investigation on Damage to Main Engine of *Cyclops*, 4 February 1918, W.B. Caperton.

Report of William J. Malestrom RE: conversation over Charles Hillyer and s.s *Amalco*, between Lieutenants Scott and Laning, June 5, 1918.

Richards, John K. Lieut. Commander, US Navy Recruiting Station, Kansas City, MO, 15 March 1920: Possible explanation of loss of U.S.S. *Cyclops.*

Rio de Janeiro newspapers

A Epoca   April 15, 1918: "O desapparecimento do Cyclops"

A Lanterna April 15, 1918: "Teria naufragado o Cyclops?

A Noite   April 15, 1918: O desapparecimento do Cyclops

A Noticia   April 15, 1918: "Estara perdido o Cyclops"

A Razao   April 16, 1918: O Mysterio da perda do transporte de Guerra Cyclops."

A Rua   April 15, 1918: Rio de Janeiro: "O Desapparecimento Mysterioso Do Cyclops."

A Seleta   April 20, 1918: Corerreio Parta os Estados.

A Tribuna   April 23, 1918: O Mysterio Do Cyclops Uma Personal-idade Necessaria.

A Tribuna   April 15, 1918: I Cyclops Foi Mesmo A Pique.

Correio de Manha   April 16, 1918: "Parece estar Absolumtamente

Perdido o Cyclops.

Gazeta de Noticias Onde anadara o Cyclops & Victima dos boches?

Journal do Commercio April 15, 1918: Infelizmente parece perdido o Cyclops.

Journal de Commercio April 16, 1918: A Falta De Noticias Sobre o Transporte de Guerra Cyclops."

Journal do Brazil April 15, 1918: No Mar: o naufragio do Cyclops.

Fon Fon, April 20, 1918 O Consul Geral dos Estados Unidos no Brasil.

Rio journal April 15, 1918 "Afunda-se entre as Antilhas e os Estados Unidos o transporte de Guerra Americano Cyclops.

————

Roberts, Corporal Paul, Camp MacArthur, Waco, Texas, May 20, 1918, to Office of Naval Intelligence, Washington DC, Subject: Naval Collier Cyclops USN.

Roosevelt, F.,   Acting Secretary of the Navy, letter to A.I. Taylor acknowledging receipt of letter of May 21, 1923.

Royal Danish Legation, letter from to Bureau of Navigation requesting information on Danish citizens as sailors aboard *Cyclops*, July 16, 1918.

Shull, H.C., Memorandum for Ensign Clark, Navy Yard, New York, May 4, 1918.

"Statement of Lieut. Commander Burkhart (Frank Tower), Commanding Officer of U.S.S. *Culgoa*, laying at foot of 35th Street, Brooklyn."

"Statement made by Lieut. Commander McKay on Board the U.S.S. *Celebes*, pier 5, Bush Docks, April 26, 1918."

Summary of investigation, *Cyclops*, 14 pages.

Supplement to #8D-22 May 13, 1918, unnamed operative reporting on W. Van Dyke and Gottschalk.

Swinyer W.W., "Dear Friends" letter sent to family of *Cyclops* crew discussing his own experiences on his June 1917 cruise.

"   "   — *A Squadron of the United States Navy: On a Friendly Cruise Around Latin America, Oakland, Calif., 1918.*

Telegram 3744 to Department of State, from Paris, April 29, 1918, Regarding U-boat activity off western coast of England.

Telephone Memorandum:
"Mr. Freeman calls June 5, 1918, informing First Naval District Boston that s.s. *Amalco* log contains reference to sighting the *Cyclops* 5 miles distance battling storm off Carolinas. Timed: 12:45 p.m. Subsequent telephone calls from agents until 5:30 p.m. same day clarifying matter."

Telegram to Bureau of Navigation, 2-13-1918, "Cyclops will sail Saturday February 16, 1918, at 9.00 .a.m. Expect to arrive at Baltimore, Md, March 8th, 1918." —George W. Worley

Telegram to Commander-in-Chief, U.S.S. *Pittsburgh*; Commanding Officer, U.S.S. Raleigh, 2-13-1918 "Cyclops sails at 9:00 a.m. Saturday February 16th, 1918."— George W. Worley.

Undersigned, to Secretary of the Navy— Subject: Request for Board of Investigation on board U.S.S. *Cyclops* (undated).

United State Department of Agriculture, Weather Bureau, Office of the Chief, Washington DC, July 2, 1918, letter to ONI, C.

Marvin, Chief of Bureau.

United States Patrol Force, Report on Search for *Cyclops*, 4-18-18.

Ward, Cabot, Lieut. Colonel, General Staff, American Expedition-ary Forces, G-2, S.O.S A.P.O 702, December 24, 1918, RE: "Myron."

Warden, D. J., of Standard Oil, Foreign Shipping Department, letter to Secretary of the Navy, April 17, 1918, regarding proper loading of manganese ore.

Whitted, William Scott, Report of Board of Investigation aboard USS *Cyclops*, August 9, 1918.

Winram, S.B, Twelfth Naval District, San Francisco, report on let-ter of Selma Worley to Mrs. Angermann, June 11, 1918.

   "   "   Report on G.W. Worley, 6-14-1918.
   "   "   Subject: Lt. Commander G.W. Worley, USNRF, 6-15-1918.

Worley, George W., Nine pages of defense to Supervisor Auxilia-ry Service, Norfolk, Virginia, August 9, 1917.

   "   "   To Commanding Officer, Commander Destroyer Force, Commander US Convoy Operations in the Atlantic, Saint Nazaire, France, 1 July 1917, Report of Passage of First Expedition-ary Force from U.S. to France.

Worley, Selma, letter to Mrs. Angermann, May 27, 1918.

Yates. I.I., Loss of the Cyclops, submission for article, Feb 20, 1920.

9 780988 850569